William J. Fay

P9-CMS-934

Where

Christology

Began

Where Christology Began

Essays on Philippians 2

Ralph P. Martin
Brian J. Dodd
editors

Westminster John Knox Press
Louisville, Kentucky

© 1998 Westminster John Knox Press

All rights reserved.
No part of this book may be reproduced or
transmitted in any form or by any means, electronic or mechanical,
including photocopying, recording, or by any information storage or
retrieval system, without permission in writing from the publisher.
For information, address Westminster John Knox Press,
100 Witherspoon Street, Louisville, Kentucky 40202-1396.

Grateful acknowledgment is made for permission to reproduce material from
"Re-Enter the Pre-Existent Christ in Philippians," by L. D. Hurst,
New Testament Studies 32 (1986): 449–57. Reprinted with the
permission of Cambridge University Press.

Book design by Jennifer K. Cox
Cover design by Brooke Griffiths

First Edition
Published by Westminster John Knox Press
Louisville, Kentucky

This book is printed on acid-free paper that meets the
American National Standards Institute Z39.48 standard. ∞

PRINTED IN THE UNITED STATES OF AMERICA
98 99 00 01 02 03 04 05 06 07 — 10 9 8 7 6 5 4 3 2 1

Library of Congress Cataloging-in-Publication Data

Where Christology began : essays on Philippians 2 / Ralph P. Martin and Brian J.
Dodd, editors — 1st ed.
    p.   cm.
  Includes bibliographical references.
  ISBN 0-664-25619-8 (alk. paper)
  1. Bible N.T. Philippians II, 5–11—Criticism, interpretation, etc.   2. Bible.
N.T. Philippians II—Criticism, interpretation, etc.—History.   3. Jesus Christ—
Person and offices.
I. Martin, Ralph P.   II. Dodd, Brian J., date.
BS2705.2.W48   1998
227′.606—dc21   97-44957

CONTENTS

CONTRIBUTORS

RICHARD J. BAUCKHAM, Professor of New Testament Studies, Saint Mary's College, University of Saint Andrews

COLIN BROWN, Professor of Systematic Theology, Fuller Theological Seminary

BRIAN J. DODD, Assistant Professor of Leadership, Asbury Theological Seminary

JAMES D. G. DUNN, Lightfoot Professor of Divinity, University of Durham

STEPHEN FOWL, Associate Professor of Theology, Loyola College (Maryland)

GERALD F. HAWTHORNE, Emeritus Professor of Greek, Wheaton College (Illinois)

LINCOLN D. HURST, Associate Professor of Religious Studies, University of California, Davis

LARRY J. KREITZER, Tutor of New Testament, Regent's Park College, University of Oxford

RALPH P. MARTIN, Distinguished Scholar in Residence, Fuller Theological Seminary, Haggard Graduate School of Theology of Azusa Pacific University, and Logos Evangelical Seminary (California)

ROBERT MORGAN, Reader in New Testament Theology and Fellow of Linacre College, University of Oxford

ABBREVIATIONS

ABD	David N. Freedman, ed., *Anchor Bible Dictionary,* 6 vols., Nashville, 1992
ANRW	*Aufstieg und Niedergang der römischen Welt,* ed. H. Temporini and W. Haase, Berlin, 1972–
BAGD	W. Bauer, W. F. Arndt, F. W. Gingrich, and F. W. Danker, *Greek-English Lexicon of the New Testament,* 2d ed., Chicago, 1979
BECNT	Baker Exegetical Commentary on the New Testament
BWANT	Beiträge zur Wissenschaft vom Alten und Neuen Testament
BBR	*Bulletin of Biblical Research*
BDF	F. Blass, A. Debrunner, and R. W. Funk, *A Greek Grammar of the New Testament and Other Early Christian Literature,* Chicago, 1961
BZNW	Beihefte zur Zeitschrift für die neutestamentliche Wissenschaft
CBQ	*Catholic Biblical Quarterly*
CD	Cairo (Genizah) Damascus Document
DLZ	*Deutsche Literaturzeitung*
DPL	*Dictionary of Paul and His Letters,* Downers Grove, Ill., 1995
ET	English translation
ExpTim	*Expository Times*
FRLANT	Forschungen zur Religion und Literatur des Alten und Neuen Testaments
FS	Festschrift
HTR	*Harvard Theological Review*
HzNT	Handbuch zum Neuen Testament
JB	Jerusalem Bible
JBL	*Journal of Biblical Literature*
JSNT	*Journal for the Study of the New Testament*
JSNTSup	Journal for the Study of the New Testament Supplement Series
JTS	*Journal of Theological Studies*
KEK	Kritisch-exegetischer Kommentar über das Neue Testament
KJV	King James Version
LAB	Liber Antiquitatum Biblicarum

LCL	Loeb Classical Library
LSJ	H. G. Liddell, R. Scott, and H. S. Jones, *A Greek-English Lexicon,* Oxford, 1940
LXX	Septuagint
MM	Moulton and Milligan, *The Vocabulary of the Greek Testament*
NCB	New Century Bible
NEB	New English Bible
n.F.	neue Folge (new series)
NICNT	New International Commentary on the New Testament
NIGTC	New International Greek Testament Commentary
NIV	New International Version
NovT	*Novum Testamentum*
NRSV	New Revised Standard Version
n.s.	new series
NTOA	Novum Testamentum et Orbis Antiquus
NTS	*New Testament Studies*
OTP	James H. Charlesworth, ed., *Old Testament Pseudepigrapha,* 2 vols., Garden City, N.Y., 1983–85
RB	Revue Biblique
REB	Revised English Bible
RSV	Revised Standard Version
SBL	Society of Biblical Literature
SBLMS	Society of Biblical Literature Monograph Series
SBT	Studies in Biblical Theology
SHR	Studies in the History of Religions
SJLA	Studies in Judaism in Late Antiquity
SJT	*Scottish Journal of Theology*
SNTSMS	Society for New Testament Studies Monograph Series
Str-B	H. L. Strack and P. Billerbeck, *Kommentar zum Neuen Testament aus Talmud und Midrasch,* 6 vols., Munich, 1922–61
TB	*Theologische Bücherei*
TBl	*Theologische Blätter*
TDNT	*Theological Dictionary of the New Testament*
THKNT	Theologischer Handkommentar zum Neuen Testament
TLZ	*Theologischer Literaturzeitung*
TWNT	*Theologisches Wörterbuch zum Neuen Testament*
WBC	Word Biblical Commentary
WMANT	Wissenschaftliche Monographien zum Alten und Neuen Testament
WUNT	Wissenschaftliche Untersuchungen zum Neuen Testament
ZNW	*Zeitschrift für die neutestamentliche Wissenschaft*
ZTK	*Zeitschrift für Theologie und Kirche*

1.
Carmen Christi Revisited

RALPH P. MARTIN

The history of interpretation relating to Paul's writing in Philippians 2:5–11 has, in my judgment, two monumental landmarks that stand out as impressive guideposts in any bid to come to terms with a problem text. I refer to E. Lohmeyer's *Kyrios Jesus* (1928) and E. Käsemann's "Kritische Analyse von Phil. 2,5–11" (1950). Some will be inclined to nominate, as a third pointer to an eluci- dation of the verses, N. T. Wright's essay on ἁρπαγμός (*harpagmos*) in *JTS* 37 (1986).[1] Together these three contributions stand out as breaking new ground, pointing the reader in novel directions.

By any reckoning Lohmeyer's lecture in its printed form serves as a decisive starting point in the twentieth-century interpretation of the passage. Käsemann paid tribute to his predecessor:

> Lohmeyer's works mark a turning-point in that they lift us out of the old ruts, and so have compelled the exegetical community and their usual readers to face new and suggestive questions.[2]

E. Käsemann himself felt drawn to the passage in Philippians 2:5–11 for some- what the same reason, namely that it is in the interests of a desire to clarify to our- selves the progress and condition of exegesis to have to wrestle with a specific example. In so doing we become aware of the problems not only that are inherent in the material (the text) but also in the task of exegetical inquiry itself.[3] The pur- suit of the exegetical inquiry is one that is ongoing in every generation, as Wright's essay illustrates, though it is just as clear that the last word on Philippians 2 has not been spoken. The text is still the occasion of much debate. This should not sur- prise us, since (to take a recent modern example) understanding D. H. Lawrence has yielded three quite different viewpoints by scholars (see Mark Kinkead- Weekes, ed., *Triumph to Exile, 1912–1922,* Cambridge: Cambridge University Press, 1996).

The suggestion that a book should chronicle this ongoing discussion, appraise the merits of the often bewildering sets of arguments pro and con on disputed points of exegesis, and so push forward the frontiers of our knowledge met with ready acceptance. For this purpose the editors were gratified to enlist a team of contributors whose work follows and is now offered to those who wish to learn of

1

the *status quaestionis* in this area of biblical studies. It falls to this opening chapter to say why Philippians 2:5–11 continues to engage scholarly interest, and what the prospective readers may expect to find in the subsequent pages.

I

There is a formidable list of reasons why this Pauline period should continue to be the focus of interest, even as we acknowledge that the text has not yet yielded its full secrets. First, Philippians 2:5–11 taxes the skill of the translator, as many of the key words, especially to do with the presentation of Christ's role in the text, baffle the lexicographer's mind and offer a wide, often puzzling, variety of choice and interpretation. This lack of agreement as to the precise nuance—or even the meaning—of words such as μορφή, ἁρπαγμός, and ὑπερύψωσεν—is evident from even a cursory examination of the modern commentaries from Dibelius to Fee.[4] And it is a feature of these essays that on such crucial exegetical matters there is no common agreement. Many of the terms under examination are rare in biblical Greek and even rarer in the Pauline vocabulary; hence the translator's difficulty is compounded. For this reason, Philippians 2:5–11 is frequently prescribed in Greek and English exegesis courses in the university, seminary, and college curriculum. A handbook of essays like this one is bound to be of service to both teachers and students seeking to keep abreast of current lexical and interpretative trends in research.

Second, the literary form of the passage gives rise to the suggestion that here we are in touch with the worshiping life of the early Christians. Questions of authorship and literary genre have figured largely in previous generations of study, with little precise agreement, though it would be fair to conclude that there is a measure of concurrence. The agreed conclusions are that Philippians 2:6–11 gives us a window into the liturgical beliefs and practices of Christian groups that either antedated Paul or were contemporary with his ministry. If the former, then we are in the twilight zone of "pre-Pauline" Christianity, whose formulations of Christ's role the apostle took over, with a measure of redactional modification and adaptation. To be sure, Paul's use of the passage places his mark of approval on what we have in the text, but that obvious statement does not exclude the possibility that the verses existed in an earlier draft that Paul may well have added to as he took it over.

There is another issue which is still discussed, though now the extent of the agreement is wider and (I would add) more securely based. The passage is commonly treated as poetic and/or hymnic, capable of being laid out in lines, couplets, and strophes, and so providing a stately composition of well-rounded and carefully modulated ideas to form a rhythmically balanced christological psalm (as Lohmeyer's pioneering analysis professed to show and as C. Brown's essay demonstrates). Our knowledge of early Christian hymnody is strictly limited, aside from the clear evidence that the churches of the New Testament period were in the habit of using "psalms, hymns, and songs of the Spirit" (Col. 3:16//Eph. 5:19) and that at least some of such specimens were addressed liturgically to the exalted Christ (e.g., Rev. 5:1–14; Pliny's report of *carmenque Christo quasi deo dicere*[5]). If the evidence of Philippians 2 is a pointer to such an example of christology-in-worship, then we may conclude that the same data show how the enthroned Lord was hailed as on a par with Israel's covenant God as worthy of liturgical praise. At least two of the essays (by L. J. Kreitzer and R. J. Bauckham) tackle this theme, and wrestle with the paradox of Christian belief in "one God" (respecting the church's Jewish heritage) and the placing of Jesus Christ in the divine court where all sentient creatures acknowledge him as Lord (*kyrios*).

Third, in our day christology is a topic of perennial interest and import. Philippians 2 has been regarded by a host of interpreters (from Jeremias to Hengel[6]) as providing a fixed starting point for all later development. It was the presence of this weighty agreement that prompted the title of the book, though (the editors hasten to add) none of the essayists should be held accountable for the title to a greater extent than to assent to the importance of the passage in New Testament understandings of who Christ was/is. The title *Where Christology Began* should be interpreted in this sense, and read in the light of the placing of the verses in a liturgical setting (which, we believe, would command more general agreement by our contributors). This phrase is a reminder that early christological thinking and formulation arose within a context (*inter alia*) of the Christians' worship of God now believed to be disclosed in the coming of Jesus of Nazareth and his exaltation to God's presence following his earthly life and obedient submission to death.

The far-reaching issues of whether or how he existed prior to his earthly life (popularly known as his preexistence, but more accurately described as his pretemporal existence) and the attributing to him of "equality with God" (whether in that postulated prior state or subsequently) continue to engage scholars. The latest phase of debate can be seen in J. D. G. Dunn's and G. F. Hawthorne's pieces; the latter picks up N. T. Wright's argument that the "hymn" is more theocentric than christological, and the former rehearses and extends his earlier reasons for finding little clue to (later) preexistence teaching here since the passage reflects a model or metaphor of Adam christology. Dunn's earlier views were challenged by L. D. Hurst, whose revised contribution is included as a service to the reader.

Finally, we turn to the interrelation of what the hymn portrays of Christ's "way" (from "being in the divine μορφή" to his acclamation as *kyrios*) to Paul's pastoral and paraenetic purpose in appealing to this story or saga. It is the issue of how Philippians 2:5–11 contributes to Paul's ethical admonitions to the local Philippian assembly. Ernst Käsemann (in 1950) regarded the hymn as dominated by the mythical scenario of the redeemer figure who, coming from God, is now taken up to share God's life, and found this a difficult question to negotiate. He turned away from the so-called "ethical idealism" (which he found in Lohmeyer as well as earlier Protestant scholars in the European liberal tradition) and took the novel turn of denying the appeal to the ethical example of "*imitation of Christ.*" Instead the key is sought in 2:5 where ἐν Χριστῷ Ἰησοῦ does not (he avers) speak of Christ as *exemplum ad imitandum* but refers to Christians' being in Christ's domain (*im Bereich des Christus*) and so obedient to his lordship, now proclaimed as universal over all spirit-powers (2:10–11).[7] In spite of the mythological setting, Käsemann was able to see in Christ's confessed lordship the ground of Paul's ethical appeal (a leap R. Morgan's discussion questions).

Käsemann's denials have provoked some fierce discussion (among traditional Anglo-Saxon and some Scandinavian scholars) and have split the "exegetical community" that Lohmeyer—and Käsemann—had in view. It is good, therefore, to have some reflections on how the story of Christ functions in the broader context of the Philippian scene, and the role model played not only by the Pauline christological story but by Paul's own paradigmatic example and that of his colleagues. Here S. E. Fowl and B. J. Dodd offer insights on the way a passage like 2:5–11 may contribute to Christian ethics.

II

In recent discussions E. Käsemann's essay of 1950 is often cited, and its English translation appeared in 1968. Yet the rendering left many students asking for more, and in particular for a greater nuanced and interpreted commentary on Käsemann's work. The desire was to know how to set it in the frame of German scholarship in the twentieth century. Robert Morgan has provided such timely help, and his essay will light up several dark places of the English translation as well as offer fresh interpretations of what Käsemann's theological agenda really was.

On a broader front, we return to E. Lohmeyer. He too is a writer whose sententious discussion cries out for elucidation and background material in both theology and philosophy. Colin Brown has done well to meet these needs, and since Lohmeyer's weighty booklet has never been translated, interested readers can thread their way through Lohmeyer's often abstruse reasoning with clear guidance provided along the way. In addition, they will be helped by Brown's own insights into the text in the light of recent scholarship.

III

One essay speaks of the "strategies and categories . . . appropriate for understanding"[8] a problem text such as Philippians 2:5–11. The editors venture to think that this volume will be of service in offering just such an answer to the quest for the meaning of the Pauline period "for our own generation"[9] (as Käsemann hoped his work might do a half-century ago).

NOTES

1. E. Lohmeyer, *Kyrios Jesus: Eine Untersuchung zu Phil. 2, 5–11.* Sitzungsberichte der Heidelberger Akademie der Wissenschaften, Philosophisch-historische Klasse, Jahrgang 1927/1928, 4. Abhandlung (Heidelberg: Carl Winter, Universitätsverlag, 2. Auflage 1961).

E. Käsemann, "Kritische Analyse von Phil. 2, 5–11," *ZTK* 47 (1950): 313–60, reprinted in his *Exegetische Versuche und Besinnungen* 1 (Göttingen: Vandenhoeck & Ruprecht, 1960), 51–95 (page references are to the later version). Translated by Alice F. Carse as "A Critical Analysis of Philippians 2:5–11," in *God and Christ: Existence and Province,* ed. R. W. Funk, *Journal for Theology and Church* 5 (New York: Harper & Row, 1968), 45–88.

N. T. Wright, "ἁρπαγμός and the Meaning of Philippians 2. 5–11," *JTS* n.s. 37 (1986): 321–52, with a later version, "Jesus Christ is Lord: Philippians 2. 5–11," in his *The Climax of the Covenant: Christ and the Law in Pauline Theology* (Edinburgh: T. & T. Clark, 1991; Minneapolis: Fortress Press, 1992), 56–98. Reasons for hesitations regarding the cogency of Wright's position are given in my *A Hymn of Christ: Philippians 2:5–11 in Recent Interpretation* (3d ed. of *Carmen Christi*) (Downers Grove, Ill.: InterVarsity Press; Leicester: Tyndale Press, 1997). This new edition attempts to survey recent studies devoted to Philippians 2:5–11.
2. Käsemann, "Kritische Analyse," 53.
3. Ibid., 51.
4. M. Dibelius, *An die Thessalonicher; an die Philipper* HZNT (Tübingen: Mohr, ²1923, ³1937); G. D. Fee, *Paul's Letter to the Philippians* NICNT (Grand Rapids: Eerdmans, 1995).
5. See, for Christ hymns as a subgenre, M. Hengel, "The Song about Christ in Earliest Worship," in *Studies in Early Christology* (Edinburgh: T. & T. Clark, 1995), 227–91.
6. J. Jeremias, "Zur Gedankenführung in den paulinischen Briefen," in *Studia Paulina in honorem J. de Zwaan,* ed. J. N. Sevenster and W. C. van Unnik (Haarlem: Bohn, 1953), 146–54 (154); Hengel, "Song about Christ," 289.
7. Käsemann, "Kritische Analyse," 57, 91.
8. R. Morgan, "Incarnation, Myth, and Theology" (see below, p. 68).
9. Käsemann, "Kritische Analyse," 51.

2.

Ernst Lohmeyer's *Kyrios Jesus*

COLIN BROWN

In a memorial tribute to Ernst Lohmeyer, Oscar Cullmann observed that future elucidation of Phil. 2:6–11 must take as its starting point Lohmeyer's insights into this "passage which is perhaps the most rich in christological content in the New Testament."[1] Few would dissent from Cullmann's verdict with regard to the passage itself or Lohmeyer's contribution.[2] The work in question is Lohmeyer's *Kyrios Jesus* (1928), which has never been published in English translation.[3] Lohmeyer's identification of Phil. 2:6–11 as a pre-Pauline psalm is well known. However, the form-critical analysis that led to this conclusion was by no means the sole contribution. Lohmeyer proceeded to suggest theories concerning its place in the eucharistic worship of the Jerusalem church, its role in development of christology, and its relationship to other literature. All this was done within the context of a metaphysic that Lohmeyer saw not only as the key to understanding the humiliation and exaltation of the figure in the psalm, but as the motive for Christian living.

My study is offered as a tribute to one of the great New Testament scholars of our time, and was completed shortly after the fiftieth anniversary of Lohmeyer's judicial murder on September 19, 1946.[4] The analysis of *Kyrios Jesus* in part 1 will follow Lohmeyer's outline, though for the sake of clarity I have adopted a modern scheme of numbering and have supplied headings, which are absent from the original. The comments in part 2 focus on selected issues.

1.   Analysis
1.1.   Form and Structure
1.2.   Analysis of the Stanzas
    1.2.1. Primordial Temptation
    1.2.2. Self-Emptying of the Servant
    1.2.3. Death of the Son of Man
    1.2.4. Exaltation and Bestowal of the Name above Every Name
    1.2.5. Universal Worship in the Name of Jesus
    1.2.6. Universal Acclaim That Jesus Christ Is Lord
1.3.   Use of the Psalm in the Eucharist

1. ANALYSIS

1.1. Form and Structure

Impetus for Lohmeyer's study came from the debate inspired by Bousset's *Kyrios Christos*.[5] At issue was the meaning of the primitive confession: "Jesus is Lord" (Rom. 10:9; 1 Cor. 12:3; Phil. 2:11). Was the application of the title "Lord"—*Kyrios*—the appropriation of a Hellenistic term, as Bousset maintained? If so, Jesus had been divinized in the same way that the Greeks and Romans divinized their heroes. Or was the use of "Lord" the application of the familiar designation for God in the Greek version of the Hebrew Scriptures? Or did the truth lie somewhere in between? Lohmeyer replied that neither Jewish nor non-Jewish parallels could answer these questions. What was beyond dispute was the fact that the title was applied to Jesus, and that it was embedded in the carefully constructed passage in Phil. 2:6–11, which provides the earliest documentation for *how* it was used.

Numerous predecessors had observed the sentence structure that stands out from the rest of the letter.[6] Building on their work, Lohmeyer divided the psalm into two strophes, each consisting of three three-line stanzas.[7] He began by examining the conjunctions. διὸ καί ("and therefore," v. 9), which introduces the fourth stanza, divides the two strophes. In both strophes two conjunctions tie the syntax together. In the first there is ἀλλά ("but") and καί ("and") in v. 7–8; in the second ἵνα ("so that," v. 10) and again καί (v. 11). Thus there is a corresponding pattern in which the resulting action is introduced by καί, which is governed either by ἀλλά or ἵνα. The first strophe is characterized by a series of subordinate participles: ὑπάρχων ("existing"/"being"), v. 6; λαβών ("having taken") followed by γενόμενος ("having become"[8]), v. 7; εὑρεθείς ("being found") followed again by γενόμενος, v. 8. In the first strophe the servant figure is the subject, and in the second strophe God is the subject and the servant figure the object of God's actions. The sentence structure that Lohmeyer detected could only be consciously devised.

(1) [6]Ὃς [9]ἐν μορφῇ θεοῦ ὑπάρχων
οὐχ ἁρπαγμὸν ἡγήσατο
τὸ εἶναι ἴσα θεῷ

(2) [7]ἀλλὰ ἑαυτὸν ἐκένωσεν
μορφὴν δούλου λαβών
ἐν ὁμοιώματι ἀνθρώπων γενόμενος

(3) καὶ σχήματι εὑρεθεὶς ὡς ἄνθρωπος[10]
[8]ἐταπείνωσεν ἑαυτόν
γενόμενος ὑπήκοος μέχρι θανάτου
[θανάτου δὲ σταυροῦ][11]

(4) [9]διὸ καὶ ὁ θεὸς αὐτὸν ὑπερύψωσεν
καὶ ἐχαρίσατο αὐτῷ
τὸ ὄνομα τὸ ὑπὲρ πᾶν ὄνομα

(5) [10]ἵνα ἐν τῷ ὀνόματι Ἰησοῦ
πᾶν γόνου κάμψῃ
ἐπουρανίων καὶ ἐπιγείων καὶ καταχθονίων

(6) [11]καὶ πᾶσα γλῶσσα ἐξομολογήσηται
ὅτι κύριος Ἰησοῦς Χριστὸς
εἰς δόξαν θεοῦ πατρός.

At this point it may be useful to give an English rendering. Rather than reproduce one of the current English versions, I base the translation on my understanding of Lohmeyer's interpretation in *Kyrios Jesus* and on his German translation in his commentary.[12] Inevitably we shall not be able to preserve the poetic meter of the Greek. Although the rendering may be literalistic, we may nevertheless capture something of the ideas that Lohmeyer heard.

(1) [6][The one][9] existing in the form of God
considered it not plunder *miseris booty – Lohmeyer*
to be like God,

(2) [7]but sacrificed himself,
having taken the form of a slave,
having become an image of humanity;

(3) and [though] being found "as Son of Man"[13]
[8]he humbled himself,
having become obedient unto death [death on a cross].[11]

(4) [9]And therefore God exalted him highly
and bestowed on him
the name above every name,

(5) [10]that in the name of Jesus
every knee should bow
in heaven, earth, and the underworld,

(6) [11]and every tongue acclaim:
  "Jesus Christ is Lord"
  to the glory of God, the Father.

Each stanza contains a single predicate, usually with one verb. The fourth stanza (v. 9) adds a second verb, but both verbs express a single **divine** act. Each stanza has lines of approximately the same length.[14] The chief **apparent** exception occurs in the third line of the third stanza ("death on the cross"), which Lohmeyer identified as a Pauline gloss.

The stanzas exhibit a logical sequence that on examination turns out to be a sorites (German, *Kettenschluss*).[15] In logic a sorites is a chain of propositions in which the predicate of a statement forms the subject of the next, and the conclusion unites the subject of the first proposition with the predicate of the last. In the psalm words and phrases are echoed, and each three-line stanza expresses a consequence that becomes the ground of the action in the next.[16] The stanzas thus build upon each other, leading to the conclusion that the one who did not exploit his divine form by seeking to be like God is universally acclaimed with the divine name to the glory of the Father.

The first three stanzas are characterized by the framing of the verb by two participles, except that the first has an infinitive verb as a noun ("to be equal with God") instead of a participle. In the last three stanzas nouns take the place of the participles. The wording is unique, and does not correspond to Paul's customary style. The first stanza (v. 6) refers to the remote object before the immediate one. In the second stanza (v. 7) the participles are juxtaposed asyndectically without conjunctions in the second and third lines. The fifth stanza (v. 10) separates the genitives in the Greek ("in heaven and on earth and under the earth") from the nouns to which they belong. The sixth stanza (v. 11) interrupts the connection between the first and third lines with the cry: "Jesus Christ is Lord."

Content corresponds to structure. The emphatic "And therefore" (v. 9) which governs the last three stanzas introduces a new turn. The first three stanzas depict Christ's way from heaven to earth and death, and the last three his exaltation. Just as the two strophes are formally divided by key particles, so is the content. The first and the fourth stanzas speak of a divine act. In both cases what follows—the course of Christ's life and the creation's worship (both characterized by two verbs)—is the consequence of what has been depicted.

These observations force the conclusion that the passage is no ordinary piece of letter writing or even rhetorical prose, but a carefully crafted poem, "a *carmen Christi* in the strict sense."[17] It is not a fragment of some larger whole, for it begins and ends in eternity. In content it is complete, even if an introductory or concluding call to the praise (as in most *Odes of Solomon*) has become detached. But how did it come to be written and find its way into the apostle's letter?

The psalm could hardly have been composed to address the envy and rivalry that form its immediate context (Phil. 2:1–5). Nor is it likely that it was composed by the apostle, for its strophic form is far more rigorously structured than other Pauline compositions, such as the celebration of love in 1 Corinthians 13. Then there is the unique vocabulary. οὐχ ἁρπαγμὸν ἡγήσατο ("he did not consider it plunder") is found nowhere else in the New Testament. ἐκένωσε ("emptied"), ὑπερύψωσεν ("exalted"), μορφήν ("form"), and σχήματι ("likeness") are used here in senses not found elsewhere in Paul. The threefold division of the cosmos—heaven, earth, and underworld—is found only here. εὑρεθεὶς ὡς ("found as") is not only un-Pauline but un-Greek. In Lohmeyer's view, the apostle's sole contribution was the insertion of θανάτου δὲ σταυροῦ ("death on a cross"), which spoils the meter but expresses Paul's characteristic emphasis. Lohmeyer concluded that the psalm was written in Greek, but by a poet whose mother tongue was Semitic.[18] In other words, it is a Jewish-Christian psalm comparable with other instances of this genre.[19]

In one other important respect Lohmeyer differed from his predecessors and successors. The NRSV translates τοῦτο φρονεῖτε ἐν ὑμῖν ὃ καὶ ἐν Χριστῷ Ἰησοῦ (v. 5) as: "Let the same mind be in you that was in Christ Jesus." Lohmeyer considered such a translation impossible on the grounds that the demonstrative τοῦτο always has a retrospective reference in Paul. It can refer to something following only if it is followed by a substantive, an infinitive, or a clause introduced by ὅτι, ἵνα, etc.[20] Lohmeyer concluded that the two segments of v. 5 were self-contained. τοῦτο φρονεῖτε ἐν ὑμῖν ("Think this among yourselves") sums up the *previous* exhortation. ὃ καὶ ἐν Χριστῷ Ἰησοῦ ("What [was] in Christ Jesus") is a quotation formula that introduces the psalm.[21]

1.2. Analysis of the Stanzas

Lohmeyer's structural analysis was accompanied by an analysis of content in terms of a metaphysic of being.[22] The contrasts between divinity and humanity are described in terms of *form*. It is not sinfulness and holiness, mutability and immutability, or might and impotence that are juxtaposed but divine and human form. The human form is accompanied by death as by a dark shadow. The divine figure is necessarily bound to that of life. From this first contrast a second follows. The divine figure dwells in the sphere of *being,* and the human figure in that of *becoming,* first in human existence and then in death. *Becoming and death* define the human figure; *being and life* define the divine figure. The unifying concept which makes possible these contrasts is that of the figure or form [German, *Gestalt*]. The one who overcomes does so through the pure, divine act. The essence of this figure is determined by his act, and his act by his form.

When Lohmeyer sought a historical source for this metaphysical conception of two worlds standing in dialectical contradiction, he found "only one material analogy on Near Eastern soil: the message of Zoroaster."[23] Here the norm of the moral was posited as the ultimate determination of all existence. The religious ethical act determined the form and meaning of divine existence, and likewise the religious existence of the believer.

1.2.1. Primordial Temptation

ἐν μορφῇ θεοῦ ὑπάρχων ("existing/being in the form of God," v. 6) designates the initial essence of the bearer of the subsequent action. The Old Testament never refers to "the form of God." The revelations of God or his angels do not occur in the form of a figure, but in the indeterminate formlessness of cloud and wind, burning bush, smoke and fire. The epiphany of Yahweh before Elijah (1 Kings 19:11–12) is typical. In later Judaism it became possible to speak of heavenly figures. The visions of Enoch and Levi translated to heaven offer further evidence.[24] This trend is also found in Philo.[25] We cannot explore what motivated this change. More important is the idea expressed in the phrase "being in the form of God." "Form" cannot denote the element "in which" a being exists or the substrate from which something particular is formed. It is itself a particular. Yet the preposition "in" requires the formless indeterminateness of an element that conceals within itself the possibilities of having form.

ἐν μορφῇ θεοῦ ὑπάρχων thus refers to two facts: the indeterminateness of the substrate and the determinateness of the one who acts. The colorless generality of the expression serves the thought that all being comes about only through the pure act. The genitive "form of God" implies that it is not God himself who is the subject of the pure action. Yet the act is characteristic of God. Thus the bearer of this action is "like God," yet is distinct from God. He has at his disposal the uniqueness of an essential relation to God, yet it still lies in the twilight of indeterminateness. It is, as it were, posited as the possibility that will only become actual reality through the specific deed. The two expressions "being in the form of God" and "being like God" are alike, but for that reason different.

Lohmeyer found confirmation in the declaration οὐχ ἁρπαγμὸν ἡγήσατο τὸ εἶναι ἴσα θεῷ ("considered it not plunder to be like God"). In classical Greek, nouns formed by adding -μος or -μα to the verbal stem almost never denote a future deed but one completed in the past. In Koine Greek the usage may be less rigid but has sunk to the realm of jocular triviality. Examples of the somewhat rare ἁρπαγμός suggest booty, plunder, something obtained to which one was not entitled.[26] But this in itself did not settle the question whether "being like God" was something to be possessed in the future or something already possessed. Lohmeyer saw elements in both and found resolution in Iranian cosmology.[27]

At this point difficulties in discussing Lohmeyer's analysis are compounded by conflicting interpretations of Zoroastrianism.[28] According to Lohmeyer, two beings—"twins"—stand over against each other: Ahura Mazda and Angra Mainyu, or Ohrmazd and Ahriman. Both have "divine form." That they separate into the antithesis of light and darkness, truth and lie, good and evil has its ground in the fact that both stand under the idea of the good. The one has chosen it; the other has rejected it. Their decision has made them what they are. The one has obtained its being as the Lord of the divine realm of light; the other his being as Lord of the satanic realm of darkness. One is the epitome of the good and the divine; the other the epitome of evil and the satanic. The two are locked in mortal combat.

Lohmeyer saw in this mythical picture a profound perception of reality. The idea of the good appears as the condition of a dialectical process. Ohrmazd, the good, becomes the object of his own decision; his being is determined by his deed. In the same way, the figure in the psalm is determined by his deed. Through his determination not to treat being "like God" as "plunder," he ultimately is given that which he refused to steal. To put it more generally in the language of Goethe: Strive to possess what you have inherited.[29] In Christian terms, "the idea of temptation is none other than a religious formula for the dialectical stuggle between good and evil."[30] In positing "the idea of the good as a transcendent reality," faith experiences itself and the world as God's creation. Temptation accompanies the idea of creation "like a dark shadow."

οὐχ ἁρπαγμὸν ἡγήσατο does not refer to an event in history but points to a primordial myth that alludes to the origin of evil. It implies a possibility that was rejected on a pretemporal level. The fact of choice and decision points to questions of the origin of evil and the relationship of hostile powers to God. The possibility of being "like God" is alluded to in the creation narrative (Gen. 3:5), which also deals with primeval history. But it is the late Jewish belief in Satan, which Lohmeyer also traced to Iranian influence, that provides the antithesis for the figure in the psalm.[31] Satan is "the power that strives to be like God."[32] He rules the earth by dint of stolen power. He is the prince of the world and the "God of our age" (2 Cor. 4:4; cf. Rev. 13:4). In the temptation stories he offers to bestow on Jesus authority over the kingdoms of the world in return for worship of himself (Matt. 4:8–9; Luke 4:6–8). In the New Testament Jesus' task is "to break the rule of Satan."[33]

The first stanza is awesome, but its meaning is indeterminate. In retrospect Lohmeyer discerned a dialectic that corresponds to the three phases of the existence of the servant figure: preexistence, earthly existence, and postexistence. "The first stanza presents the thesis: the original being of the divine figure. Two stanzas present the antithesis: historical existence in human lowliness. Three stanzas declare the synthesis: the revelation of the *Kyrios* to whom the universe bows."[34]

1.2.2. Self-Emptying of the Servant

The second stanza moves from pretemporal existence on the divine plane to temporal existence in history. The adversative particle ἀλλά ("but") governs both this stanza (v. 7) and the next (v. 8). The decision between seizing and not seizing has analogies with the teaching of Zoroaster, but humiliation unto death introduces a new element. With it the psalmist introduces a burning problem for Jewish piety since the Babylonian exile. How may the suffering of the people of God be reconciled with the conviction of divine election? He answers it by means of a pair of concepts—humiliation and exaltation—which express "the law that governs this divine process."[35] Thereby "the divine meaning of history is disclosed, and all suffering becomes a step along the way to the full reality of this meaning. Thus . . . all suffering is resolved [German, *aufgehoben*] in the well-known double sense of the word: it is simultaneously negated and preserved."[36] The action of the one who empties himself thus fulfills "a law which flows from the very being of God." To put it in a religious rather than a philosophical way, God opposes the proud but gives grace to the humble (Prov. 3:34; 1 Peter 5:5). He exalts the meek (Luke 1:52). Therefore, the children of God have a moral obligation to humble themselves (Matt. 23:12; cf. Luke 14:11; 18:14).

The word "emptied" (ἐκένωσεν) evokes the image of a vessel that retains its form after the contents have been poured out. But to Lohmeyer the term could be understood only in the sense of total surrender and self-sacrifice. "Form" is not something external to content. "What is internal is also external, and what is external is also internal."[37] It is meaningless to ask what "substance" was emptied. "The two realms of the divine and the human are indeed substantially separate. There can be no bridging of this substantial separation. What alone overcomes this deepest chasm is the purity of the moral act. Yet the act of this self-sacrifice occurs through a divine figure. For this reason the figure has to create for himself a substantial new existence in the self-giving. It is 'the form of a servant.' "[38]

This servant role is not to be understood in the general sense in which Israel saw itself as the servant of Yahweh. The psalm makes it clear that δοῦλος means "slave," and is the antithesis of κύριος, "Lord." The term "can only imply that the most extreme human degradation is necessary and is required for the divine significance of this figure." The paradigm for such a figure is given in the Servant Songs of Deutero-Isaiah, especially of Isaiah 53. "For this reason these lines can remain far removed from any concrete historical significance. We cannot even say that the words refer to birth. They continue to live entirely by the purity and generality of divine meaning, as laid down as prophecy in the songs of Deutero-Isaiah."[39]

1.2.3. Death of the Son of Man

The third stanza (v. 8) stands in parallel to the second. Both strophes are governed by the ἀλλά ("but") in v. 7. Whereas the second stanza describes the beginning of the subject's historical life, the third describes his end. In so doing it presents death, not as the inevitable natural termination of life, but as a moral act in fulfilment of obedience. But the opening line presents grammatical difficulties. One might have expected a genitive following σχήματι (i.e., "in form of . . .") parallel to the references to the "form of God" and "form of a servant." Moreover, the juxtaposition ὡς ἄνθρωπος is "linguistically impossible" in Greek.[40] Lohmeyer sought to resolve these difficulties by proposing to translate the expression back into Aramaic. Thus the ὡς corresponds to כְּ ("like") as in the expression כְּבַר אֱנָשׁ, "like a son of man," i.e., "like a man." The term could serve as a designation either for a human being or a divine emissary. Lohmeyer suggested that כְּ was inserted in the visions of Daniel, the books of Enoch, and the Apocalypse of Ezra to remove ambiguity when referring to a transcendent figure.[41]

The awkward phrasing of the opening line of v. 8 highlights the sorites that Lohmeyer detected in the correspondence between the last line of the second stanza and the first line of the third. At the same time it points to "the activity of the divinely sent redeemer" who in obedience embraced death.[42] The being and actions of this "Son of Man" figure were determined by the "law of God," which decrees that "the way to the highest glory of existence as *kyrios* leads through the humiliation of death. . . . The entire poem rests on the perception that human humiliation is the inalienable precondition of divine exaltation."[43]

Just as ἐκένωσεν implies entry into the human realm, ἐταπείνωσεν implies entry into the realm of death. In the first half of the psalm the divine figure journeys through three realms: the heavenly, the earthly, and the under-the-earthly.

This journey anticipates the return journey in the second half and the worship of all in heaven, earth, and under the earth (v. 10). At this point Lohmeyer drew a distinction between what he considered to be the theology of the poem and the theology of Paul.[44] For the author of the poem, like the authors of John and Hebrews, death is the dark, divine riddle through which access is gained to the Father. The hour of death is the hour of glorification. For Paul, on the other hand, the manner of Christ's death is the ultimate offense and folly. Death belongs to the sphere of the human. Only in the resurrection, which does not belong to death but occurs after it by a divine miracle, does Christ's death on the cross become for believers the sign of "the power of God and the wisdom of God" (1 Cor. 1:24).

Paul's insertion of θανάτου δὲ σταυροῦ interrupts the meter and upsets the balance of the stanza. At the same time it brings the psalm into closer relationship with Paul's preaching of the cross (cf. 1 Cor. 1:17–18, 23; 2:8; Gal. 3:1; 5:11; 6:12; Col. 1:20; 2:14). The insertion is comparable with the comment in 1 Cor. 15:56 added to the catena of quotations in 1 Cor. 15:54–55 (Isa. 25:8 LXX; Hos. 13:14). It also fits the paraenetic concerns of the epistle, where martyrdom and the possibility of sharing a shameful and painful death like Christ's confronted both Paul and his readers (cf. Phil. 1:12–24, 27–30; 2:17; 3:17–21).

1.2.4. Exaltation and Bestowal
of the Name above Every Name

διὸ ("therefore") marks the midpoint of the psalm, linking the two strophes and changing the direction. In the first half, the "Son of Man" was the subject and object of his own actions as he made his way through the realms of divinity, humanity, and death. But now God is the subject of a twofold action that directly affects the "Son of Man" and as a consequence the entire universe. The sequence of events gives expression to "a rational necessity,"[45] which was veiled at the beginning, but which reaches its climax in the final strophe.

ὑπερύψωσεν ("exalted highly") is a hapax legomenon.[46] Strictly speaking, the psalm contains no direct mention of resurrection. It celebrates what elsewhere is depicted as the seating of Christ at God's right hand. In quoting the psalm Paul allows his characteristic proclamation of the raising of Christ to be displaced by "an inherited, non-Pauline interpretation of the fact of the resurrection," which reappears also in the Johannine writings. In building a bridge between Paul and John, the psalm is the seedbed of both theologies.[47]

The exaltation and bestowal of the name above all names appear susceptible to "adoptionist" interpretations comparable with Acts 2:36. In the first strophe, however, the figure is already said to be in the form of God. What is striking is the fact that the first strophe is characterized by emphasis on "form," while the second is characterized by emphasis on "name." The two terms correspond. But the figure does not simply receive back what he surrendered. He gains the honor and status of being *Kyrios*. "The *Kyrios*-thought, that was veiled at the beginning and extolled in the middle, is thereby unveiled as the kernel of the poem, and emerges with increasing clarity at the end in direct words stripped of all veiling."[48]

Form and name "constitute the totality of an appearance."[49] As in the Apocalypse, visions are accompanied by names, so here the bestowal of the name completes the reality of the figure. A counterpart in the Fourth Gospel is "flesh and spirit" (John 6:63). But these pairs are not to be identified with form and reality, as in Greek philosophy. They belong not to philosophy but to oriental myth. "The name which God bestows is doubtless *Kyrios*."[50] It denotes the totality of the divine reality, its form as well as its being. But "name" has also the function of denoting "the inner essence of this figure."

> *Kyrios* is as it were the side of Christ that is turned towards the world; πνεῦμα and λόγος are the sides turned primarily towards God. The former denotes the divine reality, the latter which contain within them the μορφὴ θεοῦ denote the divine meaning. Both are contained in the designation τὸ εἶναι ἴσα θεῷ. Therefore, in the words of the older expositors they can be both the *res rapta* [the thing seized] and the *res rapienda* [the thing to be seized]. With the figure of the *Kyrios* there is also posited that of the "Son of Man."[51]

Similar conclusions follow from Lohmeyer's analysis of the term "name" in the Old Testament and Judaism. God's name is praised, blessed, or feared. It is a freestanding expression of God's eternal presence and revelation.[52] Likewise, the "name" is important in primitive Christianity.[53] The identity of "name" and "word" is attested by Philo,[54] which points Lohmeyer to the origin of "name" theology in Logos speculation. But there is also a related development in those areas of primitive Christianity that celebrated the risen Christ's reception of the Spirit. In Phil. 2:9 God bestows upon the exalted Christ "the name above every name." In Acts 2:33 the exalted Christ receives the Spirit.[55] In the Christ-hymn in 1 Tim. 3:16 he is said to be "vindicated in the Spirit." One might be tempted to treat "name" and "Spirit" as identical terms, but Lohmeyer warns against it. "Name" and "Spirit" do not have identical functions. "Through the concept of the 'name' the exalted one is the medium between God and the world—in the most comprehensive sense of the word—through the concept of the Spirit he is the medium between God and the church."[56]

1.2.5. Universal Worship in the Name of Jesus

The final two stanzas are governed by ἵνα ("that," v. 10), which is the counterpart to the ἀλλά ("but," v. 2). Both are followed by two clauses linked by καί ("and"), echoing a theme from Deutero-Isaiah:

> By myself I have sworn,
> > from my mouth has gone forth in righteousness
> > a word that shall not return:
> "To me every knee shall bow,
> > every tongue shall swear."
> > [ὅτι ἐμοὶ κάμψει πᾶν γόνυ
> > καὶ ὀμεῖται πᾶσα γλῶσσα τὸ θεόν]"
> > > (Isa. 45:23 NRSV; Greek LXX)

The quotation occurs in slightly different form in Rom. 14:11, where it is introduced by γέγραπται γάρ ("For it is written") and conflated with ζῶ ἐγώ ("As I live").[57] To Lohmeyer, there was an element of timelessness in the confession. But the introduction of the name of Jesus transforms the quotation. Whereas in the Hebrew Bible it is not uncommon to approach God in his name,[58] the psalm declares that all creation will approach God "in the name of Jesus [ἐν τῷ ὀνόματι Ἰησοῦ]." Thus the crucified and exalted Jesus is the ground of the universe's access to God and also the object of its praise.[59] The threefold division of the cosmos as heaven, earth, and hell corresponds to similar divisions in Rev. 5:3 and Ignatius, *Trall.* 9.1. It is striking that the psalm contains no reference to the church. Indeed, the entire epistle makes only two passing references to the church.[60] The psalm, like the epistle, is concerned with the cosmic significance of Christ's lordship.

1.2.6. Universal Acclaim that Jesus Christ is Lord

The voiceless posture and uttered confession represent the response of humanity: past, present, and future. "Jesus Christ is Lord" is not simply the confession of the believing community (as in Rom. 10:9 and 1 Cor. 12:3; or the Maranatha prayer, 1 Cor. 16:22; Rev. 22:20; *Did.* 10.6; and possibly Phil. 4:5). As in the briefer form "Jesus is Lord" (1 Cor. 12:3) there is no limiting "our." Yet there can be no doubt that it preserves an old liturgical tradition. Jesus is not simply Lord of the community, but Lord of the world. What is new is the title *Christ.* Nothing in the psalm has hinted at the messianic office of Christ in the specific sense. Hence Lohmeyer concluded that "Christ" is used here like a proper name, as the word order also indicates.[61]

The final line leads the solemn praise to its ultimate ground and goal. It corresponds to Jewish practice that was also followed by the early church. Here it has a particular ground, for the act of God is the turning point of the poem. It alone has created the possibility of confessing the "Lord Jesus Christ." The act initiated in the first stanza, whereby the figure did not grasp at being like God, is paradoxically consummated in the sixth with the universal acclaim of Jesus as Lord. The sorites is thus completed.

Lohmeyer went on to note a further puzzling feature: the addition of the anarthrous πατρός in the final line. The insertion might be due to rhythmic considerations, so that "Father" counterbalances "Christ" in the previous line. But why the word "Father" in particular? It cannot refer to the Father of the faithful, for the poem nowhere speaks of believers. "Father" of Christ? Thus there would be an allusion to the primitive title of Jesus: "Son of God." Lohmeyer left open the possibility that it might refer to the "Father of the world." Admittedly the expression is rare (cf. Eph. 3:15). The substance, if not the term, is found in the Johannine writings and occasionally in Paul. The early Christian need to find a surname for God is understandable. The title *Kyrios* that otherwise in Jewish belief is bestowed upon God has now been bestowed upon Jesus. This bestowal means that the world is freed from the yoke of the devil, brought back to the unity with God celebrated in the praise of the universe's confession. For this unity, which ultimately goes back to the act of God, a more appropriate word than "Father" can scarcely be found. The replacement of κύριος ὁ θεός by θεὸς πατήρ attests a fundamental difference between Jewish and primitive Christian thought.[62]

1.3. Use of the Psalm in the Eucharist

Unlike many Old Testament psalms, this psalm contains no reference to the psalmist. In this regard it might be compared with the Prologue of the Fourth Gospel or some of the Solomonic and Gnostic odes. The absence of personal reference is also a feature of other early Christ-songs such as 1 Tim. 3:16; 1 Peter 3:18, 22; Ignatius, *Trall.* 9 and *Eph.* 19.2–3; the concluding doxology of the *Didascalia;* the prayer of thanksgiving in the *Apostolic Constitutions;* and the confession of faith at baptism in Hippolytus's *Apostolic Tradition.*[63]

Clearly this creation of a nameless poet and prophet possessed a "prophetic" authority prior to Paul. Its eschatological orientation—culminating in universal adoration—suggested to Lohmeyer that it enjoyed a status more elevated than the impromptu hymns, lessons, revelations, tongues, and interpretations that were shared at routine church gatherings (1 Cor. 14:26). A more appropriate setting would be the Eucharist (Acts 2:46–47). The Palestinian character and the authority enjoyed by the psalm confirmed Lohmeyer in his belief that the psalm had its origin in the eucharistic liturgy of the Jerusalem church. The celebration of Christ's death in the Eucharist coincided with the theme of martyrdom that runs through Philippians (1:12–25; 2:17; 3:17–21; 4:13). Thus Paul could hold up the psalm "as an act of sacred worship and service to which believers are now likewise called on the way to martyrdom." Lohmeyer saw a link with the Johannine Prologue: "We beheld his glory" (John 1:14). But the psalm was prior to both Paul and John. "It is thus one of the most precious documents of primitive Christianity and an illuminating example of the rich, manifold forces that were alive in it."[64]

1.4. The Origin of the Psalm's Christology

The ultimate result of Christ's historical existence is lordship over the world. In this regard, the psalm may be compared with the confession of Rev. 11:15: "The kingdom of the world has become the kingdom of our Lord and of his Messiah, and he will reign for ever and ever." Lohmeyer traced the origin of this type of christology to the universal dominion given to "one like a son of man" in Dan. 7:13–14. As already noted, Lohmeyer detected traces of this christology in the expression "found as a man" (Phil. 2:7).[65] However, the figure in the apocalyptic vision in Daniel is evidently an angelic being who appears "*like* a son of man." Moreover, in Daniel there is no mention of him coming down to earth and certainly no hint of his death. For these elements we have to turn to the Servant Song of Isaiah 53.

It is not a question of the meaning of the Servant Song in the context of Deutero-Isaiah, but of its later interpretation.[66] The element of abasement comes to the fore in the LXX. *1 Clement* 16.3–14 quotes extensively from the LXX version of Isaiah 53 with reference to Christ, though without apparent reference to Philippians.[67]

Still later, rabbinic sources depicted the messiah in terms of the paradigm in Deutero-Isaiah.[68] Lohmeyer concluded that the Son of Man tradition was probably united with that of the Servant of the Lord in pre-Christian times. At the very least, the Servant Songs provided impetus for the thought of redemption through the suffering and death of a divine emissary.

1.5. Pre- and Postexistence

In common with many interpreters, Lohmeyer took the opening stanza to allude to "pretemporal temptation."[69] The resolve not to treat his status as plunder is undertaken on the level of pure possibility as a "preexistent act" on the plane of "timeless reality" in the context of a "dualistic metaphysic."[70] As such, the one who is "in the form of God" is less concrete than the preexistent Son in Paul and Hebrews, or the preexistent Logos in John. Preexistence corresponds to postexistence, separated by the life and death of the servant whose actions in history give expression to "a divine law." The psalm does not speak, like the Fourth Gospel, of Jesus' "going to the Father" by his own deliberate act (John 16:10). Rather, as the archaic language of Acts 2:36 puts it: "God has made this Jesus . . . Lord and Christ." Nor does it speak of a Jesus who like others was a historical human being, but of one who in his humanity was "the Son of Man." There is no thought, as in Paul, of the Son of God who was the same in his earthly and heavenly existence. Rather, we are confronted with what Lohmeyer perceived to be a more primitive christology in which the two forms of Christ's life are determined by a single act of God.[71]

1.6. The Psalm and John's Logos Christology

Although the ultimate metaphysical roots of the psalm lie in a Zoroastrian understanding of good and evil, Lohmeyer was convinced that over the centuries they had taken root in Judaism. Thus the christological features of the psalm, like Paul's cosmic christology in 1 Cor. 8; 2 Cor. 8:9; and Col. 1:15–20, are not products of "acute 'Hellenization,' but direct Jewish heritage."[72] This conclusion is confirmed by the way that the psalm juxtaposes and correlates "Son of Man" and *Kyrios.* Nevertheless, the psalm embodies a metaphysic in which one "who was in the form of God," and thus different from God, is "found as the Son of Man," and is exalted by God as *Kyrios.*

> The unity of the poem is substantially the divine law: *per aspera ad astra.* Or to put it in a Jewish way: through human lowliness to divine majesty. . . . Through this law now given of the unity of human lowliness and divine exaltation this act of God becomes one and the same revelation. Cosmology and soteriology are thus identical.[73]

"This bearer" of "the meaning of the history of the world" is the full revelation of "the primal image of God and at the same time the revealed example for the world of its process and being, its action and life. In Johannine language he is the λόγος τοῦ θεοῦ, or in short, the Logos."[74]

1.7. The Psalm and the Epistle to the Hebrews

The mighty chord sounded at the beginning of Hebrews presents Christ as the end of a series of revelations, because he was their beginning and center. He is the heir of the universe, because he was mediator of its creation. He is the eternal image of God and reflection of his glory (δόξα, Heb. 1:3), and is therefore superior to the angels. All this finds a parallel with our psalm. Lohmeyer found it significant that the word δόξα also occurs in the last stanza of the psalm.[75] In the psalm Jesus is humbled and dies as Son of Man and slave, and is exalted as Kyrios; in Hebrews he dies as sacrificial victim, and enters God's presence as high priest and becomes heir of the universe. In both Philippians and Hebrews Christ is the example, and both share the common theme of the rejection of a primordial temptation. Thus the readers of Hebrews are exhorted to look "to Jesus the pioneer and perfecter of our faith, who for the sake of the joy that was set before him endured the cross, disregarding its shame, and has taken his seat at the right hand of the throne of God" (Heb. 12:2; cf. 2:14; 4:15).

It has often been remarked that Hebrews does not speak of the resurrection of Jesus, but links his death with entry into the heavenly sanctuary. Whereas in Philippians death and exaltation are united by the divine act, in Hebrews Jesus the high priest makes his way through death directly into the sanctuary where he is exalted as savior (Heb. 9:11–12, 24–28; 10:19–22; 12:12). The uniqueness of Hebrews lies in the way that it presents in terms of cultic law the dialectic of the psalm.[76] The psalm hints indirectly at what in Hebrews is identifed as the divine purpose in the sending of the Son: "that through death he might destroy the one who has the power of death, that is, the devil" (Heb. 2:14). Whereas the psalm celebrates the universal lordship of Christ, Hebrews focuses on the believing community, first in the history of Israel and then in the Christian church.[77]

1.8. The Psalm and the Synoptic Gospels

The principal link with the Synoptic Gospels is the Son of Man theme. But the Gospels introduce a new element "in order to solve the mystery of the Son of Man figure. It lies in the concept of the Spirit of God."[78] This theme underlies the narratives of the baptism and temptation of Jesus, as well as numerous sayings. It may be argued that the Spirit is constitutive for the title Christ: that is, the one anointed by the Spirit at his baptism. However, Lohmeyer felt that he could not pursue this theme in the context of his monograph. He concluded that in confessing Jesus Christ as Lord the psalm brought together the cosmic Son of Man theme and national messianic expectations. The psalm "stands purely on the side of belief in the Son of Man, and preserves messianic faith principally in the title Christ which is reduced to a personal name."[79]

1.9. Metaphysics and Myth

Lohmeyer sought to set the psalm in its broadest religious and metaphysical context. Jewish piety rests on a metaphysic that separates God from the world. In the course of history, as relations with other peoples and cultures became acute,

God's relationship to the world became increasingly enigmatic, and the world became transformed into the scene of alien and ultimately ungodly powers. While metaphysics appear to undermine the foundations of Judaism, according to which Israel is the sole nation chosen by God, metaphysics are nevertheless posited by God's existence insofar as God is bound to Israel and to the world. For Deutero-Isaiah, Israel was the historical, visible link between God and the world. As God's servant, the Jewish nation stood eternally with God and against the world. The coincidence of suffering and grace, distress and salvation revealed the divine meaning of history through God's divine deed.

To Lohmeyer, this perspective contained all the problems of later Judaism.[80] Historical reality called into question Israel's status. The nation saw itself as the pious guardian of the values and laws for the world. But in practice they were never found in purity. Almost every page of Jewish sacred literature laments their absence and condemns the failure of the people to do the will of God. The apocalyptic figure of the Son of Man is to be understood against this background, for it presents one, though not perhaps the mainstream, solution to this problem. The ultimate solution to the problem of the meaning of God and the world is to be found in God himself in some way entering the human condition, embracing suffering and death. "[F]or the sake of the ultimate actualization of this meaning, it requires that the one who performs this act—it is a kind of second creation of the world— become "like God," i.e., become the "Lord of the world."[81]

> [In this perspective] which sees the figure of the Son of Man realized in the historical person of Jesus, lie as enclosed in a kernel the manifold forms of christology which suddenly unfold in primitive Christianity. It establishes the right of Jesus to the title of *Kyrios*. In a profound sense it is the Old Testament name for God that is applied to him. It gives rise to the possibility of a Logos perspective, for Logos is the evident meaning of God in the world and in history. It explains the riddle and miracle of his birth and death. And it may do all this because it is bound by an indissoluble spiritual tie to the mother soil of Jewish piety. It is that metaphysic of two worlds which is preserved after as before.[82]

This Christ-hymn is truly the *locus classicus* of primitive christology, for it brings together the most diverse lines of primitive Christian theology and piety and the fundamental problems of faith in a clear, unified picture of "*classic* greatness."[83]

2. RETROSPECTIVE COMMENTS

2.1. Form, Structure, and Purpose

Numerous scholars have accepted the view that the passage contains a hymn or psalm, but they have differed over its precise structure. We shall now look at some of the proposals.

2.1.1. Psalm, Hymn, or Rhetorical Prose?

Ralph P. Martin suggests that the psalm consisted of six couplets that could be chanted antiphonally.[84] But to achieve this order several lines have to be removed and treated as secondary additions: θανάτου δὲ σταυροῦ ("death on a cross"), ἐπουρανίων καὶ ἐπιγείων καὶ καταχθονίων ("in heaven and on earth, and under the earth"), and εἰς δόξαν θεοῦ πατρός ("to the glory of God, the Father"). Otfried Hofius also saw in the psalm a series of parallel couplets in metrical order with beats, comparable with psalms in the Old Testament and the *Odes of Solomon*.[85] He divided them into two corresponding halves, each of which ended with an additional line: θανάτου δὲ σταυροῦ and εἰς δόξαν θεοῦ πατρός. Likewise, Martin Hengel regards these lines as an integral part of an "inspirational song," consisting of seven double verses mostly in Semitic *parallelismus membrorum*. By such "inspired songs about Christ" the *"Christological confession* of the early Christian congregation was advanced."[86]

The variety of proposals has prompted Morna D. Hooker to question the idea of tracing the section back to a pre-Pauline hymn.[87] Gerald F. Hawthorne sits on the fence. He acknowledges "the basic hymnic structure" of the passage but declines "to specify the precise strophic structure of its composition."[88] Most recently Werner Kennel has undertaken a massive investigation of the common genre, or *Gattung,* of the early Christian hymn.[89] Once one raises the question of genre it is apparent that most subsequent writers have done what Lohmeyer did: they use the terms "hymn," "psalm," and "song" indiscriminately.[90]

In order to remedy this defect and place the study on a more scientific basis, Kennel proposes development of a typology that combines grammatical structure with semantic considerations. To examine Kennel's methodology here would take us too far afield. It must suffice to note that, when he applies it to three major candidates for the *Gattung* of "hymn," the Magnificat (Luke 1:46–55), Phil. 2:6–11, and Rev. 19:1–8, Kennel discovers considerable diversity. While all three texts make use of poetic features such as repetition, parallels, chiasm, and triplets, they do so in their own ways. The Magnificat maintains the tradition of Old Testament psalmody and has a doxological character, and the great Hallelujah of Rev. 19:1–8 qualifies it as a literary hymn. But Kennel is less sure about Philippians. "In Phil. 2,6–11 a doxological intention cannot be excluded, on the other hand it cannot be claimed either since a doxological introduction is lacking. But doxology may well be intended in v. 11b."[91] Although it exhibits features comparable with the other hymns, Phil. 2:6–11 shows most divergence from the *Gattung* of the hymn.

Others have compared the passage with the pagan hymns of the Graeco-Roman world. In his magisterial review, Klaus Berger observes that the pagan hymn corresponds to what in the New Testament is a prayer, and thus Phil. 2:6–11 is not to be placed in the ancient *Gattung* of ὕμνος.[92] It is more like an encomium.[93] Michael Lattke also doubts whether it has the form of a classical hymn, since it lacks a doxological opening.[94] In his brief but valuable overview, Edgar Krentz protests that, since we cannot be sure that any of the hymns cited in the New Testament are complete, the absence of traditional introductory invocations, petitions for aid, and concluding prayers does not mandate the rejection of our text as a hymn. Although our passage corresponds to Seneca's sequence of topics, some items are notably absent.[95] In light of these considerations and Lohmeyer's cogent argument for the essential completeness of our passage,[96] it seems doubtful whether Phil. 2:6–11 can be said to correspond to the hymn form of *pagan* antiquity.

In the meantime, Robert H. Gundry has recommended abandonment of the hymn theory. He argues that, "when we divide Phil. 2:6–11 according to its participial and finite verbal phrases, there comes to light *an overall concentric structure of meaning,* which receives additional emphasis from a number of chiasms, some of them unnoted before, as well as from other parallels often noted in early studies."[97] Gundry divides the passage into paired couplets, noting assonance and euphony, and concludes that it "represents an example of Paul's own exalted prose . . . rather than an early Christian hymn whose lines of fairly equal length Paul has disequalized with additions."[98] This structural analysis is patently linked with a theological agenda that includes Pauline authorship, the interpretation of the self-emptying as death and not incarnation, and above all a defense of preexistence based on the following chiasmus:

A. Preexistent divine being (I–II [6a and 6bc])
  B. Slave-like death (III–IV [7a and 7b])
    C. Incarnation as a human being (V–VI [7c and 7d])
  B′. Death on a cross (VI–VIII [8a and 8bc])
A′. Postexistent acknowledgment as divine (IX–XII [9a; 9b; 10a, 10b, 10c; and 11a, 11b, 11c])[99]

Space does not permit examination of Gundry's elaborate analysis. However, consideration of Gundry's outline points up problems. The segments are very unequal in form and length.[100] This example of "exalted prose" is curiously lopsided. In order to achieve this arrangement, the center of the chiasmus is made to consist of two participial clauses that lack main verbs (ἐν ὁμοιώματι ἀνθρώπων γενόμενος [7c], and εὑρεθεὶς ὡς ἄνθρωπος [7d]). The preceding segments consist of a verse and half a verse, while the final two segments consist of a verse and three verses respectively. Whereas Lohmeyer's analysis arranged the verses into two equal halves, each with its own theme (the servant's self-humiliation; God's exaltation of him), Gundry's analysis puts the entire second half into the fifth and final section of the chiasmus, which he labels "Postexistent acknowledgment as divine (IX–XII)." In the process, God's exaltation of the servant is subsumed under postexistent acknowledgment of his divinity. God does not figure at all in the outline. One cannot but wonder how much the conservative theological agenda has driven the radical formal analysis.

In the face of this variety of proposals two considerations appear to vindicate Lohmeyer with regard to the form of the passage. The first turns on the possibility of translating the passage back into Aramaic, implying that it first existed in Aramaic prior to the Greek version in Philippians. Such an attempt was made by Paul P. Levertoff and was printed in W. K. Lowther Clarke's early review of Lohmeyer's work, which was perhaps the first study in English to recognize its importance.[101] More recently Joseph A. Fitzmyer has made a fresh attempt, which differs from previous attempts by trying to use Aramaic contemporary with the first century.[102] Fitzmyer observed that "One of Lohmeyer's notable contributions to the study of Phil. 2:6–11 was to set forth the hymn in two strophes of three verses each (vv. 6–8 and 9–11). Key to the division of the passage into strophes and verses was the three-beat line."[103] But as Lowther Clarke noted, the theory works until the last two stanzas, when the pattern is disturbed by the allusion to Isa. 45:23. In the final stanza the beat appears to be correct, but it is at the expense of rhythm.

These problems together with the difference in length of lines gave rise to the sundry proposals to remove phrases and to turn the hymn into a series of couplets to be recited antiphonally. Nevertheless, Fitzmyer preferred to remain with Lohmeyer's proposal of an eighteen-line composition divided into two strophes of three-lined stanzas, "provided one recognizes that it is not possible to arrive at a perfect pattern of three beats to a line. If this attempt to retrovert Phil. 2:6–11 into a form of contemporary Aramaic is seen to be valid, it will at least support the contention that the passage represents a pre-Pauline rhetorical composition of Jewish-Christian origin."[104]

The other consideration that helps to vindicate Lohmeyer's reconstruction is his demonstration that the passage exhibits the logical form of a sorites.[105] This observation seems to have been almost universally ignored by Lohmeyer's successors, who have concentrated their enquiries on questions of rhythm, beat, and whether the alleged hymn could be sung antiphonally. But if every three lines form a unit of thought, which in turn constitutes the premise for the next three lines, the passage has a logical structure that requires the three-line arrangement Lohmeyer discovered in it.

To say this is not to deny that the passage could not have been rearranged in couplets to be sung or chanted antiphonally. After all, the variety of forms of the Lord's Prayer (Matt. 6:9–13; Luke 11:2–4; *Didache* 8) are best accounted for by the suggestion that the addition or subtraction of phrases was dictated by differing community usages.[106] But if the passage *as we have it in Philippians* has the logical structure that Lohmeyer discerned, other questions inevitably follow. Does not this form suggest some kind of mnemonic or teaching device for Christian instruction? Such a work could be recited or sung at the eucharist, but perhaps it was first learned by the convert as a *confession embodying a Christian interpretation of Jesus' life and death.* If the passage was originally a confession, rather than a hymn or psalm, absence of a doxology and reference to the psalmist's tribulations are readily understandable.

2.1.2. Sorites, Strophe, Antistrophe, Confession

Although they may seem anticlimactic, some further comments are required. We begin with reflections on the sorites and logical structure.[107] My first observation has to do with how one defines sorites. If we think of sorites as a logical, deductive argument about a single subject, some qualification is called for. We do not have a continuous subject. The *one who did not seek to be like God* is the subject of the first strophe, and *God* who exalts him is the subject of the second. Nevertheless, the one who sacrificed himself figures in every stanza in a progression that links the first with the last. He who was the visible expression of God, and did not exploit his status so as to be like God, is universally acclaimed as "Lord" to the glory of God the Father.

The argument is not a series of logical deductions from a self-evident premise.

The first strophe is not a logical demonstration but an *interpretation* of the life and death of Jesus. The second strophe concerning events in the world beyond is also an *interpretation*. In this regard, I would want to express things somewhat differently from Lohmeyer. While it is correct to say that the passage does not speak of resurrection as such, nevertheless the divine exaltation celebrated in the fourth stanza must have been linked to the conviction that Jesus was in some sense alive. Otherwise the passage would at best be a celebration of a slain martyr who had been mistakenly crucified as a blasphemous seducer. At worst it would be the mistaken celebration of one who was rightly condemned. The argument is not presented as a series of syllogisms of a kind that Cicero and Sextus Empiricus found faulty. It is a confession of faith in poetic form with its own hermeneutical commitments and interpretations which challenge those of the church's adversaries. Nevertheless, these interpretations trace a series of connections with events that are both logical and doxological.

We have used the term *strophe* to denote the two sets of three corresponding stanzas. The first strophe describes humiliation resulting in death; the second describes exaltation resulting in universal acclaim. In view of this pattern, it might be better if we could revive Greek usage and speak of the first three stanzas as the strophe and the second three as the antistrophe.[108] For the second strophe, or antistrophe, represents a return movement that answers to the movement of the strophe. Just as the three stanzas of the strophe unfold the narrative from the decision not to exploit divine status, to the assumption of the role of a slave, and to death as the ultimate act of obedience, so the corresponding three stanzas of the antistrophe unfold the narrative of God's reversal and vindication from the bestowal of the name above all names, to the universal reverence in the name of Jesus, and finally to his acclaim as Lord to the glory of the Father. That which he refused to seize at the outset is freely bestowed at the conclusion. Thus the passage is Greek in language and form, yet its content is thoroughly Jewish in its images and metaphors.

The confession embodies and elaborates the most primitive Christian confession of all, "Jesus is Lord" (1 Cor. 12:3; cf. 8:6; Rom. 10:9). In 1 Cor. 12:3 this confession is presented as the antithesis or counter-confession to Ἀνάθεμα Ἰησοῦ ("Let Jesus be cursed"). The latter is best explained as the slogan of Jesus' adversaries, linked to the fact that Jesus had died the death of one who was under the curse of God (Deut. 21:22–23; Gal. 3:13; cf. 11QTemple 64:6–10).[109] The demand to curse Jesus was a ready test of whether one adhered to the orthodoxy, which condemned Jesus, or whether one was a Christian. To Paul, both the demand and compliance with it were proof that whoever uttered such words was not speaking by the Spirit of God. Conversely, to confess that "Jesus is Lord" is a sign that one is speaking by the Spirit. To the author of our passage, the death of Jesus was to be understood not as a curse, but as the outcome of obedience which received its due vindication. What we have in this passage is—to reiterate Fitzmyer—"a pre-Pauline rhetorical composition of Jewish Christian origin." Its purpose was to give a Christian interpretation and confession of Jesus' death in a form that could be memorized and remembered in dark hours and also used in worship.

Whether one would want to trace such a Hellenized form of confession and praise back to the Jerusalem church would depend on how Hellenized one judges that church to have been. If the work was a confession used in the Jerusalem church, one might have expected to have found other traces of it. Yet if Lohmeyer was right in seeing connections with other New Testament literature, one would have to admit that the ideas of the passage, though not its format, were seminal. Lohmeyer suggested Damascus and Antioch as possible places of origin. One might envisage either city as more hospitable to Hellenistic rhetoric. While attempts to identify a place of origin must be speculative, it is not impossible that Philippi itself was the place. If "What was in Christ Jesus" was a quotation formula,[110] Paul may have been reminding his readers of a confessional poem that they already knew.

2.2. Metaphysics and Myth

Lohmeyer's work was not only a brilliant essay in form-critical analysis. Literary study was integrated with the study of the history of religions, which was set in the context of a philosophical worldview. Lohmeyer's work invites comparison with that of his predecessor at Breslau, Rudolf Bultmann. Though they shared common concerns, the two were poles apart. Lohmeyer was committed to an idealist philosophy indebted to that of his friend and colleague, Richard Honigswald. Bultmann worked within a philosophical framework that was shaped by Marburg Neo-Kantianism and Heidegger's existentialism.[111]

Even before publication of *Kyrios Jesus,* differences had come to a head through Lohmeyer's review of Bultmann's *Jesus.*[112] To Lohmeyer, Bultmann's work was "a book about Jesus without Jesus" (col. 433). Bultmann reciprocated with the complaint that Lohmeyer's *Vom Begriff der religiösen Gemeinschaft* was not theology but philosophy.[113] Like Lohmeyer, Bultmann traced what he perceived to be the salvation myth of the New Testament to the Iranian myth of the primal man and the cosmic conflict of good and evil. But he gave it a radically different interpretation. "The *oriental-Gnostic redeemer-myth,* that goes back so far as we can see to the Iranian primal-man myth, penetrated more strongly than other motifs of different origin. . . . Already for Paul, Christ is the eternal Son of God, who left the heavenly world, in order—clothed as a man and thus concealed from the demonic rulers of the world—to achieve his redemptive work through death and resurrection and then be exalted as Lord (1 Cor. 2:7–8; Phil. 2:6–11)."[114] Bultmann went on to launch his celebrated demythologizing program with his essay on "New Testament and Mythology" (1941). Lohmeyer responded in a lecture on "The Right Interpretation of the Mythological" (1944).[115]

To Lohmeyer, Bultmann's program called for the abandonment of the mythological thought of the New Testament "like an empty and useless husk. . . . For existentialist philosophy is concerned with man, whereas myth is concerned with God and gods. The only truth behind myth is therefore, as Bultmann says, the understanding of human existence which its imagery enshrines."[116] Lohmeyer took a diametrically opposite view. "[M]yth is the mode in which God reveals himself, and . . . the apparently empty and worn-out husk is the symbol of the historicity of that eschatological revelation of God in which 'the Word became flesh.' . . . But the language of myth is not that of science. In the one we have imagery, parable, and the reality of a divine-human event: in the other, the abstract concept and the truth of historical fact."[117] The subject matter of a discipline must determine its methods. In this regard, existentialism has no more right "to pontificate" about theology than about physics.[118]

In retrospect, it would appear that Bultmann and Lohmeyer were using "myth" in somewhat different senses. To Bultmann, myth appears to have been what Earl R. MacCormac termed "the false attribution of reality to a suggestive metaphor."[119] Consequently, the ancient supernatural myths have to be stripped away to lay bare the truths of existence. To Lohmeyer, myth was more like metaphor that cannot be turned into nonmetaphorical truth.[120] It might embody and exemplify what Lohmeyer peceived to be laws which govern life. But in the nature of the case, faith must make its affirmations and express its commitments through image and metaphor. In this regard, it is Lohmeyer's approach that appears to be vindicated by current study.[121]

2.3. Exegetical Issues

If Phil. 2:6–11 is essentially a Jewish-Christian confession, any satisfactory interpretation must be congruent with that context in three areas: (1) the Jewish monotheism out of which the church grew; (2) the location of key terms in semantic fields appropriate to that setting; and (3) the fact that Jesus was charged with being a satanic seducer and that the manner of his death suggested he was under a divine curse. With this in mind I shall focus on some key issues in Lohmeyer's discussion and the current debate.

2.3.1. ἐν μορφῇ θεοῦ

Instead of seeing v. 6 as an incongruous allusion to a preexistent state, several scholars have argued that "being in the form of God" is another way of saying "in the image of God." They point out that μορφή ("form") and εἰκών ("image") are used as interchangeable terms in the LXX and are regarded as synonyms elsewhere.[122] Others note that "form" is also a way of expressing "glory" (δόξα).[123] Stephen E. Fowl observes: "In the LXX the visible form of God is often described in terms of God's δόξα, God's glory and splendor, by which the majesty of God is made manifest to humanity. . . . It seems most adequate, then, to take the μορφή of God as reference to the glory, radiance and splendor by which God's majesty is made visible. By locating Christ in this glory, it conveys the majesty and splendor of his pre-incarnate state."[124] On the other hand, James D. G. Dunn contends that "of all the contexts or paradigms of thought within which the text may be read in the endeavour of historical exegesis (Son of God, Servant, Wisdom, Gnostic Redeemer myth), the one which provides the most coherent and most complete (the claim is relative) reading is Adam christology."[125]

Dunn sees five points of comparison, and notes the Christ/Adam paradigm elsewhere (Rom. 5; 1 Cor. 15; Heb. 2). However, of the last three points of comparison—"enslavement to corruption and sin," "submission to death," and "exalted and glorified"—the first fits the biblical Adam but not Christ, and the last two fit Christ but not Adam.[126] The first two are more substantive. If we grant that "in the form of God" is another way of saying "in the image of God" (Gen. 1:27), we may have an *indirect* allusion to Adam.[127] Dunn's other point of comparison is also substantive. The temptation to grasp equality with God (τὸ εἶναι ἴσα θεῷ, Phil. 2:6b) appears to echo the thought, if not the exact language, of Adam's temptation to be "like God" (ὡς θεοί, Gen. 3:5 LXX).

Two considerations suggest that the image/Adam allusion should be recognized. The first is the fact that attempts to translate our passage back into Aramaic draw on image terminology in their reconstructions.[128] The second is the growing awareness of the role of intertextuality. Instead of speaking about quotations, paradigms, and intentional allusion, it is often more appropriate to speak of the transposition of images, metaphors, and sign systems. On this level we are not talking about explicit reference, but about what Richard B. Hays calls "symbolic fields," "the embedding of fragments," "intertextual echoes," and "resonance."[129] On this view, we are concerned with hearing sensitivity and with reckoning that words and phrases may contain multiple allusions that invite attention and response.

When looked at in this light, our passage is replete with intertextual echoes that the author deploys to represent Jesus and to evoke imitation and worship. We need only recall how Lohmeyer brought together the images of the servant of the Lord and the Son of Man, which he reinterpreted in the light of Jesus' death on the cross. Similarly, our passage reinterprets christologically the universal worship of Yahweh in Isa. 45:23 and the title *Kyrios*. We do not have to choose between interpretations of ἐν μορφῇ θεοῦ that require us to see an allusion either to the glory of God or to Adam as God's primeval image. There seem to be echoes of both, especially in the traditions which link the two.[130] In Pauline thought Christ, the Son, is preeminently the image of God and also the manifestation of his glory (2 Cor. 4:4; cf. 3:18; Rom. 8:29; 1 Cor. 15:49).

Nevertheless, we must recognize that μορφή and εἰκών are not exact synonyms.[131] μορφή connotes visible appearance, whereas εἰκών is less specific.[132] If μορφή denotes visible appearance, the shape or form in which someone or something appears, use of μορφή in Phil. 2:6 suggests more than a simple comparison between Christ and Adam. While the biblical Adam was the image of God, he was not the visible appearance of God or the form which God took. Use of μορφή would be compatible with a vision or an epiphany in heaven (cf. *Pseudo-Clementine Homily* 17.7), but it would be equally compatible with *the visible* form or expression of God on earth. Thus, ἐν μορφῇ θεοῦ could very well allude to *one whose earthly life was a manifestation of God*.

Since our passage purports to celebrate the life *of the earthly Jesus* as the ground of his exaltation, we may ask what other traditions—especially traditions related to the cross and resurrection—may resonate with it and help us to hear it better. First, we may mention the tradition of Jesus' temptations.[133] Mark reports that Jesus "was in the wilderness forty days, tempted by Satan" (1:12). In Matthew and Luke the temptations are elaborated and given specific form (Matt. 4:1–11; Luke 4:1–13). Two of the temptations—to turn stones into bread and to perform a death-defying leap from the temple—are predicated on the premise, "If you are the Son of God. . . ." The remaining temptation is the offer of "all the kingdoms of the world and their glory [δόξα]," if only Jesus will worship Satan. In short, the essence of the temptations is *to be like God,* either through use of his authority as *Son of God,* or through obeisance to Satan in return for the dominion that God gave originally to Adam. By rejecting temptation and remaining faithful unto death, Jesus is given all authority in heaven and on earth (Matt. 28:18; cf. Luke 24:46–47).

In this light, ἐν μορφῇ θεοῦ ὑπάρχων[134] may be a counterpart to εἰ υἱὸς εἶ τοῦ θεοῦ (Matt. 4:3, 6; Luke 4:3, 9). "Son of God" alludes to the identification by the voice from heaven following Jesus' baptism and anointing by the Spirit (Matt. 3:17; cf. Luke 3:22). In the Synoptic context with its intertextual echoes of Psalm 2:7 and Isa. 42:1, the title refers to the newly anointed messianic king on whom God has put his Spirit, and who *as such* is God's Son.[135] There are strong grounds for seeing the image of God in terms of kingship and the role of God's representative.[136]

Two facets of the Gospel accounts may be noted. The first is the sequence in Luke's narrative. Between the baptism—which culminates in the pronouncement by the voice from heaven—and the temptation of Jesus, Luke inserts his genealogy. All three segments focus on sonship. Whereas Matthew traces Jesus' genealogy *from* Abraham to Joseph (Matt. 1:16), Luke traces his genealogy *backward* through Abraham down to "Adam, son of God" (Luke 3:38).[137] In other words, Luke draws attention to the implied connection and contrast between Adam and Christ, as son of God and king of the earth. The other facet of the Gospel accounts is the fact that Satan's εἰ υἱὸς εἶ τοῦ θεοῦ reappear in only slightly modified form in Peter's confession of Jesus as "the Messiah, the Son of the living God" (Matt. 16:16) and the high priest's question, "Are you the Messiah, the Son of God?" (Matt. 26:63).[138] Temptation, confession, and accusation all turn on the question of divine sonship.

In addition to the temptation tradition, we may mention the rumbling echoes of charges that Jesus was setting himself up as God.[139] The ensuing Beelzebul charge insinuated that Jesus had in fact entered into a pact with Satan.[140] It implied that Jesus was a seducer, empowered by an alien deity, and as such should be put to death (Matt. 10:24; 12:24; Mark 3:22; Luke 11:15; cf. Lev. 20:27; CD 12:2–3). Finally, there is the anathematization that we have already noted.[141] In view of these negative traditions, I see Phil. 2:6 as a repudiation of charges against Jesus, and vv. 7–8 as a Christian counterinterpretation. Jesus did not seek to exploit his status and authority to be "like God" in the manner to which Adam succumbed and to which Satan sought to induce him. Nor was he guilty of the charges leveled against him. As the visible manifestation of God, he sacrificed himself in obedience which led to the cross.

Thus my interpretation both questions and confirms that of Lohmeyer. It questions his situation of v. 6 on the level of pretemporal existence, but it confirms his belief that our passage has its roots in the conflict between good and evil, epitomized in the tradition of the personal conflict between Christ and Satan.[142]

2.3.2. ἁρπαγμός

So far we have not examined the term ἁρπαγμός, which some see as a decisive reason for situating v. 6 in the sphere of pretemporal decision. A case in point is N. T. Wright's detailed discussion.[143] Wright agrees with Dunn in asserting that "Adam-christology is central to the passage," and in seeing a contrast between Christ's obedience and Adam's sin, but he rejects Dunn's attempts to exclude allusions to the incarnation of a preexisting divine son. Wright wants to combine "Christ as Adam, Christ as Servant, and Christ the pre-existent one."[144] The way to do this lies in following R. W. Hoover's interpretation of ἁρπαγμός as "taking advantage" of something that one already possesses.[145] Thus the RSV gives the wrong idea in its translation: "did not count equality with God a thing to be grasped." It implies that Jesus was tempted to grasp at something that he did not yet possess. Wright prefers the NRSV: "did not regard equality with God as something to be exploited."[146] The passage means that "the one who, *before becoming human,* possessed divine equality did not regard that status as something to take advantage of, something to exploit, but instead interpreted it as a vocation to obedient humiliation and death."[147]

The interpretation of Hoover and Wright has not gone unchallenged.[148] It may well be that in context Wright is correct in treating ἁρπαγμός as "taking advantage" of something that one already possesses. The fallacy lies in assuming that this "something" *must* be personal, pretemporal existence. Just as other examples of ἁρπαγμός do not imply exploitation on a pretemporal plane, so it is here. In the context of our discussion of the temptation tradition, we saw that the temptations consisted precisely in the temptation to take advantage of Jesus' status as the messianic Son of God, which he had acquired through his anointing by the Spirit after his baptism. Thus the interpretation of ἁρπαγμός as not "taking advantage of" is fully consistent with treating Phil. 2:6 in terms of the narrated history of Jesus' life and activity.

Although ἁρπαγμός is found in the New Testament only in Phil. 2:6, there is perhaps a later echo. This suggestion is strengthed by the fact that some of the characteristic vocabulary of chap. 2 reappears transposed in chap. 3, where Paul reviews his life.[149] Just as Christ did not *consider* his status as something to be taken advantage of, so now Paul no longer considers an advantage the status that he formerly prized. Circumcision on the eighth day, membership of the people of Israel, of the tribe of Benjamin, a Pharisee, zealous in persecution, and blameless in observance of the law (Phil. 3:5–6)—all these Paul now considers (vv. 7 and 8 twice) as loss. He has lost all things, and considers them as loss and excrement,[150] compared with gaining Christ (vv. 9–11).

2.3.3. κύριος

If the weight of ἁρπαγμός falls on exploitation, we must nevertheless reiterate, with Lohmeyer and Martin,[151] that there is a progression in our passage. The conclusion of the passage is not merely—in the words of R. H. Gundry[152]— "postexistent acknowledgment [of Jesus] as divine." At the beginning he was ἐν μορφῇ θεοῦ, but he was not κύριος. The title κύριος is bestowed by God in the antistrophe only on the grounds of what Jesus is said to have done in the strophe. Universal acclaim of Jesus as Lord is possible only because of what he is said to have done in vv. 6–8.

If we ask what this might mean, we might seek to answer this question from the standpoint of Gentile and Jewish hearers of the epistle. Gentiles might hear κύριος and situate it in the world of imperial Rome, drawing comparisons between Christ and mighty lords of the past like Alexander the Great, divine heroes like Heracles, or seemingly all-powerful emperors like Caligula or Nero.[153] They might also draw the conclusion that Jesus has conquered the powers of the underworld in view of the bending of the knee of the καταχθονίων, which may well include subterranean beings and powers.[154] As Lohmeyer observed, Christ is not depicted as Lord of the church. He is Lord of the universe, and will be acknowledged as such even by those who now deny it. To Jewish hearers, the acclamation of Jesus as Lord might suggest that a second throne had been set up in heaven alongside Yahweh's. Such a suggestion was later proposed by Rabbi Aqiba on the grounds that Daniel 7 implied a throne for the messianic son of David.[155] Orthodox rabbis dismissed the idea as heretical, but our passage seems to point in that direction, or perhaps to the belief that Jesus, now dignified with the divine name, was seated with God on God's throne.[156]

If we ask in the manner of Lohmeyer how this idea might relate to other New Testament texts, three possible connections come to mind. First, there are the Synoptic passages that speak of being seated at the right hand of God. They occur in the debate about the implications of Psalm 110 (Mark 12:35–37; Matt. 22:41–46; Luke 20:41–44) with its allusions to κύριος and the issue of being seated at the right hand of God. The account of the hearing before the Sanhedrin represents Jesus declaring that his interrogators "will see the Son of man seated at the right hand of Power, and coming with the clouds of heaven" (Mark 14:61–62; cf. Matt. 26:64; Luke 22:69; cf. Dan. 7:13). The thought of Phil. 2:6–11 appears to have a counterpart in Rom. 14:9–12 and perhaps 2 Cor. 5:10–21 (both of which passages contain references to the judgment seat).[157] Thus in both the Synoptics and Paul there are links between the "Lord" traditions and throne traditions. Second, we might note accounts of preaching in Acts that stress that salvation is given in no one else, for there is no other name under heaven given among mortals whereby they may be saved (Acts 4:12). Here as elsewhere the theme of Christ's authority is set against the backdrop of the wrongful crucifixion (cf. Acts 4:10; 2:22–24, 34–36 [recalling Psalm 110 and concluding that "God has made him both Lord and Messiah, this Jesus whom you crucified"]; 5:30–31; 10:36–34). Third, we might recall with Lohmeyer the cultic interpretation given by the Epistle to the Hebrews, which construes the exaltation of Christ in terms of the action of the high priest in entering the Holy of Holies on the Day of Atonement.

In view of these connections I would be reluctant to identify Phil. 2:6–11 as the beginning of christology. Philippians is one of the later Pauline letters, and Paul had already articulated a developed christology in Romans and his Corinthian correspondence which appears to *anticipate,* rather than *echo,* themes in our passage.[158] While the dating of Philippians represents the *terminus ad quem* for the dating of our passage, we have no idea of when it was actually composed. What we can say is that Phil. 2:6–11 forms a web of belief that reaches back to other confessions and beliefs—including those of the adversaries of the church. Intertextual echoes of words, thoughts, and symbols that we find here were concurrently shaping Christian belief in other contexts, traditions, and writings. But if we cannot say that our passage is the foundation document of christology, we can say that it brings together like no other the central issues of christology which defined Christianity and led to its separation from Judaism.

NOTES

1. "Ernst Lohmeyer † (1890–1946)," in *Vorträge und Aufsätze, 1925–1962,* ed. Karlfried Fröhlich (Tübingen: Mohr [Siebeck]; Zurich: Zwingli Verlag 1966), 665.

2. Cf. R. P. Martin, *Carmen Christi: Philippians ii. 5–11 in Recent Interpretation and in the Setting of Early Christian Worship,* SNTSMS 4 (Cambridge: Cambridge University Press, 1967; rev. ed. Grand Rapids: Eerdmans, 1983; with new title, *A Hymn of Christ,* Downers Grove, Ill.: InterVarsity, 1997).

3. Ernst Lohmeyer, *Kyrios Jesus: Eine Untersuchung zu Phil. 2,5–11,* Sitzungsberichte der Heidelberger Akademie der Wissenschaften, Philosophisch-historische Klasse, Jahrgang 1927/1928, 4. Abhandlung (Heidelberg: Carl Winter, Universitätsverlag, 2. Auflage 1961).

4. Ernst Lohmeyer (1890–1946) in 1921 succeeded Rudolf Bultmann at Breslau, where he remained until 1935. An opponent of the Nazis, he was removed from his position, but obtained an appointment at Greifswald. He saw military service in both world wars. In 1945 he was appointed rector of the university, but was arrested on the eve of the reopening. He was executed by the communist regime the following year, though confirmation of his death was delayed for almost five years.

   Appreciations and studies include Erik Esking, *Glaube und Geschichte in der theologischen Exegese Ernst Lohmeyers: Zugleich ein Beitrag zur Geschichte der neutestamentlichen Interpretation,* Acta Seminarii Neotestamentici Upsaliensis 18 (Kopenhagen: Ejnar Munksgaard; Lund: Gleerups, 1951); Werner Schmauch, ed., *In Memoriam Ernst Lohmeyer* (Stuttgart: Evangelisches Verlagswerk, 1951); Wolfgang Otto, ed., *Freiheit in der Gebundenheit: Zur Erinnerung an den Theologen Ernst Lohmeyer* (Göttingen: Vandenhoeck & Ruprecht, 1990); Ulrich Hutter-Wolandt, "Theologie als Wissenschaft: Zu Leben und Werk Ernst Lohmeyers (1890–1946): Mit einem Quellenanhang," *Jahrbuch für Schlesische Kirchengeschichte* 69 (1990): 1–46, reprinted in Hutter-Wolandt, *Die evangelische Kirche Schlesiens im Wandel der Zeiten: Studien und Quellen zur Geschichte einer Territorialkirche,* Veröffentlichungen der Forschungsstelle Ostmitteleuropa an der Universität Dortmund, Reihe B 43 (Dortmund: Forschungstelle Ostmitteleuropa, 1991), 237–81; Günter Haufe, *Gedenkvortrag zum 100. Geburtstag Ernst Lohmeyers,* Greifswalder Universitätsreden n.F. 59 (Greifswald, 1991); James R. Edwards, "Ernst Lohmeyer—ein Schlusskapitel," *Evangelische Theologie* 56/4 (1996): 320–42.

   Kyrios Jesus was followed by Lohmeyer's commentary, *Die Briefe an die Philipper, an die Kolosser und an Philemon,* KEK 9 (Göttingen: Vandenhoeck & Ruprecht, 1930; 9th ed. [drawing on Lohmeyer's handwritten papers], ed. Werner Schmauch, 1953). Schmauch also contributed a *Beiheft* to the commentary (1964).

5. Wilhelm Bousset, *Kyrios Christos: Geschichte des Christusglaubens von den Anfängen des Christentums bis Irenaeus* (Göttingen: Vandenhoeck & Ruprecht [1913], 2. Auflage 1921); Eng. tr. by John E. Steely, *Kyrios Christos* (Nashville and New York: Abingdon, 1970).

6. *Kyrios Jesus,* 4.

7. Ibid., 5–6. Lohmeyer used the German *Strophe,* which can mean "stanza," "verse," or "strophe." To avoid confusion with the verses of the biblical text, I shall use the word "stanza" to denote the short three-line divisions which Lohmeyer detected in the composition, and "strophe" to denote the two groupings of verses, each consisting of three stanzas. In Greek choral and lyric poetry στροφή ("turning") denoted the movement of the chorus from right to left, and ἀντιστροφή the return movement from left to right. In logic antistrophe negates strophe.

8. NRSV and other versions translate γενόμενος (v. 7) as "being born," whereas in v. 8 it has the sense of "having become." γίνομαι is capable of having both meanings. Lohmeyer recognized the ambiguity of the Greek, and saw a parallel with John 1:14 (*Kyrios Jesus,* 37).

9. Lohmeyer thought that ὅς ("who") did not belong to the song itself, and substituted the definite article ὁ, giving the translation, "The one existing in the form of God. . . ." However, J. C. O'Neill has suggested that in similar contexts ὅς stands for "he it was who" by analogy with Sirach 46:1; 48:1–2; 48:12; 49:8; 50:1 ("The Source of the Christology in Colossians," *NTS* 26 [1980]: [87–100] 90).

10. *Novum Testamentum Graece*[27] (1993) and NRSV make the stanzas correspond to verses. Lohmeyer's division appears linked with his identification of sorites (note 15).

11. The bracketed phrase indicates that it was inserted into the psalm by Paul.

12. Lohmeyer, *Der Brief an die Philipper,* 90.

13. Lohmeyer, *Kyrios Jesus,* 43, cf. 39–40.

14. Ibid., 6.

15. Ibid. cf. Johannes Weiss, "Beiträge zur Paulinischen Rhetorik," in the Festschrift for Bernhard Weiss, *Theologische Studien* (Göttingen: Vandenhoeck & Ruprecht, 1897), 190ff. Lohmeyer noted the sequential repetition of μορφῇ ~ μορφήν; γενόμενος ~ γενόμενος; ἐν ὁμοιώματι ἀνθρώπων ~ ὡς ἄνθρωπος; τὸ ὄνομα τὸ ὑπὲρ πᾶν ὄνομα ~ ἵνα ἐν τῷ ὀνόματι Ἰησοῦ.

σωρίτης, also σωρείτης, lit. "a heap," is a technical term in logic, and is so-called from the question of when the addition (or subtraction) of grains constitutes (or ceases to constitute) a heap. Its origin was attributed to Eubulides of the school of Euclides (Diogenes Laertius, *Lives of Eminent Philosophers* 2.108). Cicero considered it fallacious, though not refutable, for there were no rules to determine the first or last point in the process of increasing or diminishing (*Academica* 2.49, 92–94, 107, 147). Sextus Empiricus questioned the validity of drawing logical inferences by means of sorites concerning unobservable objects (*Outlines of Pyrrhonism* 2.253; 3.80; *Against the Logicians* 1.416; *Against the Physicists* 1.182, 190). This applied particularly to arguments asserting divinity. Sorites was satirized by Lucian (*Symposium* 23).

16. The predicate of the first stanza (v. 6), the refusal to exploit what it might be "to be like God" becomes the subject of the second stanza, which expresses the consequences of the first. The taking of the form of an image of humanity and slave results in self-sacrifice (v. 7ab). The consequence of this self-sacrifice is obedience unto death described in the third stanza (vv. 7c, 8).

The obedience unto death in the third stanza results in the high exaltation and bestowal of the name above all names in the fourth stanza (v. 9). The consequence in the fifth stanza (v. 10) is the worship of all creation in the name of Jesus. This leads in the sixth stanza to the universal acclaim that Jesus is Lord to the glory of God the Father (v. 11). The conclusion unites the subject of the first stanza with the predicate of the last: the one who declined to be like God is universally acclaimed with the divine title to the glory of the Father.

17. *Kyrios Jesus,* 7. Lohmeyer adopted the term used by Pliny to describe the practice that he had uncovered (111–112 C.E.) of Christians meeting "on a stated day before dawn and singing alternately a hymn to Christ as to a god [*stato die ante lucem . . . carmenque Christo quasi deo dicere secum inuicem*]" (*Epistles* 10.96; cf. Martin, *Carmen Christi,* 1).

18. The aorist participle in μορφὴν δούλου λαβών ("having taken the form of a slave") does not express an incidental fact (as is usual with a second participle), but amplifies the self-emptying. While it is un-Greek for the second line of the stanza to be in the form of an aorist participle, it is possible for a finite verb to be continued by means of a participle in Semitic languages (*Kyrios Jesus,* 9; cf. BDF §339; GKC §120). ὡς ἄνθρωπος is "linguistically impossible" in Greek, and represents a literalistic attempt to translate the Aramaic of "like a [son of] man" into Greek (*Kyrios Jesus,* 38–40; cf. §1.2.3., below).

19. The stanzas have three lines mostly with the triple beat of Semitic poetry (*Kyrios Jesus,* 9–10; cf. Hermann Gunkel, *Kommentar zu den Psalmen,* passim). Whereas the stanza of Aramaic poetry typically had four lines, the three-line stanza with similar metrical form is found in Eph. 5:14; *Odes Sol.* 4:7, 9 and often; and 1 Tim. 3:16 (with two beats as sometimes in our psalm and Rev. 18:21–24). Recent study of the *Odes of Solomon* confirms Lohmeyer's contention concerning three-line stanzas, but not necessarily in the instances that he cited (*OTP* 2:736–37; Majella Franzmann, *The Odes of Solomon: An Analysis of the Poetical Structure and Form,* NTOA 20 [Freiburg: Universitätsverlag; Göttingen: Vandenhoeck & Ruprecht, 1991], 24–26).

20. *Kyrios Jesus,* 12; cf. BDF §290. The point is exemplified by Phil. 3:15, which uses the demonstrative with the same verb: ῞Οσοι οὖν τέλειοι, τοῦτο φρονῶμεν· καὶ εἴ τι ἑτέρως φρονεῖτε, καὶ τοῦτο ὁ θεὸς ὑμῖν ἀποκαλύψει. Cf. 1:17; 2:2; 3:19; 4:2, 10.

21. Lohmeyer noted a parallel use of ἐν in the quotation formula in Rom. 11:2: ἢ οὐκ οἴδατε ἐν 'Ηλίᾳ τί λέγει ἡ γραφή (lit. "Or do you not know what the Scripture says in Elijah?"). He took the ἐν to correspond to ב as a means of introducing quotations well attested in rabbinic literature (*Kyrios Jesus,* 13; cf. Str-B 3:288). *Der Philipperbrief,* 91, notes, *T. Sim.* 4:5 as a further parallel: ἡ καθὼς ἴδετε ἐν 'Ιωσήφ. Thus the poem may have been known as "Christ Jesus."

22. *Kyrios Jesus,* 14.

23. Ibid., 17. Lohmeyer used the more authentic Zarathustra. Zoroaster is used here on account of the term Zoroastrianism.

24. *1 Enoch* 70–71; *T. Levi* 5.

25. *De Vita Mosis* 1.66.

26. *Kyrios Jesus,* 20–22, for discussion of ἁρπαγμός and the somewhat more common ἅρπαγμα.

27. Ibid., 23.

28. Carsten Colpe, *Die religionsgeschichtliche Schule: Darstellung und Kritik ihres Bildes vom gnostischen Erlösermythus,* FRLANT 60 (Göttingen: Vandenhoeck & Ruprecht, 1961), 62, 126.

In some accounts of Zoroaster's teaching Ahura Mazda, the Wise Lord, is the father of two spirits who are divided into opposing principles through their choices and decisions. In later Zoroastrianism dualism reappears. Ahura Mazda, now called Ohrmazd, is opposed by Ahriman, the Destructive Spirit and the Lie. At the beginning of time the world was divided into the dominion of good and evil. Human beings must choose the rule of Ohrmazd or Ahriman. R. C. Zaehner termed this later dualism "reformed Zoroastrianism" as contrasted with the "primitive Zoroastrianism" of Zoroaster himself, and the paganization of the prophet's message through the readmission of old gods which he called "catholic Zoroastrianism" (*The Dawn and Twilight of Zoroastrianism* [London: Weidenfeld & Nicolson, 1961], 81–82). However, Mary Boyce appears to support Lohmeyer's analysis in attributing to Zoroaster the vision of Ahura Mazda and Angra Mainyu as two equally uncreated beings, "two primal Spirits, twins, renowned to be in conflict" (*Zoroastrians: Their Religious Beliefs and Practices* [London: Routledge & Kegan Paul, 1979], 20, citing Yasna 30.3).

29. *Kyrios Jesus,* 24; cf. *Faust,* part 1, Night.
30. *Kyrios Jesus,* 25.
31. Ibid., 28.
32. Slavonic Enoch tells of an archangel who set his throne higher than the clouds, "that he might become equal to my [God's] power" (*2 Enoch* 29:4).
33. *Kyrios Jesus,* 29.
34. Ibid., 30. Lohmeyer noted a parallel in the late tenth-century messianic appendix to the *Pesikta Rabbati* 36 (161a) (*Kyrios Jesus,* 30–31; cf. Str-B 2:287–89, 347–49). It represents a dialogue between God and the preexistent messiah concerning his ordeals.
35. *Kyrios Jesus,* 32.
36. Ibid., 33.
37. Ibid., 34.
38. Ibid., 35.
39. Ibid., 36.
40. Ibid., 38.
41. Ibid., 40. ὅμοιος υἱὸς ἀνθρώπου (Rev. 1:13; 14:14) reflects the underlying Aramaic. The Gospels avoid the כ which apparently veils but in reality points to the divine messenger. For them the term no longer hovers in apocalyptic hope, but designates the figure of Jesus.
42. *Kyrios Jesus,* 41; cf. Ernst Lohmeyer, "Die Verklärung Jesu nach dem Markusevangelium," *ZNW* 21 (1922): 188–91. "Translation," as in the legends concerning Enoch and Elijah, was not an option for the servant.
43. *Kyrios Jesus,* 41.
44. Ibid., 44–46; cf. also Ernst Lohmeyer, *Grundlagen Paulinischer Theologie* (Tübingen: Mohr [Siebeck], 1929; reprint, Nendeln: Kraus, 1966), 90–94.
45. *Kyrios Jesus,* 47.
46. Ibid., 48. The intensive ὑπερυψοῦν is found only in Phil. 2:9. ὑψοῦν is applied to Christ in John 3:14; 8:28; 12:32, 34; Acts 2:33; 5:31 (cf. *Odes Sol.* 41:12). In Acts it results in Christ being seated at the right hand of God. Elsewhere ὑψοῦν is applied to believers in a positive or negative sense (Acts 13:17; 2 Cor. 11:7; James 4:10; 1 Peter 5:6).
47. Ibid., 49. Lohmeyer notes that ἀνάστασις is found in the Johannine writings in the sense of the general resurrection and of particular believers, but is never used of Christ (John 5:29; 11:24–25; Rev. 20:5–6). ἐκ νεκρῶν ἀναστῆναι is found only in a reference to a "Scripture" (John 20:9). ἐγείρειν occurs only in narratives (John 2:22; 5:21; 21:14). It occurs once in Hebrews, where it does not refer to Christ (11:19).
48. Ibid., 51.
49. Ibid., 52.

50. Ibid., 52.

51. Ibid., 53.

52. Ibid., 53–54; cf. LXX Deut. 2:25; 10:8; 12:3, 5, 11; 14:23–24; 16:15; 18:5, 7; 3 Kings 18:24–26; Tob. 3:11; 5:11; Pss. 5:11; 7:17; 9:2, 10; 12:6; 21:22; 32:21; 43:8; 48:11; 51:9; 58:11; *Test. Zeb.* 9:8; *Test. Levi* 5:5.

53. *Kyrios Jesus,* 54; cf. Acts 5:41; 3 John 7; Ignatius, *Eph.* 3.1; *Hermas* 3.2.1; Justin, *1 Apology* 4.3; Tertullian, *Apology* 2.

54. "But if there be any as yet unfit to be called a Son of God, let him press to take his place under God's First-born, the Word, who holds eldership among the angels, their ruler as it were. And many names are his, for he is called 'the Beginning,' and the Name of God, and His Word, and the Man after His image, and 'he that sees,' that is Israel" (Philo, *De Confusione Linguarum* 146, LCL).

55. "Being therefore exalted [ὑψωθείς] at the right hand of God, and having received from the Father the promise of the Holy Spirit [τοῦ πνεύματος τοῦ ἁγίου], he has poured out this that you both see and hear" (Acts 2:33).

56. *Kyrios Jesus,* 55–56; cf. the role of the Spirit in the confession of Jesus as Lord in 1 Cor. 12:3.

57. ζῶ ἐγώ, λέγει κύριος, ὅτι ἐμοὶ κάμψει πᾶν γόνυ καὶ πᾶσα γλῶσσα ἐξομολογήσεται τῷ θεῷ (Rom. 14:11).

   Here κύριος denotes the God of the Old Testament. For the ζῶ ἐγώ formula see, e.g., Isa. 49:18; Jer. 22:24; Ezek. 5:11.

58. See, e.g., 1 Kings 8:43; 18:24; Pss. 20:5, 7; 44:8, 20; 63:4; 105:3; 116:17.

59. Lohmeyer's interpretation rightly challenges the familiar translation "at the name of Jesus every knee shall bow." Jesus is the *ground* of the universe's worship of God the Father. In Isa. 45:23 and Rom. 14:11 the object of veneration is denoted by a simple dative. If the name of Jesus were the object of worship, we might have expected it to be likewise expressed by a dative, rather than by ἐν ("in").

   ἐν τῷ ὀνόματι Ἰησοῦ is found only here in the New Testament (*Kyrios Jesus,* 58), though the addition of Χριστοῦ (e.g., Acts 3:6; 4:7) or κυρίου (e.g., 1 Cor. 5:4; 6:11; Eph. 5:20) is more common. ἐπὶ τῷ ὀνόματι Ἰησοῦ (Acts 4:18; 5:40) is used by opponents, and πρὸς τὸ ὄνομα Ἰησοῦ τοῦ Ναζωραίνου occurs on the lips of Saul, the persecutor (Acts 26:9).

60. Phil. 3:6 ("as to zeal, a persecutor of the church"); 4:15 ("no church shared with me in the matter of giving and receiving, except you alone").

61. *Kyrios Jesus,* 61.

62. Ibid., 62.

63. Ibid., 63–64. Lohmeyer noted the pioneering work of C. F. Burney in identifying poetic forms particularly in regard to reminiscences of the *Odes of Solomon* in the letters of Ignatius (*The Aramaic Origin of the Fourth Gospel* [Oxford: Clarendon Press, 1922], 161–66). Burney's examples illustrate both types of psalm. Some contain personal reference, while others do not.

64. *Kyrios Jesus,* 67.

65. Ibid., 40, 69; see above §1.2.3.

66. *Kyrios Jesus,* 36, 69; see above §1.2.2.

67. *Kyrios Jesus,* 69; cf. D. A. Hagner, *The Use of the Old and New Testaments in Clement of Rome,* NovTSup 34 (Leiden: Brill, 1973), 49–50. Clement uses ταπεινοφρονεῖν (*1 Clem.* 16:1, 2, 17) which is not found in the New Testament. However, Paul repeatedly uses φρονεῖν (Phil. 1:7; 2:5; 3:15, 19; 4:10), and ταπεινοῦν figures in the psalm and in Paul's self-description (Phil. 2:8; 4:12).

Whereas the title κύριος is bestowed on Christ *after* his humiliation in the psalm, Clement appears to use it indiscriminately when he writes "if the Lord humbled himself in this way . . ." (*1 Clem.* 16.17; cf. 16.2).

68. *Kyrios Jesus*, 69, cf. 30–31; Gustaf Dalman, *Jesaja 53: Das Prophetenwort vom Sühnleiden des Gottesknechts mit besonderer Berücksichtigung der jüdischen Literatur* (Leipzig: J. C. Hinrichs, 1894); Str-B 2:274–340 (on Luke 24:26).

69. *Kyrios Jesus*, 70.

70. Ibid., 71.

71. Ibid., 73.

72. Ibid., 73.

73. Ibid., 74–75.

74. Ibid., 75.

75. Ibid., 77.

76. Ibid., 81.

77. Ibid., 82–83.

78. Ibid., 84.

79. Ibid., 84.

80. Ibid., 86.

81. Ibid., 87.

82. Ibid., 88.

83. Ibid., 89.

84. *Carmen Christi*, 36–38.

85. *Der Christushymnus Philipper 2, 6–11*, WUNT 17 (Tübingen: Mohr [Siebeck], [1976] 1991), 8–9.

86. "The Song about Christ in Earliest Worship," in Hengel, *Studies in Early Christology* (Edinburgh: T. & T. Clark, 1995), (227–91) 288–89. Hengel likewise traces this "christological confession" to the "*messianic psalmody*" at eucharistic worship in the Jerusalem church (289, italics his).

87. Morna D. Hooker, "Philippians 2, 6–11," in E. E. Ellis and Erich Grässer, eds., *Jesus und Paulus: Festschrift für W. G. Kümmel* (Göttingen: Vandenhoeck & Ruprecht, 1975), 151–64.

88. G. F. Hawthorne, *Philippians* (Waco, Tex.: Word, 1983), 77. In *The Presence and the Power* (Dallas, Tex.: Word, 1991) Hawthorne embraces a Spirit christology, which he sees as "the key to kenosis" (199–225).

89. Werner Kennel, *Frühchristliche Hymnen? Gattungskritische Studien zur Frage nach den Liedern der frühen Christenheit,* WMANT 71 (Göttingen: Vandenhoeck & Ruprecht, 1995).

90. Kennel, *Frühchristliche Hymnen?* 25; cf. Lohmeyer, *Kyrios Jesus,* 13 and passim. While acknowledging Lohmeyer's achievement in identifying the autonomous character of the text and in raising the basic question, Kennel notes that Lohmeyer was incorrect to maintain that "Each strophe has lines of approximately equal length" (*Kyrios Jesus*, 6). Kennel points out that the lines vary between 5 and 16 syllables or between 2 and 5 words (*Frühchristliche Hymnen?* 25n110).

91. Kennel, *Frühchristliche Hymnen?* 289; cf. 185–224.

92. Klaus Berger, "Hellenistische Gattungen im Neuen Testament," *ANRW* 2.25.2 (1984), (1031–1432) 1151. (See Addendum after note 158 below.)

93. Cf. Klaus Berger, *Formgeschichte des Neuen Testaments* (Heidelberg: Quelle & Meyer, 1984), 240, 345, 367.

94. Michael Lattke, *Hymnus: Materialen zu einer Geschichte der antiken Hymnologie,*

NTOA 19 (Freiburg: Universitätsverlag; Göttingen: Vandenhoeck & Ruprecht, 1991), 233.

95. Edgar Krentz, "Epideiktik and Hymnody: The New Testament and its World," *Biblical Research* 90 (1995): (50–97) 91; cf. 89. Items absent are: discoveries for humans, ancient exploits as handed down by tradition, honor from descent.

96. See §1.1.

97. Robert H. Gundry, "Style and Substance in 'The Myth of God Incarnate' according to Philippians 2:6–11," in Stanley E. Porter, Paul Joyce, and David E. Orton, eds., *Crossing the Boundaries: Essays in Biblical Interpretation in Honour of Michael D. Goulder* (Leiden: Brill, 1994), [271–93] 271–72 (emphasis mine).

98. Gundry, "Style and Substance," 288; cf. G. D. Fee, "Philippians 2:5–11: Hymn or Exalted Pauline Prose?" *BBR* 2 (1992): 29–46.

99. "Style and Substance," 274. Gundry arranges the phrases in couplets numbered I–XII. The verse numbers are inserted here for reference.

100. Ibid., 272–73.

101. Paul P. Levertoff, "The Epistle to the Philippians," in W. K. Lowther Clarke, *New Testament Problems: Essays—Reviews—Interpretations* (London: SPCK, 1929), 141–50. The transliterated version on p. 148 was turned into Hebrew characters by Martin (*Carmen Christi,* 40–41). A subsequent attempt was made by P. Grelot, "Deux notes critiques sur Philippiens 2,6–11," *Biblica* 54 (1973): 169–86. Grelot's version called for restructuring of the hymn.

102. Joseph A. Fitzmyer, "The Aramaic Background of Philippians 2:6–11," *CBQ* 50 (1988): 470–83.

103. Ibid., 482.

104. Ibid., 483. This conclusion falls short of demonstrating that the work was *originally composed* in Aramaic. It shows only that it is possible to retrovert it into contemporary Aramaic, using words, forms, and ideas that fit an Aramaic *Sitz im Leben.* Whether the work was originally composed in Aramaic or whether, as Lohmeyer thought, it was composed in Greek by an author whose native language was Aramaic, remains an open question.

105. See notes 15 and 16.

106. Cf. Ernst Lohmeyer, *The Lord's Prayer* (London: Collins, 1965), 30–31; Joachim Jeremias, *The Prayers of Jesus,* SBT Second Series 6 (London: SCM Press, 1964), 82–107. Luke omits: "Our . . . in heaven," "Thy will be done, On earth as it is in heaven," "But deliver us from evil." Luke has "sins," where Matthew has "debts."

107. See notes 15 and 16.

108. See note 7. The strophe and the antistrophe would seem to contain a chiasmus of the form:
    A. Though in "divine form" he did not consider it plunder "to be like God" (v. 6)
       B. Having taken the form of a slave, having become an image of humanity (v. 7)
          C. As "son of man" he sacrificed himself and became obedient unto death (v. 8)
          C.′ Therefore, God highly exalted him and gave him the name above all names (v. 9)
       B.′ So that every knee shall bow in his name (v. 10)
    A.′ And every tongue shall acclaim "Jesus Christ is Lord" to the glory of God the Father (v. 11).

109. Cf. Otto Betz, "Jesus and the Temple Scroll," in James H. Charlesworth, *Jesus and the Dead Sea Scrolls* (New York: Doubleday, 1992), 75–103; J. Duncan M. Derrett, "Cursing Jesus (1 Cor. xii. 3): the Jews as Religious Persecutors," *NTS* 21 (1975):

544–54; reprinted in *Studies in the New Testament* (Leiden: Brill, 1978), 2:194–204. J. M. Bassler notes a possible autobiographical allusion to Paul's previous career as a persecutor of the church (1 Cor. 15:8–10; Gal. 1:13–16; Phil. 3:6; cf. "1 Cor. 12:3— Curse and Confession in Context," *JBL* 101/3 [1982]: 415–18).

110. Cf. note 21.

111. Cf. Erik Esking, *Glaube und Geschichte,* 109–21; Dieter Lührmann, "Ernst Lohmeyers exegetisches Erbe," in Wolfgang Otto, ed., *Freiheit in der Gebundenheit,* 53–87. On Bultmann see Roger A. Johnson, *The Origins of Demythologizing,* SHR 28 (Leiden: Brill, 1974).

112. Rudolf Bultmann, *Jesus* (Berlin: Deutsche Bibliothek, 1926); reviewed by Lohmeyer in *TLZ* 52 (1927): 433–39.

113. Ernst Lohmeyer, *Vom Begriff der religiösen Gemeinschaft,* Wissenschaftliche Grundfragen, herausgegeben von R. Hönigswald, 3 (Leipzig: Teubner, 1925); reviewed by Bultmann in *TBl* 6 (1927): 66–73.

114. Rudolf Bultmann, in *RGG*² 4 (1930): 393.

115. Hans-Werner Bartsch, ed., *Kerygma and Myth: A Theological Debate,* tr. Reginald H. Fuller, vols. 1 and 2 combined (London: SPCK, 1972), 1–44, 124–37.

116. Ibid., 125.

117. Ibid., 130, 131–33

118. Ibid., 133.

119. Earl R. MacCormac, *Metaphor and Myth in Science and Religion* (Durham, N.C.: Duke University Press, 1976), viii.

120. Janet M. Soskice, *Metaphor and Religious Language* (Oxford: Clarendon Press, 1985), 67–96. Soskice gives the following "working definition": "*metaphor is that figure of speech whereby we speak about one thing in terms which are seen to be suggestive of another*" (15, italics hers). Eva Feder Kittay observes: "Metaphor achieves its cognitive aims not by positing new existents but by forcing a reconceptualization of what is already given" (*Metaphor: Its Cognitive Force and Linguistic Structure* [Oxford: Clarendon Press, 1987], 302).

121. Soskice, *Metaphor and Religious Language,* 142–61.

122. Martin, *Carmen Christi,* 102–20; cf. Friedrich-Wilhelm Eltester, *Eikon im Neuen Testament,* BZNTW 23 (Berlin: Töpelmann, 1958); J. Jervell, *Imago Dei: Gen. i. 26f. im Spätjudentum und in den Paulinischen Briefen,* FRLANT 76 (Göttingen: Vandenhoeck & Ruprecht, 1960); Jerome Murphy O'Connor, "Christological Anthropology in Phil. 2.6–11," *Revue Biblique* 83 (1976): 25–50; Seyoon Kim, *The Origin of Paul's Gospel* (1981; reprint, Grand Rapids: Eerdmans), 200–205; Morna D. Hooker, "Philippians 2.6–11," in *From Adam to Christ: Essays on Paul* (Cambridge: Cambridge University Press, 1990), 80–100; J. D. G. Dunn, *Christology in the Making: A New Testament Inquiry into the Origins of the Doctrine of the Incarnation* (London: SCM Press [1980] 1989), xii–xix, 114–25, and his contribution to the present volume; C. K. Barrett, *Paul: An Introduction to His Thought* (Louisville, Ky.: Westminster John Knox Press, 1994), 105–9; G. B. Caird, *New Testament Theology,* ed. L. D. Hurst (Oxford: Clarendon Press, 1996), 96–100.

εἰκών renders דְּמוּת in Gen. 5:1, and צֶלֶם in Gen. 1:26–27; 5:3; 9:6. εἰκών renders the Aramaic צְלֵם in Dan. 2:31; 3:1, and the emphatic צַלְמָא in Dan. 2:31, 32, 34, 35. μορφή translates צְלֵם in Dan. 3:19. In *Corpus Hermeticum* 1:12–15 εἰκών and μορφή are used synonymously.

123. εἰκών and δόξα are used in the LXX translation of תְּמוּנָה. Commenting on 1 Cor. 11:7, L. H. Brockington observes: "It may well be that δόξα is here virtually a synonym

of εἰκών, seeing that δόξα translates הְּמוּנָה 'form' in Num. 12:8 and Ps. 17 (16):15" ("The Septuagintal Background to the New Testament Use of DOXA," in D. E. Nineham, ed., *Studies in the Gospels: Essays in Memory of R. H. Lightfoot* [Oxford: Blackwell, 1957], [1–8], 2). "[T]here seems to be good evidence that the early church thought of Jesus as Himself the manifestation of the glory of God" (A. M. Ramsey, *The Glory of God and the Transfiguration of Christ* [London: Longmans, 1949], 150).

124. Stephen E. Fowl, *The Story of Christ in the Ethics of Paul: An Analysis of the Function of the Hymnic Material in the Pauline Corpus,* JSNTSS 36 (Sheffield: Sheffield Academic Press, 1990), 54. Fowl notes that Paul uses δόξα as the visible manifestation of God's majesty (Rom. 1:23; 1 Cor. 11:7; 2 Cor. 3:18; 4:6).

125. James D. G. Dunn, *Christology in the Making,* xviii–xix.

126. Our passage relates Christ's death to his obedience, which resulted in his exaltation and glorification. Neither observation could be applied to Adam in canonical scripture.

127. "Then God said, 'Let us make man [Adam; אָדָם; LXX ἄνθρωπον] in our image, according to our likeness [בְּצַלְמֵנוּ כִּדְמוּתֵנוּ LXX κατ᾽ εἰκόνα ἡμετέραν καὶ καθ᾽ ὁμοίωσιν]; and let them have dominion. . . . ' So God created man [Adam] in his image אֶת־הָאָדָם בְּצַלְמוֹ; LXX κατ᾽ εἰκόνα θεοῦ], in the image of God he created them [אֹתוֹ בְּצֶלֶם אֱלֹהִים בָּרָא; LXX omits the parallelism]" (Gen. 1:26–27). The identification of the Adam of Genesis 3, whose story is told in personal terms, with the generic man who is the image of God in Genesis 1 turns on a canonical reading of Genesis that unites into a continuous story material belonging to the P and JE traditions.

128. The earlier rendering of Paul P. Levertoff favored the use of דמה (cf. Gen. 1:26), while P. Grelot and Joseph A. Fitzmyer favor the צלם of Dan. 3:19 (*CBQ* 50 [1988]: 473, 475, 476, 482). Both terms may be traced to the parallelism in Gen. 1:26–27.

129. Richard B. Hays, *Echoes of Scripture in the Letters of Paul* (New Haven, Conn. and London: Yale University Press, 1989).

130. In Jewish readings of Genesis, Robin Scroggs notes that a "way of exalting Adam is to say that he possessed glory" (*The Last Adam: A Study in Pauline Theology* [Oxford: Blackwell, 1966], 26; cf. 48–49). Whether Adam was worshiped or served in some traditions depends on the translation (*Sib. Or.* 8:439–45; Life of Adam and Eve 13). Numerous texts refer to the loss of glory through the fall and its hoped-for restoration (*Apocalypse of Moses* 20–21; *1 Enoch* 50:4; *4 Ezra* 7:122; *2 Apoc. Baruch* 51:1, 3; 54:15, 21; 1QS 4:23; CD 3:20). This is a major theme of Paul in Rom. 3:23; cf. 1:23 with 8:18–21 (cf. J. D. G. Dunn, *Romans 1–8* [Dallas: Word, 1988], 168).

131. David Steenburg, "The Case against the Synonymity of MORPHE and EIKON," *JSNT* 34 (1988): 77–86. Steenburg notes that there is only one instance in the LXX where μορφή translates צלם (Dan. 3:19). He suggests that μορφή is used, not because it is synonymous with εἰκών, but because it covers a rare portion of the semantic field of צלם that εἰκών does not.

132. Steenburg, *JSNT* 34 (1988): 84. In Plato, God's μορφή is God's necessarily unchanging form (*Republic* 2.380D, 381 b.c.). The μορφὴ θεοῦ surpasses knowledge and description (Josephus, *Apion* 2, 190; Diogenes Laertius, *Lives* 1.10). However, in most cases μορφή expresses "something which may be perceived by the senses" (J. Behm, *TDNT* 4:745; cf. R. Bultmann, *Theology of the New Testament* 1:192–93; S. Kim, *The Origin of Paul's Gospel,* 196–205; *LSJ* [1996]: 1147). Our passage suggests that through the figure God was made visible, albeit in an indirect way.

133. In making this point, I am not necessarily suggesting direct literary dependence on Matt. and/or Luke. Lohmeyer noted the connection with the temptation stories, but

did not press it, presumably because he located v. 6 in the pretemporal realm (*Kyrios Jesus*, 27).

134. Use of ἐν may reflect that of בְּ in בְּצֶלֶם אֱלֹהִים (Gen. 1:27). D. J. A. Clines has made a strong case for translating it not as "in the image of God" but "as the image of God" ("The Image of God in Man," *TB* 19 [1968]: 76–80). Thus, we might render v. 6 as "He it was who existing as the visible form of God. . . ."

135. For background see James H. Charlesworth, ed., *The Messiah: Developments in Earliest Judaism and Christianity* (Minneapolis: Fortress Press, 1992); John J. Collins, *The Scepter and the Star: The Messiahs of the Dead Sea Scrolls and Other Ancient Literature* (New York: Doubleday, 1995).

136. In light of the comparative study of Near Eastern texts, Clines has shown that Babylonian kings and Egyptian pharaohs were designated as the image of their respective deities (*TB* 19 [1968]: 80–85). As the image of God, the king is God's representative. Genesis 1:26–27 appropriates this role for humankind, and describes it in terms of stewardship over the earth (cf. Psalm 8).

137. In the Greek υἱός is understood. In both the genealogy and the temptation narratives υἱός is anarthrous.

138. In Mark the words of Peter's confession and the high priest's question are identical apart from the question mark (Mark 8:29; 14:61; cf. Colin Brown, "The Hermeneutics of Confession and Accusation," *Calvin Theological Journal* 30/2 (1995): 460–71.

139. After the healing of the paralytic at Capernaum opponents asked, "Who can forgive sins but God alone?" (Mark 2:8; cf. Luke 5:7). After the healing of the paralytic by the pool Beth-zatha, the opponents sought all the more to kill him, because he not only broke the sabbath "but was also calling God his own Father, thereby making himself *equal with God* [ἴσον ἑαυτὸν ποιῶν τῷ θεῷ]" (John 5:18). The charges imply that Jesus was usurping the authority of Yahweh.

140. From the standpoint of his opponents, Jesus was a seducer of Israel who was empowered by Beelzebul (Colin Brown, "Synoptic Miracle Stories: A Jewish Religious and Social Setting," *Foundations and Facets Forum* 2/4 [1986]: 55–76; Graham N. Stanton, "Jesus of Nazareth: A Magician and Prophet Who Deceived God's People?" in J. B. Green and M. Turner, eds., *Jesus of Nazareth: Lord and Christ: Essays on the Historical Jesus and New Testament Christology* [Grand Rapids: Eerdmans, 1994], 164–80).

    The Beelzebul charge is rebutted by its self-contradictory character and the evident working of the Spirit of God in Jesus' exorcisms (Matt. 10:25; 12:22–32; Mark 3:20–30; Luke 11:14–23; 12:10). In John Jesus is said to be a Samaritan who has a demon (John 8:48; cf. 7:20; 10:20–21) and a false teacher who leads astray (7:12, 14–18, 45–49; 9:24–34; 18:12–24).

    From the standpoint of the evangelists, Jesus was the anointed Son and agent (שָׁלִיחַ, cf. Berakot 5:5) of his Father. Thus, Jesus the Son has authority to act on his Father's behalf (Peder Borgen, "God's Agent in the Fourth Gospel," in J. Neusner, ed., *Religions in Antiquity* [Leiden: Brill, 1968], 137–48, reprinted in John Ashton, ed., *The Interpretation of John* [London: SPCK; Philadelphia: Fortress Press, 1986], 67–78; Jan A. Bühner, *Der Gesandte und sein Weg im 4. Evangelium: Die kultur- und religionsgeschichtlichen Grundlagen der Johanneischen Sendungschristologie sowie ihre traditionsgeschichtliche Entwicklung*, WUNT 2 [Tübingen: Mohr (Siebeck), 1977]; Anthony Harvey, "Christ as Agent," in L. D. Hurst and N. T. Wright, eds., *The Glory of Christ in the New Testament* [Oxford: Clarendon Press, 1987], 239–50).

141. 1 Cor. 10:3; Gal. 3:13; cf. Deut. 21:22–23; 11 Q Temple 64:6–10 (see §2.2).
142. Following his discussion of the Zoroastrian roots of the conflict between good and evil, and of the meaning of ἁρπαγμός, Lohmeyer asks: "But what is the religious significance of the picture? It is, in brief, the thought of temptation" (*Kyrios Jesus,* 25).

   My interpretation of the role of Satan differs from that of Isidore of Pelusium, Theodore of Mopsuestia, and Ethelbert Stauffer (J. M. Furness, "Behind the Philippian Hymn," *ExpTim* 79 [1967–68]: 178–82; Stauffer, *New Testament Theology* [London: SCM Press, 1955], 64). Whereas they see a contrast between Satan's attempt to usurp power and Christ's refusal to do so, my interpretation follows the Synoptic tradition, which depicts Satan as the instrument of Christ's temptation.
143. "Jesus Christ is Lord: Philippians 2:5–11," in *The Climax of the Covenant: Christ and the Law in Pauline Theology* (Edinburgh: T. & T. Clark, 1991; Minneapolis: Fortress Press, 1992), 56–98.
144. Ibid., 90–91; cf. 95.
145. Ibid., 82–86; R. W. Hoover, "The Harpagmos Enigma: A Philological Solution," *HTR* 64 (1971): 95–119.
146. *Climax,* 82.
147. Ibid., 97 (italics mine).
148. J. C. O'Neill, "Hoover on *Harpagmos* Reviewed, with a Modest Proposal Concerning Philippians 2:6," *HTR* 81 (1988): 445–49; cf. C. K. Barrett, *Paul,* 106–8. O'Neill favors "robbery" as the most common meaning (cf. Lohmeyer, *Kyrios Jesus,* 20–22), and Barrett notes three meanings which are linguistically possible: "a prize possessed," "a prize desired," "an act of seizing; banditry, unlawful taking and possessing."
149. ἡγεῖσθαι, which is applied to Christ (v. 6), is applied by Paul to himself in Phil. 3:7 and again twice in 3:8. φρονεῖν (v. 5) is repeated in 3:15 (twice), 19. μορφή (only in the New Testament in vv. 6 and 7, apart from Mark 16:12) reappears in συμμορφίζεσθαι (only in the New Testament in 3:10) and σύμμορφος (3:21; elsewhere in the New Testament only in Rom. 8:29: συμμόρφους τῆς εἰκόνος τοῦ υἱοῦ αὐτοῦ). σχῆμα (only in v. 7 and 1 Cor. 7:31) reappears in μετασχηματίζειν (3:21). κύριος is found often in the epistle (2:11; 3:8, 20). ταπεινοῦν (Phil. 2:8; cf. 4:12; and ταπεινοφροσύνη in 2:3) has its counterpart in ταπείνωσις (3:21), where the idea is also associated with mortality. δόξα (v. 11) is used in an eschatological sense in 3:21 in a conclusion which recalls 2:6–11, bringing together several of these terms: "He will transform the body of our humiliation that it may be conformed to the body of his glory, by the power that also enables him to make all things subject to himself."
150. It may be that the thought of excrement (σκύβαλα, 3:8) was suggested by the medical use of κενόω (2:6), which has the sense of "to excrete," "evacuate" (Hippocrates, *Aphorisms* 2.51; Galen, *On the Natural Faculties* 1.13.42; 1.16.64; 2.9.139).
151. Lohmeyer, *Kyrios Jesus,* 74–75; Martin, *Carmen Christi,* 147, 233–37; *pace* Wright, *Climax,* 67.
152. *Crossing the Boundaries,* 274.
153. Peter Oakes, "Philippians: From People to Letter," *TB* 47.2 (1996): 371–74; J. M. Furness (above, note 142). Jews might also reflect that images (εἰκόνας) of Caligula had been set up in Jewish "places of prayer," and that Caligula had ordered the erection of his statue in the name of Zeus in the Jerusalem temple (Philo, *Embassy to Gaius,* 134, 188; Josephus, *War* 2.184–87, 192–203). The threat was preempted by Caligula's death.
154. BAGD, 420; Hawthorne, *Philippians,* 93 (cf. Col. 1:16, 20; 2:15; Eph. 3:10).

155. *Hagigah* 14a; *Sanhedrin* 38b. Cf. Alan F. Segal, *Two Powers in Heaven: Early Rabbinic Reports about Christianity and Gnosticism,* SJLA 25 (Leiden: Brill, 1977); Marc Philonenko, ed., *Le Trône de Dieu,* WUNT 69 (Tübingen: Mohr [Siebeck], 1993).

156. Cf. Martin Hengel, " 'Sit at My Right Hand!' The Enthronement of Christ at the Right Hand of God and Psalm 110:1," *Studies in Early Christology,* 119–225. Hengel suggests that "the name that is above every name" is the tetragrammaton YHWH for which κύριος was already substituted in the LXX. "God gave his unspeakable name to the Crucified and Exalted One. If the Exalted One is given the same unique name as God in Phil. 2:9, so also—presumably already in Rom. 8:34, but in any case in later texts, which speak of '*sitting* at the right hand of God'—he participates in the unique throne of God, the *kisse' hakkabôd,* that is, also in the kingdom of God" (*Studies,* 156–57). In a lengthy footnote (156n81). Hengel rejects the suggestion that the use of κύριος for the tetragrammaton in the LXX was due to Christian influence, and insists that the LXX played a significant role in the introduction of the title κύριος into christology. Earlier Hengel has observed that, "Paul places the granting of the title 'κύριος,' that is, the holy name of the God of Israel, in place of the *sessio ad dexteram*" (153; cf. Rom. 14:9). Reference to "the only son/God who is in the Father's bosom" (John 1:18) appears to the Johannine counterpart.

157. Romans 14:9 looks like a briefer statement of our passage: "For to this end Christ died and lived again that he might be Lord of both the dead and the living." It is followed by a recommendation concerning conduct (not to judge each other), "For we will all stand before the judgment seat of God [τῷ βήματι τοῦ θεοῦ]" (v. 10; cf. 2 Cor. 5:10). It is reinforced by a citation from Isa. 45:23 (cf. Phil. 2:10; see above §1.2.5.). It concludes with a general recommendation as to how Christians should live (v. 12; cf. Phil. 2:12–13). Although the views of Christ's exaltation that we have noted might appear adoptionistic, they were not so for Paul: "All this is from God who reconciled the world to himself through Christ . . . that is, God was in Christ reconciling the world to himself" (2 Cor. 5:18–19).

158. Unless we conclude that passages noted in note 156 actually allude to our passage.

Addendum. The view taken by Klaus Berger that Phil. 2:6–11 is more like an *encomium* than a hymn (see notes 92, 93) is supported by Ralph Brucker, *"Christushymnen" oder "epideiktische Passagen": Studien zum Stilwechsel im Neuen Testament und seiner Umwelt,* FRLANT 176 (Göttingen: Vandenhoeck & Ruprecht, 1997), 304–19. However, because of the single focus and brevity of the passage (as compared with the *encomium* which celebrates numerous deeds and virtues), Brucker prefers to use the terms *epainos* or *laus Christi* ("praise" or "praise of Christ"). The ancient genre of ἔπαινος celebrated someone's ἀρετή (virtue). This may be the sense of its use in Phil. 4:8 which the apostle commends to his readers for their consideration.

3.

Incarnation, Myth, and Theology

Ernst Käsemann's Interpretation of Philippians 2:5–11

ROBERT MORGAN

Ernst Käsemann's "Kritische Analyse von Phil. 2:5–11"[1] begins with a general observation that "from time to time it is necessary to clarify for ourselves the course and condition of exegesis in our own generation by means of a concrete example." He finds this a "fruitful and sometimes exciting procedure because it makes us acutely aware of the problems not only in the material but also in exegetical work itself." These opening remarks prepare the reader for what anyone familiar with Käsemann's work will in any case expect: that what follows is not only commentary on a difficult passage but a passionate engagement with the contemporary German theological scene, aiming to clarify the meaning and truth of Christianity in Käsemann's own day. His descriptive work is at the same time prescriptive, and fuses first- and twentieth-century concerns in a way that less theologically interested exegetes and less hermeneutically oriented theologians are more likely to call a confusion than a fusion of horizons.

Neither its engagement with the writings of a generation that has now itself become history, nor the widely disputed theory of New Testament theology that lies behind it, makes this essay easily accessible to anyone reading it half a century later, and from outside its German Protestant context. But problems of historical and theological distance are the daily diet of biblical scholars, and rereading a classic of biblical interpretation is itself a "fruitful and sometimes exciting procedure," making us aware of problems in the essay itself and in the text it seeks to elucidate, and also in New Testament exegesis and theological interpretation at the end of the twentieth century. Even if it should prove impossible to offer a definitive interpretation of the hymn and to determine the correctness or otherwise of Käsemann's attempt, the investigation may tell us something about interpretation in general and New Testament interpretation in particular.

The theological motivation of Käsemann's essay is plain from its central thesis: that the Christ-hymn of Phil. 2:6–11 is not to be understood in ethical terms as providing an example of humility for Christians to imitate, but rather in kerygmatic terms as a drama of salvation. The dialectical theology's repudiation of liberal Protestantism's ethical idealism stands as godfather to this interpretation. The same interest accounts for the weight given to Karl Barth's dogmatic interpretation of the hymn. As a New Testament specialist Käsemann registers some reservations, but he is far more positive about it than most exegetes would be. Conversely, he is surprisingly negative about the interpretation of Martin Dibelius, who shares his own academic background as an heir and successor of the history of religions school, but who is weighed in theological scales and found wanting. Third, the theological judgment passed on Lohmeyer is revealing. It is one thing to argue, as any exegete might, that "the entire framework of Lohmeyer's construction collapses" in his account of v. 7 (75, ET 69). It is quite another to say that Lohmeyer's dissolution of soteriology into cosmology and metaphysics is "theologically intolerable" and "from a Christian point of view" inadequate, falling short of Paul's justification of the ungodly (56, ET 50). Unlike many exegetes who have discussed the Christ-hymn, Käsemann is here engaging in Christian theology, and that means contemporary (1950) Christian theology. We may prefer a more disinterested discussion of the text, but we need to be clear at the outset about the genre of Käsemann's essay. It is New Testament theology, understanding that controverted term in a way that gives due weight to the noun "theology", as a reference not to any scholarly discourse that happens to use the word "God" but to our attempts to express a religious conviction coherently and critically. As the scriptures named in the phrase are Christian, New Testament theology is a form of Christian theology. The less that Käsemann's style of doing Christian theology is understood or approved of in much of the English-speaking world, the more it is necessary to draw attention to his understanding of the relationship between biblical studies and contemporary theology, expressed in his practice of New Testament theology, before turning to the essay itself.

A more common understanding of this relationship between biblical studies and Christian theology is that classically enunciated by William Wrede a century ago. Wrede thought that even the most theological branch of biblical studies "has to investigate something from given documents—if not an external thing, still something intellectual. It tries to grasp it as objectively, correctly and sharply as possible. That is all. How the systematic theologian gets on with its results and deals with them—that is his own affair. Like every other real science, New Testament theology has its goal simply in itself, and is totally indifferent to all dogma and systematic theology."[2]

The conceptual problem with Wrede's view is that the "intellectual something," namely, early Christian religion, which he elucidates so admirably within the limits of his historical reason, is itself contested territory. Even *describe* a religion well one needs some theory of religion. Presuppositions are not easily escaped. They had better be declared and argued for rationally. There is no reason at all to accept Wrede's claim that "New Testament theology has its goal simply in itself." Like medical research, practitioners are often motivated by goals other than scientific knowledge. The history of religion does have historical goals, as Wrede observed, and it may even be relatively disinterested. But theology is not simply history, however inescapably it is wedded to historical study.

Käsemann's participation in the German theological revolution that broke with Wrede's liberal theology is an essential aspect of his essay. But like his teacher Bultmann he remained firmly committed to the tradition of radical historical criticism represented by Wrede, and in particular to the approach pioneered by the history of religions school to which Wrede also belonged. This dual background of the Bultmann school in the dialectical theology and in history of religions research (including form criticism) provides the starting point of both this essay and Käsemann's other academic writing.

The most important contribution to the interpretation of the Christ-hymn in Philippians was and remains Ernst Lohmeyer's short monograph *Kyrios Jesus* (1927/8). As well as being a brilliant exegete Lohmeyer also was guided by strong theological interests and drew deeply on philosophy, though a very different one from the Marburg theologians, namely, Platonism. Bultmann's critical engagement with this worthy opponent, his successor at Breslau (where Wrede had also taught), was part of Käsemann's formation in the late 1920s. He learned to admire the exegetical boldness and theological aims of Lohmeyer while repudiating the particular philosophical medium adopted and adapted for theological interpretation.

Rival philosophies and competing theologies notwithstanding, Lohmeyer and the Bultmannians shared a critical exegetical background and history of religions approach, with its emphasis on the Jewish and/or Hellenistic and/or Gnostic background to the mythological motifs found in the New Testament. Classicists and orientalists—notably Reitzenstein, Norden, and Cumont—had studied religious texts, and it was history of religions research that gave birth to form criticism. The life setting of some texts in the cult (Gunkel on the Psalms), the identification of formal stylistic traits (Norden's *Agnostos Theos,* 1913), the interest in early Christian worship stimulated by Bousset's *Kyrios Christos* (1913, ²1921) and Lietzmann's analysis of *[The] Mass and the Lord's Supper* (1926), all stood in the background, but it was Lohmeyer's monograph and 1930 commentary that gave the decisive stimulus to the study of early Christian liturgical materials.

Käsemann's dissertation *Leib und Leib Christi,* submitted in 1931 and published in 1933, had explored the history of religions background of Paul's "body" language, and had proposed a Gnostic origin. His second book, on the epistle to the Hebrews, *Das wandernde Gottesvolk* (1939, ET *The Pilgrim People of God,* 1984) remained firmly committed both to the Gnostic hypothesis and to his own theological interest in ecclesiology. In the 1930s, Otto Dibelius's phrase, "the century of the Church" had not yet turned sour, and in addition to the contributions to ecclesiology made by these two books Käsemann had also written on the Eucharist (1937, responding to Jeremias) and (Paul's) ministry (1942).

After fifteen years as a pastor and latterly a soldier, he returned in 1946 to a university post in Mainz, to contribute there to the postwar task of reconstruction, and to the preservation of the critical theological heritage in a church always tempted to discard this in periods of conservative reaction. He wrote more on the ministry in the New Testament (1949, ET 1964), contrasting a protestant Paul with an early catholic Luke and Pastorals, and on "The Pauline Doctrine of the Last Supper" (1947/8, ET 1964). By taking up again the question of liturgical materials in the New Testament, Käsemann could build a bridge to the classical period of German historical scholarship that had emerged from the First World War and subsequent economic disaster, only to suffer more serious damage in the political crisis and war of 1933–45. His form-critical investigation and theological interpretation of these liturgical texts would help rejuvenate theology and church, advancing also the dominant Bultmannian synthesis that combined the liberal legacy in historical criticism with the more ecclesial, neo-Reformation, kerygmatic, or dialectical theology of the 1920s. Immediately before writing on Philippians 2 Käsemann had worked on the New Testament hymns, with an essay for the first Bultmann Festschrift (1949) on Col. 1:15–20. At the time he considered it "an early Christian baptismal liturgy," composed out of a non-Christian, Gnostic source.

Two features of the period must also surely have directed Käsemann's attention to the mythological language of the New Testament. This was the time when the demythologizing controversy sparked by Bultmann in 1941 was raging most bitterly in the German church, and the memory of the demonic powers, experienced most horrifically in Germany, was still strong. It must have seemed a matter of ecclesial responsibility to clarify the mythological character of much biblical language in opposition to a mindless conservatism, but also to interpret it correctly and especially to get the measure of the realities to which it pointed more satisfactorily than Bultmann's existentialist theology seemed able to achieve.

Käsemann's criticism of Bultmann's theology was still muted, and mainly implicit, in this essay on Philippians 2. At the time that Bultmann was carrying the flag of critical theology in the face of ecclesiastical condemnation it was important to be in solidarity with him. Käsemann was also at this time shipping wine from Mainz to Marburg, in return for books. But the good pupil does not need to ape the master, and Käsemann's criticisms became direct and explicit in 1953 in his Marburg lecture to the old boys on the problem of the historical Jesus. Pointers in this direction may in retrospect be found at the end of the earlier essay on Philippians 2. While sharing most of his teacher's literary and historical assumptions, Käsemann had even as a student had theological reservations. He had never shared the school's enthusiasm for Heidegger, and his excitement over Luther and over Barth's *Romans* (^{2}1921) suggests a style and christological content somewhat removed from Bultmann's cool philosophical or phenomenological analysis.

Käsemann's friendly but deadly serious differences with his teacher were later to loom large. They should not, however, be overstated, even though they are implicit as early as his dissertation. The two scholars were on the same side, and Bultmann's hostility to myth in 1941 may have been sharpened by the use made of myth by the Nazis.[3] But Käsemann shows more awareness of the trans-subjective reality and experience of evil expressed in the New Testament by myth.

These largely forgotten factors need to be kept in mind when turning to Käsemann's essay. Recognition that every theological interpretation of scripture is constructed for a particular place and time should make us hesitate before ruling his proposals out of court from the vantage point of a supposedly superior knowledge. Käsemann himself takes it as self-evident at the outset that "individual results and total understanding of a passage alike are determined [*sic*] by the perspective of the exegete" (51, ET 45). "The ideal of a science without presuppositions is probably nowhere now asserted" (ibid.). On the other hand, that old liberal ideal had stood for something which Käsemann both as theologian and as biblical scholar is desperate to defend: a determination to see what the text was saying, and not read into it our own arbitrary and uncritical conclusions or intuitions. Unlike Barth he is not a postmodernist before his time. Like Bultmann he wants strict critical methods to keep the church's proclamation attentive to the biblical text. Now that Protestant exegesis is no longer oriented to a firm doctrinal tradition, he says, it is up to critical exegesis to maintain a true seriousness about the subject matter of the New Testament and to preserve the critical potential of the gospel (ibid.).

A generation or two later, the capacity of historical exegesis alone to keep Christian theology in tune with the gospel appears more than doubtful. Käsemann was writing from within a Christian theological context, even now remarkably intact in Germany and Switzerland, where New Testament exegesis of the most academically rigorous kind could presuppose the general validity of what the texts were saying. Outside that German, Protestant, and latterly also Roman Catholic context, this combination of linguistic expertise, critical historical questioning, and theological commitment has seldom produced such a religiously potent exegesis. Many in Britain and North America would repudiate that ecclesial ideal in biblical studies as inappropriate to the pluralism of contemporary culture. Today it is necessary to take Käsemann's truism about "individual results and total understanding (being) determined by the exegete's point of view" more seriously than Käsemann himself intended, and to build it into our accounts of New Testament theology. Not all presuppositions are equally valid, but the theological subject matter of a New Testament passage is unlikely to find adequate contemporary expression unless the exegete's pre-understanding plays some part, however tacit, in the work of interpretation. Engagement with religious texts is a personal as well as a scholarly matter, without thereby necessarily becoming eisegesis. Is this still exegesis? That word privileges the grammatical at the expense of the wider, hermeneutical considerations. The word "interpretation" gives more weight to the interpreter. Attempts to articulate the Christian gospel through New Testament exegesis are therefore more naturally called "theological interpretation," than "theological exegesis"[4] or *Sachexegese*. The legitimacy and criterion of *Sachkritik* will be considered by Käsemann when he refers to the demythologizing controversy. That will reinforce the present point that Käsemann, unlike many New Testament scholars who have discussed the Philippians passage, is writing Christian theology, and writing it in a mode not universally accepted, that is, as New Testament theology. He deserves first to be evaluated in those terms.

He makes several exegetical proposals, some of which are more persuasive than others. His interpretation of the whole is built up of these, and if enough of them fail to persuade then the whole construction will collapse. But the whole construction is what gives some of his exegetical proposals the weight they possess. There is some progress in exegesis; a particular proposal may be shown to have been mistaken. But very often the exegetical options remain open, and choices are made on the basis of one's total interpretation of a passage or text. These total interpretations are not always able to be judged right or wrong. A variety of readings may be thought appropriate and all more or less different from what the author intended (could that be known). This general feature of literary criticism has a special relevance for theological interpretations, because theology is more conditioned by its time and place than most interpretative disciplines. Käsemann's interpretation should not be dismissed too quickly, even if it were to be found unpersuasive today. It might have been an appropriate word in 1950.

Käsemann himself would not welcome this kind of defense. He would not acquiesce in the skepticism that is tempting today when one considers the range of more or less plausible interpretations of this passage. He would expect the continuing discussion among exegetes with shared assumptions to lead to progress, even where certainties are few. But he would also agree with Bultmann[5] that all interpretation involves daring, and we may echo Karl Popper that one way in which progress is made is by daring conjectures or imaginative leaps being subject to refutation in rational argument.

Theological interpretation of scripture is part of the ongoing conversation within the church, where certain broad assumptions about the identity and truth of Christianity are shared. This model is quite different from the popular idea of a church turning to scripture for correct doctrinal and ethical answers, and of exegetes being paid to provide these. It is good that they cannot deliver such easy certainties. On the contrary, modern theologians and ethicists try to discover Christian truth by attending both to contemporary experience and to their tradition, above all the scriptural traditions. Nobody's understanding of Christianity is based on a particular exegesis of a particular text, however powerfully the gospel may on occasion be epitomized in the way a particular text is read.

In other words: Rereading a distinguished contribution to the history of research is unlikely now to mark a stage on the road to a generally accepted solution. To see in it a warning against false trails is also too little. If Käsemann's proposals are still worth pondering, the value of his discussion today lies in the way it too "clarifies the course and condition of exegesis in our own generation." It is today less clear than it appeared to Käsemann that some of the alternative solutions he reviewed are hopelessly wrong. It is surely necessary to acknowledge a plurality of possible readings, some of them "powerful misreadings" but none of them wholly persuasive, and few of them so plainly wrongheaded as he thought. That is a depressing prospect for historians who want to know "how christology began," but it need not damage the New Testament basis of Christian proclamation. Convictions about truth in Christianity sometimes emerge from the conflict of interpretations.

Käsemann was professionally interested in the historical reconstruction of early Christian theology. He was at the same time engaged in theological interpretation of scripture in and through his historical and philological exegesis. That is clear not only from his opening remarks already quoted and from his concentration on theological questions at the expense of literary analysis and history of religions detail, but also from his *theological* criticism of Lohmeyer's "dissolution of soteriology into cosmology and metaphysics," already noted. For all his rigorous and methodical critical exegesis Käsemann aims to produce an interpretation of the passage that conforms to his own understanding of the Christian gospel.

That will appear less shocking today than it would have appeared to Wrede. There is nothing disreputable about exegetes having theological interests, and so long as they observe the historical and linguistic rules they can float interpretations with which they can personally agree. New Testament theology is not a matter of digging out the one correct understanding of the gospel by means of historical exegesis. Those who are fascinated but not wholly persuaded by several of the interpretative options available for understanding Phil. 2:5–11 might well conclude that the ongoing argument and conflict of interpretations is more fruitful for Christian appropriation of scripture than a single correct reading ever could be. A classic literary text is typically open to a plurality of interpretations, and the New Testament is clearly religious literature. It is also Christian scripture, widely considered normative for the definition of Christianity. Doctrinal norms are neither impossible nor undesirable,[6] but the facts of contemporary interpretations of scripture and theological pluralism seem to indicate that the notion of doctrinal norms must be construed more loosely than was once the case. The relevance of this claim to the text (Phil. 2:5–11) and interpretation (Käsemann's) under consideration, will perhaps emerge in what follows.

II

It will help us negotiate an often "tortuous"[7] argument if the salient points of Phil. 2:5–11 in recent interpretation are briefly recapitulated. Identifying the main issues will provide a thread through the labyrinth of a passage that contains almost as many ambiguities and opportunities for different interpretations as Rom. 3:21–26, another passage signally illuminated by Käsemann at about the same time.[8]

The Christ-hymn of vv. 6–11 seems to speak of the divine "form" (or whatever μορφή means) of Jesus, his incarnation (though this has been contested[9]), his earthly lowliness and death, and his exaltation by God to receive a name (or title, presumably κύριος) and universal acclamation and worship. In the second line of the hymn, v. 6b, the meaning of ἁρπαγμόν is unclear. "Robbery" does not make sense; "prize" is preferable, whether it is to be taken in a bad sense, as booty snatched, or in a good sense, as reward. Whether it means holding on to something already possessed (res rapta) or grasping at something wanted (res rapienda) cannot be decided on linguistic grounds but will depend on one's interpretation of the hymn as a whole. The meanings of other words are also unclear in this context: ὑπάρχων (being), ὁμοίωμα ("likeness" can mean identity or only similarity, i.e., non-identity), and σχῆμα (outward appearance). Even the meanings of the common words and phrases—γενόμενος (twice: having become, or being born), εὑρεθεὶς ὡς ἄνθρωπος (found as a human), ἑαυτὸν ἐκένωσεν (emptied himself)—are debatable. The identity of those who worship (v. 10) is important and disputed, and the force of the final phrase in v. 11 is also uncertain. Answers to one or another of these questions may affect our answers to others.

Despite the possibility of argument over nuances the general drift of the passage seems at first sight clear enough. Paul exhorts the Philippians to humility and unselfishness in 2:1–4 and seems to reinforce this by speaking of the humility of Christ in vv. 6–8. The second half of the Christ passage (vv. 9–11) is less obviously relevant to his exhortation, but presumably Paul simply wants to complete the story of Christ, and his vindication perhaps implies a promise of future reward for Christians who follow his example. That commonsense first reading is precisely what Käsemann disputes. It is well to be aware of the magnitude of the task he has set himself.

On second thought it is not entirely clear whether it is the act of incarnation, or Christ's manner of life on earth, or both, which constitute a model of humility, but that scarcely troubles the casual reader of the passage. Exegetes and theologians, however, are not casual readers, and a text that speaks so powerfully of Christ has naturally been questioned more closely for what exactly it is saying. In particular, since the divinity of Christ is the central doctrine of Christianity, hammered out at length in the patristic period, this passage has been a central scriptural witness to Christian belief about Jesus. It seems to speak of his preexistence and incarnation, and that fits the church's classical doctrinal structure, drawn largely from John's gospel and in need of a wider biblical base or support.[10] This Christ hymn seems to fit, and so support, orthodox Christian belief in the divinity and humanity of Christ, in addition to its aim of encouraging Christians to find an ethical example in the One who came not to be served but to serve and to give his life a ransom for many (Mark 10:45). There is nothing about ransom here, but Christians combine various passages of scripture to build up their synthetic faith pictures.

Christian reading of a scriptural passage typically fits what is read into an already accepted doctrinal scheme without asking how far this interpretation corresponds to what exactly the author had in mind. Provided it does no obvious violence to the passage, it can be thought to correspond to Christian scripture "as a whole"—by which is meant to Christianity itself as commonly understood and taken to be based on scripture and "broadly" to correspond to its witness.

Modern biblical scholarship, on the other hand, looks more closely at each passage and seeks to understand it in its original historical context without making any assumptions about its conformity with later belief. This procedure has challenged the dogmatic structure of traditional Christianity and contributed to the greater variety of ways in which Christians understand their faith today. The discovery of doctrinal diversity in early Christianity has proved liberating, even if uncertainty about the boundaries of correct belief has also weakened Christian witness to what it claims is the truth of God for the well-being of the world.

Modern discussion of this Philippians passage begins rather late in the history of critical research, with Lohmeyer's 1927 monograph *Kyrios Jesus,* which first identified and described a pre-Pauline "hymn of Christ" in 2:6–11 on grounds of its un-Pauline language and balanced rhythmic structure. This proposal has been generally accepted. It is crucial for the interpretation of the passage because it allows and even encourages exegetes to interpret the hymn on its own terms without regard to its context in Philippians, or to Paul's intentions in quoting it. Whether this is legitimate for Christian reading of scripture, or whether that should be tied to a more contextual and canonical reading is debatable.[11] The same issue arises in the gospels, where few would want to exclude Jesus' supposed intentions and be confined to those of the evangelists. In any case this isolation of the hymn from its context is clearly legitimate, and important for the historian who wants to reconstruct the development of early Christian thought and worship. The question "How christology began" may be answered on different levels, but the historical task depends on distinguishing between different layers within early Christian tradition.

Lohmeyer's hypothesis, once accepted, refocuses the reading of this passage. Separate it from its Pauline context, and the natural assumption that it presents Christ Jesus as a model of humility to imitate is no longer so compelling. Talk of his incarnation, the form of a servant, and obedience unto death *may* imply an example of humility, but this is no longer the natural reading of the hymn, especially in view of its second half. This will prove important for Käsemann.

Lohmeyer presented what he thought was the original structure of the hymn. It contained two parts, each with three verses or stanzas, each of these containing three short lines. The phrase "even a death on a cross" at the end of v. 8 does not fit into this structure, and Lohmeyer adjudged it an addition by Paul himself. This final hypothesis of a Pauline gloss was also widely accepted, but has been challenged more recently by O. Hofius.[12] Lohmeyer's proposal about the hymn's structure has been less widely shared, though Käsemann professed himself content with it. Käsemann in fact seems not to have been very interested in how the hymn was structured; that is surprising, because this might affect the interpretation considerably, as his teacher had pointed out.[13]

The most important aspect of Lohmeyer's interpretation, after his isolation of the hymn, was his history of religions approach to its interpretation. This has, in many different forms, dominated subsequent German discussion of the hymn and is characteristic of Käsemann's essay also, whereas it has proved much less attractive outside Germany. That reflects the prominence of this line of questioning in Germany in the forty years prior to Lohmeyer's essay, and the further time lag before it became equally prominent elsewhere.

Like others before and after him, Lohmeyer found an allusion to the suffering servant of Isaiah 53 in "the form of a servant" (v. 7), but he broke new ground in seeing an allusion to the "one like a son of man" of Daniel 7 in "found as a man" (εὑρεθεὶς ὡς ἄνθρωπος, v. 7). He thought the hymn combined these two motifs, not through direct borrowing from the Septuagint (which is quoted in vv. 10f.: Isa. 45:23) but through the way they were understood in later heterodox Judaism. He saw Jewish apocalyptic rooted in Iranian myth and was clear that what we have in Philippians 2 is not a reference to Christ's earthly ministry but the myth of a preexistent being becoming incarnate and then exalted. The details are discussed by Colin Brown in chapter 2 of this volume and need no recapitulation beyond stressing that Lohmeyer's essay provides the essential background to what follows. Käsemann radicalizes some of Lohmeyer's proposals and takes issue with others. He agrees in finding here a myth of the incarnation and exaltation of a divine being, and like Lohmeyer he is keen to interpret this theologically for the contemporary church and world; but he disagrees with Lohmeyer about the general scope of the passage and about its source in the history of religions, as well as over several exegetical details.

The general structure of Käsemann's essay appears simple. After the brief introductory remarks discussed above, there are three parts. The first provides some history of interpretation, offering some incisive discussion of the German debate around this passage, mainly since the 1920s, but glancing back as far as the commentaries of E. Haupt (Meyer, 1902) and von Soden (HzNT, 1906), and F. C. Baur's *Paulus* (1845). The second and largest section contains detailed analysis or commentary on the passage, again in sharp discussion with other modern scholars; and the third section moves towards a unified understanding of the hymn as a whole, starting with some detailed discussion of the meaning of the introductory v. 5. Even this final section again provides as much about contemporary theological discussion as an overview of the hymn. The division into three sections imposes some order on a complicated, elusive, and sometimes rambling essay, but the different threads continue to weave in and out throughout the essay. It can now be summarized as it stands.

Käsemann's economical sketch of Lohmeyer's thesis sweeps through the range of new suggestions which made that monograph a turning point in the interpretation of the passage, and which made the hymn itself, perhaps eucharistic in origin, a central passage for New Testament theology. Lohmeyer thought it not only pre-Pauline but Palestinian, very early Jerusalem theology, and a stem from which the christologies of Paul, John, and the epistle to the Hebrews had sprouted. He explained the inclusion of the hymn, and the epistle to the Philippians as a whole, with reference to martyrdom as the ultimate expression of Christian existence (several years before his own execution by the Russians, or martyrdom). These suggestions had not found wide acceptance, but had forced scholars to ask new questions.

For Käsemann, it was important that Lohmeyer had established that the hymn spoke of the act of *incarnation,* and did so in the form of *myth.* Writing at the time of ecclesiastical attacks on Bultmann for speaking of "myth" in the New Testament, Käsemann observes that Lohmeyer's calling what the hymn portrayed "myth" made necessary a thematic discussion of the significance of myth for Christian proclamation (52, ET 46). He was also fascinated by Lohmeyer's theory about Paul's theology of martyrdom accounting for his use of the hymn and shaping the interpretation of Philippians. He did not accept it, but (like Bultmann on Ignatius) he could see in this existential concern a serious theological proposal. The main point, however, was that the myth projects a drama of salvation. It speaks of God, albeit in a way that a modern reader cannot simply accept, and not simply of human moral ideals, as the dialectical theology accused liberal Protestantism of doing.

Käsemann agreed that the hymn presents a myth of an incarnate being. Though he would suggest a different history of religions background from Lohmeyer's double appeal to the Old Testament, the concepts "incarnation" and "myth" would loom large in his own interpretation: the hymn speaks mythologically of the descent of a savior figure. It follows (as Lohmeyer saw) that v. 6 speaks of his pre-existence. This verse does not speak of the earthly figure of Jesus, as had been traditionally assumed, and was still assumed by Schlatter. Käsemann thought that Lohmeyer was nevertheless still influenced by that two-natures christological reading at two points: He took ἁρπαγμόν, the "thing grasped" or "to be grasped at," to mean that the preexistent one was tempted and made a free ethical choice between good and evil, and received the title "Lord" for making the right choice, unlike the fallen angels. Second, Lohmeyer took the hymn to express some law of religious relationship between lowliness and exaltation: *"per aspera ad astra,* or in Jewish terms: through human lowliness to divine majesty" (53, ET 47, quoting Lohmeyer, 74). Jesus' obedience to death is thus (according to Lohmeyer, 42) "the divine proof of an exemplary humility."

Käsemann's point is that Lohmeyer is strangely ambiguous in leaving such strong traces of the older "ethical" interpretation in his new recognition of a mythical drama in which such human attitudes are inappropriate. The thrust of his own interpretation will be to root out all traces of ethical ideas from the interpretation of the hymn. Whether that is possible remains to be seen. Lohmeyer has preserved an ethical interpretation of this christological passage, but without reading the traditional two-natures christology into it. *Kenosis* remains "a purely ethical concept despite or even because of the mythical narrative" (Lohmeyer, 34f.); that is, it depicts complete abandonment and self-sacrifice. At the same time Lohmeyer insists that the humiliated Christ also was the revelation of God. This is different from the usual ethical idealism of the old liberals, who saw here only an example for the Christian disposition. That is why he speaks of the objectivity of a divine-human or cosmic event. It is history of religions insights, says Käsemann, which allow Lohmeyer to transcend the categories of an ethic of intention. Our hymn is not about the pious individual nor even the Christian community, but about a worldwide revelation event. God and the world are the powers that control the movement of the psalm. That is why it does not speak of believers. The liberals' "principle of faith" is explicit only in the earthly existence of the divine figure, and only in the form of myth. The second part of the hymn (vv. 9–11) shows Lohmeyer that it is about victory over the world, not merely correct ethical attitude. The demonic forces that resist the eschatological consummation are eliminated.

Käsemann agrees with this as strongly as he rejects the way Lohmeyer finds in the myth an example for humans to imitate. He disputes many of the details of Lohmeyer's interpretation, especially those by which he inserts his own speculative metaphysics into the hymn. But he admires him for identifying the main problem of the hymn and trying to solve it, however incredible his particular proposals. Lohmeyer, he says, "became clear that the hymn speaks in a mythical scheme which describes the destiny of a divine being as a journey through the three stages of preexistence, incarnation, and exaltation. This poses for the exegete the question of the continuity of that being in the different stages" (54, ET 48). His violent solution of smuggling the Isaianic servant and the son of man into the horizon and even into the text maintains this continuity of the divine being through all the stages of its journey. In other words, the hymn speaks mythically of a "metamorphosis" of a divine being.

Lohmeyer interprets this myth of the incarnation of a divine being in a way that maintains the doctrine of the divinity of Christ in his incarnation (God striding across the earth, as in John's Gospel) but without using the dated categories of Chalcedon's two-natures doctrine. Like Schleiermacher and Käsemann himself, and unlike "ethical idealism," Lohmeyer accepted this one basic christological dogma of Christianity—without being committed to the time-conditioned categories in which patristic theology had articulated it. His alternative metaphysical interpretation did not impress Käsemann, but it shows that he saw the problem that Christian orthodoxy through the centuries had tried to answer: how to express the basic Christian experience of salvation from God in Jesus. Neither the ancient myth, nor the ancient metaphysical theology, nor Lohmeyer's modern metaphysical theology appealed to Käsemann, but all four were engaged in the same quest to articulate the Christian gospel of salvation in Christ. And that gospel was not adequately expressed by the old liberals' ethical interpretation of the hymn.

Lohmeyer's move from a correct recognition of the saving activity of God, expressed by the myth, to an interpretation that made of this cosmic event merely an eternal example for humans to imitate shocked Käsemann. It makes Christ the believer's leader and model (Lohmeyer, 85), and dissolves soteriology into cosmology and metaphysics. Paul admittedly goes farther than this, making Jesus the model of martyrdom in which faith shows itself victorious over the world, but all the hymn has to say (Lohmeyer, 75) is that "Believers must imitate his example. The question how this imitation is possible for the individual is not asked here. The only possibility raised here is the objective one, present in this event between heaven and earth. The psalm does not yet raise the question of subjective possibility (i.e., how it is accepted, viz., by faith); . . . it is enough that an eternal example has been established. The human task is now to do the one thing that is necessary" (85), that is, imitate it.

Käsemann responds sharply that this is not the Christian gospel as he understands it, not justification by faith. An event between heaven and earth, set up as an eternal example, does not enable us to do the one thing necessary. Lohmeyer sees here his religious "law uniting lowliness and majesty." The ethical meaning of that cosmic event lies in proving one's obedience to this law in one's own suffering and witness (Lohmeyer, *Kommentar,* 98). Käsemann takes that to mean that Christ is here made into the representative of a generally valid norm. The Philippians text is thus represented as a stage on the way to a Logos christology (Lohmeyer, 75). This is more than a mere moral attitude. It transcends the human sphere and can reveal itself objectively in an event. It is binding on the human and provides a basis for moral action. But it has absolutely nothing to do with early Christian christology, says Käsemann, because it has nothing to do with early Christian eschatology. Lohmeyer, too, ends up in an ethical idealism, however idiosyncratic and sublimated, aided by the historian's intuition and knowledge and by modern philosophy. Käsemann hopes to find more Christianity in this hymn, that is, a gospel of salvation.

The opening section of an academic thesis often describes the *status quaestionis* in a way that introduces what follows as the appropriate next step in research, if not the final truth of the matter. Like F. C. Baur, Käsemann expects truth to emerge from the conflict of opposing views. Dialectic as much as chronology makes Karl Barth an appropriate second witness.[14] The importance he attaches to this admittedly doctrinally interested interpretation of the hymn is untypical of

Barth

New Testament scholarship. For all its exegetical faults it is constitutive for Käsemann's interpretation on account of the vigor with which it excludes all those based on ethical idealism, including Lohmeyer's.

Barth had begun polemically, contradicting what many would call common sense: "Paul is not trying to support what he has said in vv. 1–4 by pointing to the example of Christ" (cf. Barth 53, ET 59). Käsemann did not in theory need to agree with Barth's apodictic and improbable assertion because his own argument is based on what the hymn originally meant, not on Paul's use of it.[15] But he does not here trade on any possible difference between the hymn and the apostle's own theology, as he does in his analysis of Rom. 3:24–26 (1950–51). For him personally, and at a deeper level than his exegetical argument, it is Paul's view that matters, not that of the tradition that Paul uses (and sometimes alters by telling additions). It would not satisfy Käsemann for the hymn alone to resist ethical interpretations. He does not himself any more than Barth want Paul to be supporting vv. 1–4 by pointing to the example of Christ, even if some of Barth's arguments for this anti-*imitatio* view are mistaken. Barth's translation of μορφή as "knowability," his talk of the resurrection, and his denial that a new stage begins with v. 9, are all wrong, and his failure to recognize the mythical character of the hymn leads him wrongly to introduce believers or the church into v. 10. But the antiliberal-idealist thrust of Barth's theological reading was what Käsemann hoped to justify exegetically.

Since this negation of the usual ethical interpretations of the hymn is Käsemann's main point, and as it will strike most English-language readers as implausible, it is worth recalling why Käsemann is so anxious to protect Paul from being thought to refer to Jesus' obedience in what seems the natural way, meaning a human moral attitude or relationship (cf. nn. 95, [99]). Nineteenth-century idealist theology had spoken of God (Spirit) by speaking of the human, and had interpreted the divinity of Christ in terms of his perfect humanity. Both philosophically and theologically this strategy had failed, at least in the opinion of the dialectical theologians. Barth's *Romans* had taught Käsemann to think of God very differently from German idealism, in a way that owed more to Luther than to Hegel, let alone Harnack and the attenuated idealism of cultural Protestantism. He was thus predisposed to interpret the hymn differently.

Exegetes without theological pretensions might well recoil from the modern theological argument going on below the surface of Käsemann's interpretation of the hymn. They can leave the dogmatically minded to worry over the scriptural bone, and as historians can make up their own exegetical minds without reference to the theological consequences. However, they cannot prevent their conclusions from having theological implications; neither can they deny the rights of others to be interested in these, and it is interesting to see why the issue is so important for some. Theological interests do not justify distorting the text to fit a theological agenda, but where much is uncertain and much is at stake, it is reasonable for theologians to look for readings of their scriptures which are religiously meaningful today. Barth and Käsemann are interested in speaking of God through their interpretations of this text, as were the older liberal interpreters, and as are most contemporary interpreters, if sometimes quite naïvely. They did not imagine, as some do today, that simply repeating scripture will solve the hermeneutical problem of speaking intelligibly of God. Reflecting on scripture involves systematic theology. Exegetes also insist on linguistic and historical controls, but their theological interpretation of scripture (if they choose to write theology) can scarcely avoid these deep waters.

Käsemann's front against idealist theology is only the negative side of what he learned from Barth's *Romans*. He also learned from Barth what he would later call "the primacy of christology" and would then press against the anthropological orientation of Bultmann's existential theology. This christological concern was no doubt another factor directing his attention to the New Testament christological hymns. But unlike Barth and in agreement with Lohmeyer (and Schleiermacher) Käsemann held no brief for the two-natures doctrine of Chalcedon. He preserved the christocentric emphasis that the dogma protected (*vere Deus, vere homo*), and which patristic theology had expressed in the language of natures and substance, but he assumed that the divinity of Christ should be articulated differently today. His own solution was in principle Bultmannian but mildly critical of Bultmann's practice: to recognize the myth of incarnation as myth, but to interpret it appropriately, as Bultmann intended to do, but more appropriately than Bultmann had achieved—that is, in terms of Paul's (and Luther's) theology of the cross, rather than in terms of Heidegger's analysis of human existence.

On one major point Käsemann agreed with Barth against Lohmeyer: on the meaning of "in Christ Jesus" in v. 5, and so on how that elliptical verse is to be understood. Lohmeyer had adhered to the traditional view, which fitted the ethical interpretation of the hymn. Like most translators, he had added *was:* Have this mind in you which *was* also in Christ Jesus. That allows the two occurrences of "in" to stand in parallel, and to mean the same thing. Barth had followed J. C. K. von Hofmann and J. Kögel[16] in supplying "which you have" or "must have," thus giving "in Christ" its technical Pauline meaning (on one "local," ecclesiological interpretation of the phrase favored by Bultmann and Käsemann): within the realm of Christ. That removes the main support of one ethical interpretation of the hymn, that is, its advocacy of Christian character, without subverting another (interpersonal relationships within the Christian community), but it also opens the door to a kerygmatic interpretation of the hymn. Christians stand where they stand on account of Christ's saving act, described in the hymn that follows.

Barth, however, understands the hymn quite differently, in terms of the two-natures doctrine. Instead of recognizing the mythical pattern of the hymn he sees the drama of the savior's progress as the unfolding of a paradox which has to be understood as dialectical: Christ is at the same time divine and human, precisely in his "humility." This paradox raises the question of how it is perceived, and who perceives it. Barth's reply is to point to the divine miracle of the resurrection, corresponding to the other miracle of the identity of God and the human in Christ. Unfortunately, remarks Käsemann drily, neither this epistemological problem nor the resurrection are dealt with in the hymn.

Käsemann's negative judgment on Barth's exegesis should not obscure his appreciation of Barth's theological insight. If he was wrong to relate the christology of the hymn to the classical two-natures christology he was right to see in it something much stronger than a human example, and to refuse to reduce the divinity of Christ to his humanity's transparency to divine glory. The christological hymn speaks in mythical terms of incarnation. The question is how to interpret the high christology of the hymn when once its mythical form is recognized. What is the truth of the myth of God incarnate? How are we to understand the doctrine of the divinity of Christ?

Käsemann's third witness is Lohmeyer's mentor, Martin Dibelius, who had published a commentary on Philippians in 1913 (2d ed. 1925), but had changed the third edition (1937) under the influence of Lohmeyer's monograph. Already in 1925 Dibelius had assembled an array of mythical motifs by pointing out numerous Hellenistic parallels. He had concluded that a myth of descent into hell had been christologically modified. He took "form of God" and "form of a servant" to refer simply to heavenly and earthly modes of existence. Paul thus preserves the classical heritage, though for him of course the mythical scheme is merely the "clothing" for his ethical concern expressed in v. 8: insofar as the humiliation of Christ is here described as an act of free obedience, the myth is moralized. What happens to Christ shows the Christian that it is not selfishness and self-assertion, but humility and self-surrender that lead to the divine glory.

Käsemann reveals his Bultmannian theological colors when he comments acidly on this interpretation that it makes absolutely no attempt to find in the mythical presentation a meaning which would still be valid for today. The myth is merely a temporally conditioned expression of the self-denial motif found in v. 8. The following verses (9–11) do not really need to be there. The whole passage is for Dibelius only an excursus, and that is how we must understand these final verses: the apostle underlines his moral teaching with a reference to the heavenly promise. Käsemann quotes W. Lueken (1917), and P. Ewald (³1917) to the same effect. Not even this latter conservative could hear Kögel's warning against this ethic of intention, or understand Kögel's sharp observation (p. 15) that "only the conclusion makes the apostle's aim clear, and shows what really matters for him."

The third edition of Dibelius's commentary shows the effects of Lohmeyer's analysis on all this tame exegesis. It accepts the hypothesis of a hymn while still thinking it likely that Paul himself was the author, and while disagreeing with Lohmeyer about the meter. Dibelius thinks it was originally independent, and sees parallels to it in 1 Peter 2:21–5 and 3:18ff. (Dibelius, 72f.), because the exaltation statements (vv. 9–11) have no moral exhortation to them and are superfluous in their present (ethical) context. The original meaning of the hymn, independent of its present context, can therefore hardly have been to make Jesus an ethical example. On the other hand, neither is the work of salvation prominent, as it usually is with Paul. That would have required a reference to believers or the church, and would have had to touch on the problem of sin (Dibelius, 34). But then what holds the hymn together and makes sense of the whole? Dibelius is at a loss; his "solution" is no solution. He suggests (73) that all this is poetry, not technical terminology—as though that were a real antithesis. Early Christian liturgical language is rich in ideas and motifs, including technical terms, even though philosophical categories are absent. Because Dibelius has no clear theory about the passage as a whole, he is at sea over the details. He admits some mythical motifs and the possibility of the Gnostic primal man myth but takes neither the myth nor the christology seriously. Instead he returns to "ethical idealism," albeit no longer basing it on v. 8 alone. For Dibelius the point of the hymn is that Christ gained his sovereignty, and Christians overcome the world, by way of renunciation not claim, humility not defiance. To Käsemann that is a thin interpretation. Lohmeyer's discovery invites stronger theological reflection.

The sharpness of Käsemann's criticism of a scholar he admires and respects is striking. Dibelius was a leading representative of the history of religions and form-critical approach maintained by Bultmann and his pupils. But beyond that, Bultmann (and so Käsemann) demands of exegetes the conceptual clarity of philosophers or systematic theologians, and they make distinctions which surely never occurred to the New Testament writers. Dibelius is criticized here for being unclear about whether being in the form of God and being equal with God are the same thing or different, and whether the "robbery" in v. 6 is *res rapta* (something held on to) or *res rapienda* (something *to be* grasped at), whether the divine form is completely laid aside or retained incognito under the form of the servant, and how the status of the exalted Lord is related to that of the preexistent being. If anyone should object that these are the questions of a modern systematic theologian, Käsemann would reply, like Barth,[17] that of course he is a theologian and that a theologian's responsibility when interpreting scripture is to make the gospel clear in the language of today. There is nothing wrong in using concepts and distinctions unfamiliar to the author. They may well be necessary. This passage has central importance for the church's christology and deserves a weighty interpretation that takes it seriously as a whole. Listing individual motifs—the paradox of humble renunciation, the factuality of Christ's humanity, his humble obedience unto death, and his new status of Lord worshiped in the cult by the whole world—does not add up to an interpretation.

The outcome of Dibelius's exegesis, according to Käsemann, was "to make visible the impasse to which the interpretation of Phil. 2 was brought by Lohmeyer" (62, ET 55). The commentary of W. Michaelis (1935) leaves its readers similarly at sea. The only idea he can see in the hymn is the obedience of Christ towards the will of the Father, and the way he works this out again fails to take the myth seriously as speaking of the work of salvation. Instead we are back with Christ as an ethical example. The various motifs present in the hymn are not convincingly integrated. Similar criticisms are made of the commentaries by Karl Staab (1950) and Gerhard Heinzelmann (1949). Their lack of precision and their edifying language are all that separates them from the older liberal interpretations, such as von Soden's (1906), which spoke more soberly and worthily to the church. Käsemann's theological judgment on all this is severe: "A Church intent on the Gospel simply cannot accept such interpretation without denying itself. And if the Church is silent about this, it should at least tone down the newly awakened protest against critical research" (64, ET 57).

The undertone is clear. At a time when conservative ecclesiastics are attacking the Bultmann school, it is we radical critics who are preserving the gospel against all the pathetic watering down of a feeble exegesis that does not even know enough to recognize its liberal ancestry. Non-German exegesis is scarcely mentioned—and is briefly swatted aside. Enough has been said to justify a new attempt at interpreting the passage. Käsemann has tried to prepare the ground for his own theological seeds by blasting away the weeds of "ethical idealism." The popularity of ethical interpretations today suggests that he was not successful.[18] Whether his attempt deserves more attention than it received outside Germany[19] is a question at issue in what follows.

III

The second and largest section of Käsemann's essay presents his own exegesis, starting with details rather than proceeding from the total structure. He was no doubt being guided in his reading of the details by his provisional and hypothetical view of the whole, but that was in turn built up from the details, and it is there that exegetical arguments can be launched.

He begins with the term μορφή, which in the Hellenistic world (he claims) had mostly lost its classical meaning of "form" or "manner of appearance." In Hellenistic religious texts it no longer means the individual entity as a formed whole, but some specified "mode of being" (*Daseinsweise*), such as divine substance and power. The "form of a servant" does not therefore justify Behm's "making visible an attitude of will."[20] Dibelius had in his second edition translated the word correctly as "mode of being," and supported that with Hellenistic parallels. He also recognized the motif of the divine form being transformed. But Dibelius's conceptuality (the contrast he develops between myth and philosophy) gets the history of ideas context wrong and fails to explain Paul's meaning. Lohmeyer had recognized that the phrase "*in* form," using a preposition of place, designates the realm in which we stand and by which we are determined, as in a magnetic field. Käsemann's later interpretation of Paul is already adumbrated, supported by a (questionable!) historical argument or assertion about how human existence was understood in the Hellenistic world. Classical Greek confidence in the capacity of reason to impose order on the world had collapsed. As in Luther's anthropology, and against the humanism of Erasmus, we are subject to powers and caught up in a cosmic struggle. That is also Käsemann's twentieth-century experience, whether or not his linguistic arguments persuade.

The exegetical conclusion that Käsemann draws is that the "form of God," and "equality with God" stand in parallel and are synonymous, or at least coordinated. They should not be analyzed separately (as in interpretations which find here a reference to Adam), and their Greek background must be recognized. However, the Greek application of equality with God to heroes or "divine men" is not relevant here because (says Käsemann) v. 6 refers exclusively to the preexistent Christ. The closest Hellenistic analogy that Käsemann can find is in the Hermetic *Corpus* 1.13f., where the primal man and savior is said to be like God, and even to show the beautiful *form* of God. It seems to Käsemann (and we note his caution—neither the words "Gnostic" nor "redeemer myth" occur here) that the myth of a divine primal man has at least influenced the terminology of Philippians 2; this background confirms his identification of "form of God" and "equality with God."

He next considers the related question of what the rest of the sentence means, especially the "not reckoning it a ἁρπαγμόν," and takes "use something for one's own benefit" (implying *res rapta*) as sufficiently established by linguistic parallels. He is astonished that even conservative exegetes are willing to accept the history of religions hypotheses involved in reading it as *res rapienda*. The idea of Christ resisting the temptation to which Adam and Satan succumbed has no basis in the text and is unnecessary. Käsemann dislikes this, or thinks others like it, because it reintroduces the notion of ethical decision, however oddly this is attached by Lohmeyer and Michaelis to the preexistent Christ. The text speaks only of an objective fact, not temptation and ethical decision. The next verse confirms the *res rapta* view, because Christ gave up what he really possessed. Philippians 3:7 also offers some kind of (antithetical) parallel. The world of ideas is that of the primal man as savior taken over from Gnosticism and used in New Testament christology (as Käsemann had argued in 1939, in his study of the Epistle to the Hebrews). It is similar to Christ as the image of God in Col. 1:15, but here the preexistent glory of Christ is simply background, heightening the paradox of the incarnation. In that sense Barth was on the right lines. All this means too that Jesus' "equality with God" can no longer be made the secret center of the hymn, as always happened when the classical christology guided its interpretation. What is described here is not the relationship of Christ to God but an event, a "drama" with its successive phases. Christology is here subject to *soteriology,* contrary to Lohmeyer's view.

This assumes that v. 7a refers to the act of incarnation, not to a decision by the preexistent Christ, and not to the historical Jesus alone. What is celebrated is God's saving act, the incarnation, not an ethical model. That whole line of interpretation is false, in Käsemann's view (following Kögel and Barth and some hints in Lohmeyer). It is discredited by the contradictions it involves. Lohmeyer was right that there is no mention here of believers or the church. The ethical interpretation needed that. The objectivity of the hymn's language suits the description of a salvation-event better than it suits moral exhortation.

If that is right, the emphasis no longer falls on the status of Christ in his different states, even if individual statements seem to suggest that. The divine glory of the preexistent Christ is mentioned only to highlight the miracle of the saving act. What follows speaks mainly of what he *did,* not of who he *was.* That distinguishes New Testament christology from the questions of patristic theology and throws light on "he emptied himself." Käsemann agrees with Oepke[21] that 2 Cor. 8:9 provides the best commentary on this word, and he sees it as a statement of the incarnation: Jesus emptied himself of his divine mode of being, and that makes it necessary to say what took its place. Later dogmatic arguments about kenosis and later worries about docetism are not yet present. These verses speak of a transition into something different, and see it as a free act of Christ. To ask about the continuity of Christ's person in the different states goes beyond the text, however inevitable (perhaps) for us. Its "but" (v. 7) simply states the contrast. The status of the incarnate One stands in the shadow of the event of incarnation. This is described in a mythical way as in other myths of divine metamorphosis. The heavenly essence ("characterized by existence in a particular sphere," 73, ET 67) is laid aside, and an earthly one put on. The miracle is simply stated, not explained.

Other views are rejected. The text speaks neither of relationship with God (Michaelis) nor (directly) of the Isaianic servant (Lohmeyer). "The form of a servant" envisages human existence as such, reflecting a Hellenistic experience of life as servitude also reflected in Pauline cosmology, anthropology, and demonology (cf. Gal. 4:3f.). This confirms for Käsemann his interpretation of v. 6. Only "essence," not character, appearance, or attitude will render μορφή or existence in a particular sphere. Verses 6 and 7 stand in sharp opposition; only a miracle of human and divine essence can connect the existence of a Lord and a slave. The background is Hellenistic. Lohmeyer's theory of a Palestinian origin for the hymn is highly improbable.

Verses 7a and 7b are thus parallel, says Käsemann. ὁμοίωμα (likeness) raises similar problems to μορφή, with which it is interchangeable (as it also is with εἶδος and εἰκών) in Hellenistic Jewish literature. Certainty is impossible but the context favors the meaning *identity* of form (as at Rom. 5:14 and 6:5) rather than *similarity,* as at Rom. 8:3, which Lohmeyer chose ("appearance"). It is true, that as the obedient one, Christ is different from other humans, and that there is an affinity with Paul's reservation at Rom. 8:3. "Likeness" would also avoid a tautology between v. 7b and 7c. But what then is the relationship between ὁμοίωμα and σχῆμα? In 1 Cor. 7:31 σχῆμα designates the essence as it appears, or mode of appearance. Käsemann surveys these Pauline parallels without considering the possible difference in understanding the term as between Paul himself and his tradition (the hymn), or the possibility of Paul living with ambiguity.

Käsemann judges that Lohmeyer's whole construction breaks down at this, for him, most important point. The argument is hard to follow and would be tedious to analyze, but we may note that when the exegetical alternatives are finely balanced it is the total view which rightly proves decisive. It is clear that "the form of a servant" is not intended to dispute the reality of Christ's humanity, but rather to emphasize it. However, this real man acted differently from others, and as at Rom. 8:3 ὁμοιώματι leaves room for that difference. In any case the passage is not christology in the sense of defining Christ's being, but simply describes a sequence of occurrences within a unified event.

"And found ἐν σχήματι as a human" in 7c could go with what precedes or with what follows. It makes no difference to the meaning, which lies not in the becoming but in the being human, "as even Dibelius admits" (note 93). Käsemann ties it with what follows to avoid spoiling Lohmeyer's hymnic structure, which he accepts. Jesus' death is the secret goal and climax of the incarnation, as the repetition of "himself" also emphasizes.

The big issue now (v. 8) is the interpretation of "he humbled himself" and "becoming obedient," the mainstays of ethical interpretations of the hymn. Käsemann bluntly denies the usual view that the verb refers to Christ's "humility." As the text did not earlier define Jesus' essence, so neither does it here suddenly speak of his moral character. Like "he emptied himself," this "humbled himself" concerns rather an objective state of affairs, namely, his becoming lowly. Note that it does not say to whom Christ was obedient. Of course it means the Father, but Barth rightly saw that it is not the relationship but "the fact that he obeys" (59, ET 65) which is important for the hymn. The same is true of the preceding verses, insists Käsemann.

It is true (so Haupt, 82) that the text does not mention believers or the church, and so does not speak of the saving significance of what is described. But that is just as embarrassing for an ethical as for a soteriological interpretation of the hymn. Käsemann repeats that there is no basis for the ethical interpretation before this verse (he does not at this point discuss Paul's context), and then he makes a crucial move, saying that this objection takes "soteriological" too narrowly, to refer to the individual and perhaps the church. Anticipating later emphases in his Pauline interpretation, and also echoing his dissertation, he insists that even apart from the book of Revelation the New Testament frequently emphasizes the cosmic dimensions of Christ's saving work. This is because early Christian preaching is eschatological, and that embraces the whole world. Käsemann finds it remarkable that the word "eschatological" has almost dropped out of modern discussion of this hymn and is replaced by the much weaker words "mythical" and "ethical." He notes that in the New Testament "humility" and "humiliation" are to a large extent the marks of the elect in the eschatological age, and that the cross of Christ is mirrored in Christian existence.[22] An ethical interpretation of the word seems natural, but it is not altogether necessary. The paradox of the highest one becoming lowest is the miraculous eschatological event. It is neither an object for inspection nor an example, says Käsemann (with Barth). Once we see that "he emptied himself" and "humbled himself" refer to the mythically described event of incarnation, not the earthly life of Jesus, the case for an ethical interpretation is weak, and even the obedience of Jesus appears in a new light.

Obedience is clearly a moral category, the first to occur in the hymn, but it should not be made into the main theme of the whole hymn, as Dibelius rightly observed. Not even the paraenetic context justifies that. And here too the hymn speaks of a fact, the event of incarnation, not moral effort or attitude. Jesus enters the human sphere of subjection, and the meaning of v. 8 must be determined by the "wherefore" which at once follows. It is not about humble resignation, as Dibelius thinks. The reversal spoken of in v. 9 (as in v. 7) can only mean that the manifestation of the humiliated and obedient one was in fact the eschatological event. Whatever its context in the epistle, this is the heart and center of the hymn.

Käsemann thinks that the failure of the usual ethical interpretation confirms this judgment, but he goes on to find support in Rom. 5:12ff. and Heb. 5:8f. In this Romans passage the eschatological event which brought life and justice to the world was the revelation of the one man Jesus Christ who, as the obedient one, stands over against the disobedient man, Adam. In Hebrews the eschatological event is the epiphany of the obedient one because he produced obedient children. Käsemann assumes, as was widely held at the time, that the Gnostic savior myth of a primal man stands behind this, but he places no weight on that hypothesis because the myth is in any case modified here to describe the descending Savior as the obedient one. The value to Käsemann of that now generally discarded theory was that it reinforced his view that the hymn was essentially soteriological. His theory of the Adam myth standing in the background of this passage through the Gnostic primeval man being identified with Adam is, of course, very different from the theory which sees Christ as second Adam here in moral terms (obedience) and disputes any myth of preexistence and incarnation. That attractive typology was taken up by Irenaeus, but it hardly does justice, as Käsemann seeks to do, to the New Testament witness to Christ as the eschatological event.

Käsemann's mythical view of the hymn takes seriously the cosmic scale of the Christ event. It shows what christological questions are *not* answered by the text but also makes some christological points of its own. The *Anthropos* remains a heavenly being and so can never be an example. He is *Urbild* not *Vorbild*, archetype not model. In this epiphany of the obedient one, incarnation and death belong together as he enters the realm of the powers (cf. Heb. 2:15), but Jesus' death is freely grasped, and this overcomes the necessity and fate to which humans are subject.

Now Käsemann turns to the second half of the hymn, hoping to find confirmation for his admittedly daring hypothesis. But first he agrees with Lohmeyer that "death of a cross" is a Pauline addition to the hymn. It disrupts the structure and is at odds with the scheme. Paul's death and resurrection scheme is different from the incarnation and exaltation pattern that he can adopt, as here. It is not necessarily opposed to it. For Paul the cross is the cause of *skandalon* and thus the revelation of life, whereas for the hymn death as such is the ultimate contrast to the preexistent one's equality with God; the mode of death is irrelevant. The hymn is closer to the gospel proclamation of Jesus' voluntary serving, whereas Paul typically focuses on his cross.

Verse 9 introduces a new stage in the savior's journey, which is the drama of salvation expressed by the myth. Christ has now become the highest, and is depicted as ruler over the cosmos and over the powers mentioned in v. 10. This heavenly enthronement motif is found also at 1 Tim. 3:16 and Heb. 1:3ff., and Käsemann sees it (again without placing any weight on this hypothesis) as a Christian variation of the savior myth of a primal man. A new name is given at this presentation at the heavenly court, as at Heb. 1:5. The *super*exaltation refers to his new visibility as Lord. The main point is again that this is an eschatological and N B soteriological event—to which the ethical interpretation (e.g. of Michaelis, 1935) cannot do justice. This confirms Käsemann's interpretation of the more difficult vv. 7–8. The divine act of enthroning Christ shows that the earthly action of the obedient one affects the whole world and is a salvation event. It is more than the ethical act of an individual; it is revelation. That is shown in the objective language of the myth, typical of early Christian proclamation.

The designation of God in the Septuagint (*kyrios*) is here applied to Jesus, and Isaiah 45:23 (which speaks of God as Lord) is quoted. Käsemann here moves beyond Bousset's thesis in *Kyrios Christos* (1912) about the cultic origins of the *kyrios* title in early Christianity. It is not the cult that is in view here, but (as Lohmeyer insisted) the world. Christ is Lord of the world, not just of the Christian community in this hymn—contrary to Paul's normal usage.

This enthronement grants to the exalted one the role of representing God in this world until the Parousia, as 1 Cor. 15:28 says. The world has to do with God only by having to do with Christ, whether it recognizes that or not. Christ is now ruler and judge. He determines the destiny of the universe and every individual being. He is *deus revelatus,* the criterion and judge of all history.

v 10-11

That is the point of vv. 10–11. The Isaiah quotation describes an act of cosmic veneration, and the threefold insertion of heavenly, earthly, and subterranean beings makes this clear. Perhaps the earthly beings includes spirit powers (so Dibelius), since these represent the cosmos in Hellenistic thought. These powers are present in the related liturgical material at Rom. 8:38f.; Col. 1:20; 1 Tim. 3:16; Heb. 1:6; and 1 Peter 3:22, wherever the universal significance of Christ's triumph is being described. (See also the liturgical formula in Ignatius *Trall.* 9.1.) Isaiah's future tense ("will bow") has been removed because the enthronement of Christ has already occurred. It is still an eschatological event, however: the beginning of the end time.

The main reason why Käsemann takes "those on earth" to refer to spiritual powers, not human beings, is that humans know of Christ's triumph only as members of the Christian community, whereas the hymn refers to the whole cosmos, and that is represented by the powers. He follows his first teacher Erik Peterson (Εἶς θεός, 1926, 317) in taking "confess" to refer to public acclamation in response to a theophany, not the personal confession of private experience. But can the demons worship Jesus? In this mythical scheme of heavenly enthronement, says Käsemann, the point is a transfer to Christ of power over the whole cosmos. This is endorsed by the prostration and acclamation of the powers. This astonishing idea is common in the early Christian hymns, and refers to an already completed fact, even in Col. 2:15.

These spiritual powers bear the destiny of the earth. The author of the hymn need not have been familiar with all this mythical background, but recalling it shows how the hymn will have been understood at the time: Christ has taken the place of *anankē,* that necessity that has humans trapped in its grip. The message is one of salvation, not humility and obedience. Christ is now the ruler of all (*Pantocrator,* says Käsemann; the Greek word does not occur here, but at 2 Cor. 6:18 and nine times in the book of Revelation), unifying what had previously been at war. As at Col. 1:20 this Lord of the triple-decker cosmos is the reconciler of the universe. That too comes from the myth of the enthroned redeemer, familiar from Virgil's fourth Eclogue. He forces the rebellious spirits to accept his peace, and rids the world of demons, as redeemer and conqueror. That is what "Jesus Christ is Lord" means in the hymn, says Käsemann. Writing in the aftermath of Hitler, he could no doubt say a modern Amen.

The concluding doxological formula is Jewish, but awkward for Käsemann. Can the powers speak of God as Father? He cannot call it a Pauline addition because he accepts Lohmeyer's structuring of the hymn. Perhaps it is colored by Christian usage. In that case here (and only here in the hymn) the community knows itself to be included in eschatological saving event.

Finally, the hymn mentions Jesus by name in v. 10, whereas the LXX had God saying "to me." This ties the myth to history, as Lohmeyer noted. Käsemann is not satisfied with that, and we note again that his dissatisfactions are usually aroused by theological considerations. If this historical reference is merely a peg on which the myth of the humiliated and exalted *Anthropos* in its Christian form is hung, we would have here a complete mythologizing of the history of Jesus. If there is something different here, it must emerge from the mythically expressed kerygma itself. The difference from the pre-Christian myth must be found in the drift of the whole hymn. Only if this is apparent can the Christian kerygma use the mythical scheme without itself turning into mere myth. The drift of the whole, as Käsemann identifies it here, is that the Obedient one is the ruler of the cosmos, and as such the criterion and judge of all history. Unlike a mere myth of apotheosis, we have here a Jesus who leads the world through its many decisions to the final question at the last judgment: whether or not we were obedient. Our destiny depends on our confrontation with the Obedient one. This is what gives world history and the life of individuals their character. That is what it means for Jesus to be Lord: that he determines our existence and that of the world. And that is what makes the Christian kerygma different from the myth of apotheosis. This meaning of obedience here has already been given with vv. 7–8: that lowliness is grasped as the possibility of the freedom to serve.

That final paragraph with which Käsemann concludes his long and detailed analysis goes beyond analysis and introduces his unified understanding of the whole hymn. His shorter final section develops that a little, but has other fundamental issues to discuss too. First v. 5: the meaning of its "in Christ Jesus," and what has to be added to make sense of the elliptical formulation. He has already touched on this in discussing Barth's exegesis (p. 56 above). The traditional ethical interpretation sees a parallel exhorted between the conduct of Christians and that of Christ. Käsemann is convinced we must treat the "in Christ" in Paul's more technical sense, and claims that despite Lohmeyer most exegetes now agree on this, following Kögel (1908). The Philippians are admonished to behave toward one another as is appropriate within the realm of Christ. Paul here draws an imperative from an indicative, as he does at Rom. 6:2ff. Thus the "in Christ" has a soteriological character. It points to the salvation-event, rather than setting Christ up as a moral example for the community. Paul read the hymn as the portrayal of the salvation event, and the second half of it is as important to him as the first. For the ethical interpretation it was merely an excursus.

But all this provides difficulties for a modern reader. Can Christian existence be based on mythical schemes? Käsemann here alludes to the demythologizing controversy, pointing out that there is plenty of mythological material in Paul apart from this *Anthropos* myth. Even the "in Christ" has its roots in Hellenistic myth and mysticism. But Paul does not himself use the formula in a mystical sense; he interprets it ecclesiologically to speak of life in the body of Christ, life in the church. In this way he makes clear that for him the church is simply the realm where Christ rules. Even here the gospel ends up in ordinary everyday language. Paul takes up these Hellenistic mythical and mystical conceptions because they enable him to speak of the presence of salvation, consisting in a close relationship with the redeemer and concerning the whole world, whereas Jewish apocalypticism sees the salvation of the world as a future event, which the Messiah only introduces. Its conceptual schemes were inadequate to express the church's missionary message: salvation for the whole world, already present *now,* and only in Christ. The myths and mysteries of the Hellenistic age offered categories to express an eschatological message of *present* salvation in Christ alone, and that is why they are taken up.

The reason for early Christian appropriation of Hellenistic myth seems to Käsemann relevant to the demythologizing controversy of his own day. If it was taken up to articulate early Christian present eschatology then this should provide the criterion in the current debate. The hymn shares the triple-decker view of the world, and of humanity enslaved to the powers. The mythical worldview that allows the miracle of metamorphosis gets in the way of the later dogmaticians' distinctions, but caused the early Christians no problems. They did, however, correct the soteriology of the mythical scheme. In the myth the end of the world brings human apotheosis through the coming of a savior. The Christian message, says Käsemann, as a theology of the cross, speaks of humiliation unto death in free obedience, not merely of God becoming human. The myth's theology of glory has no "therefore" in v. 9, says Käsemann. There the divine spark in each of us finds its true essence and is then no longer distinguished from the savior. Here the obedient one becomes the ruler of the cosmos and the world does not (as in Gnosticism) come primarily to itself but to its Lord. Redemption here means a change of lordship. The eschatological message of Christianity is the message of a new Lord of a world that had previously seen itself confronted only by the powers.

Käsemann admits that the myth also speaks of a change of ruler, as it does of the savior becoming human. That is the point of its mystical "being in" language. Human existence is here understood in terms of the world that determines us, and salvation means being transplanted out of the world of nothingness and into the heavenly world, out of slavery to the powers and into the freedom of God's rule. But there change of ruler means only freedom *from* the rule of necessity. When Christian proclamation acclaims the obedient one as cosmic ruler it speaks of a freedom *for,* and a dominion we can enter.

The "in Christ" language means the same thing, says Käsemann. It signifies the turn of the ages, where God became human to stop us wanting to be like God. In the incarnation "he humbled himself," and that kind of abasement is the law of the new age. Salvation was revealed on a cross. The world ruler is the one who puts humans where they are truly human, namely in obedience. As Lord of the new world, he puts an end to the old world and its history.

Käsemann realizes he is chancing his arm in filling out what the hymn is about. But if he is more or less right, he says, we can see why Paul can use it to support his moral exhortation to humility, and to characterize this existence as "in Christ." It is eschatological existence at the turn of the ages, the existence of the new humanity. It is then clear that this is about eschatology and soteriology, not ethics. The church and believers are not mentioned, which is why Lohmeyer insisted it was cosmic, not ecclesiastical and cultic, in scope. But it is the Christian community that pronounces and hears this hymn. Such hymns were thought of as inspired and were held to proclaim a mystery that the world did not know, a mystery concerning the end of the old world. In this hymn the Christian community on earth takes up antiphonally what is happening in the divine court where the powers are prostrate before God's throne. It is drawn into the eschatological event and on earth witnesses to the enthronement of the obedient one. The church does not have to say what is happening to itself. When it proclaims Christ as ruler of the world, the new world comes into view. It becomes clear that the obedient one is generating more obedient children. This is not cosmology. It is eschatology and soteriology. When the obedient one is proclaimed as world ruler, a boundary divides the old and the new world. The Christian community is now called afresh into the sphere in which it has to stand, act, and suffer. This sphere, "in Christ," consists in humility and obedience, in the freedom of those who are redeemed. This hymn is thus confession, and in early Christianity confession marks the boundaries between the old and the new ages, boundaries which always threatened to get blurred in everyday life. The boundaries are maintained by explicating what it means to be "in Christ." An ethical model would not get us out of the old world. What is said here is that the world belongs to the Obedient one. He is Lord so that we can be obedient. We become obedient not by imitating a model but through a word that tells us that we belong to him.

IV

Thus breathlessly and epigrammatically Käsemann summarizes what he thinks the myth is about, and what Paul is getting at in quoting it. He finds in the hymn a myth of incarnation, highlighting by its contrast the theology of the cross. The Pauline addition in v. 8 is appropriate to the early Christian hymn, though not to the underlying myth. Almost as an afterthought he adds a very short paragraph on the original setting of the hymn. A definite decision between Lohmeyer (eucharistic) and Seeberg (baptismal) is impossible, but Käsemann tentatively prefers baptism because the hymn concerns the new world and humanization. The question, like many that exercise biblical scholars, is not important to Käsemann. His interest lies in highlighting the theological message of the hymn. That he makes clear in the final few pages of his exposition.

Käsemann agrees with Bultmann that we have here a myth, and that today myth needs interpreting if the Christian kerygma is to be expressed. But it is the eschatology and soteriology of early Christianity that become visible in the transformation of a Gnostic myth in this early Christian hymn. It speaks of the Obedient one as Lord and insists that the world belongs to him. Käsemann's interpretation gives due weight to its character as a christological hymn, and to the christological character of the eschatological message of salvation.

This corrective to Bultmann is lightly applied. The main thrust of the essay is directed against ethical interpretations of the hymn that are scarcely kerygmatic at all. As these are again dominant, must we conclude that Käsemann's energetic interpretation has failed—and has little to teach a later generation?

That would be a premature judgment, possible only if his suggestions had been decisively refuted at the exegetical level and alternative interpretations were found more satisfactory. This is scarcely the case. The big questions about the identity and truth of Christianity posed by this hymn are sometimes not even asked. The exegetical difficulties cannot be said to have been resolved. The meaning of the text is still unclear, and it is still possible to deny that the hymn speaks of preexistence or incarnation. It thus remains possible to read it in very different ways. The issues are conceptual as well as exegetical. Is the passage as important as many, including Käsemann, have thought? What strategies and categories are appropriate for understanding it? Its strongly christological focus demands more attention than the ethical interpretation provides, but on closer inspection the apparent links between this passage and orthodox Christian belief will scarcely bear the weight that has been laid upon them. Even if the relation between scripture and Christian doctrine could still be thought of in terms of proof texts it is doubtful whether classical incarnational doctrine would be able to find here much support. Myth cannot simply be read as doctrine.[23] The different kinds of religious language must be distinguished, and this is made more difficult by the word "incarnation" being used in different ways. The notion of myth is surely inescapable in analyzing the hymn, but its interpretation is complicated by the conflicting attitudes to myth among modern theologians.

Granted that this is a powerful and influential passage of scripture it is surely appropriate to build a bridge from the hymn to the christological and soteriological heart of the Christian gospel, as Käsemann attempted. His negative attitude to the "ethical" interpretation, like Barth's, may seem perverse, but it deserves respect for its insistence on taking the passage more seriously as an expression of the Christian gospel. The ethical dimension cannot be swept out of Paul's field of vision, but the question remains whether a more theological reading can be drawn from the hymn.

The traditional christological reading referred vv. 6–8 to the incarnate state of the "truly God, truly human" Jesus. That strikes historical exegetes as anachronistic, but it may not be untrue, however nondemonstrable. An orthodox Christian who accepts as dogma the divinity of Christ, without claiming to know how that is to be understood, might reasonably suppose that the hymn is saying *inter alia* what later christological doctrine tried to define: the universal Christian perception that in having to do with the crucified and vindicated Lord Jesus we have to do with God who is Lord of all.[24]

That is not the route from the scriptural hymn to contemporary Christian belief and practice proposed by Käsemann, though it agrees with his route in acknowledging the mythical character of this salvation drama of Jesus' incarnation, death and exaltation, and in seeing in the recognition of mythological language a way of doing justice to its religious weight. Käsemann takes the category of myth seriously as a way of speaking of God's redemptive activity, even though as a modern German Protestant theologian like his teacher Bultmann, he wants to interpret it in a way that preserves and communicates its Christian kerygmatic impact while cutting loose of the myth itself. Like the older liberals he has little time for myth, but finds more of the Christian kerygma in this hymn than their ethical interpretations could admit. He interpreted the myth of God incarnate—and perhaps finally eliminates it—but without trivializing it. Our "perhaps" holds open the possibility that he retains more mythological language than he intends.

Käsemann worked within the history of religions paradigm, which had thrown spectacular light on the passage over the previous generation. The specific hypothesis of a Gnostic "Primal Man" myth, however, was already losing credibility, and over the next few years Käsemann himself abandoned it. His argument does not depend on it. Rather more depends on his account of the wider "world of religious Hellenism" than any specifically Gnostic savior myth, which is only briefly mentioned and does not fit the Philippians hymn well. This hymn is not interested in the fall of any primal man, involves no conversation between the redeemer and the powers, and does not present the redeemed as part of the story. The Gnostic myth does not even offer a genuine incarnation, and its hypothetical redeemer rises of his own power, unlike Jesus in Phil. 2:9. D. Georgi was therefore right to challenge Käsemann at this point and propose a Jewish wisdom myth as a better model than H. Jonas's Gnostic myth.[25]

The reason for Käsemann's interest in that history of religions hypothesis (apart from its being then still fashionable in Germany) was that it reinforced his reading of the hymn as a mythic drama of redemption. But it is compelling to read this mythic story of Jesus as implicitly soteriological, whatever its antecedents. The Gnostic myth, if confirmed for this early period, would have helped explain the origins of much New Testament christology, but its evaporation does not negate the theory that the mythic drama repeated here was thought of as a story of salvation. Even the less likely alternative hypothesis, which would eliminate the idea of preexistence by finding here reference to the Adam story, is implicitly soteriological. But the categories of myth and incarnation seem appropriate to understand the passage. It is certainly possible to dispute many of Käsemann's details, such as his claim that it is demons who worship the Lord at 2:10,[26] but those who are sympathetic to his ideal of theological interpretation[27] will admire his attempt to find an interpretation that is meaningful for himself in his own day. It is not the least of Käsemann's services to the discipline to have asked whether a more deliberate theological engagement than is now common is demanded by a text such as Phil. 2:5–11.

Whether Käsemann's own interpretation of the myth will resonate today as it did in 1950 is another matter. Like the ethical interpretation that he resisted he himself also finally turns attention on to the earthly human figure of Jesus, obedient unto death and calling others to obedience. Käsemann speaks powerfully of the lordship of Christ, but neither the hymn nor Paul's theology in general compels theological interpreters to speak of obedient discipleship by attending to the obedience unto death of the historical Jesus. Paul's "obedience of faith" is based on and determined by its object (the crucified and risen Lord), not a historical model, despite a newly fashionable interpretation of πίστις Ἰησοῦ.[28] It is even arguable that the traditional "two natures" interpretation of the hymn, which historical exegetes rightly discard, actually catches more of the meaning of the myth than modern interpretations that speak undialectically of the human Jesus. As in Wesley's hymn, "mild he lays his glory by"; but the pathos of his humanity depends on the reality of his divinity, and even as it speaks of his transformation it does not expect us to lose sight of his original status.

When Käsemann and Bornkamm speak only of Christ's humanity in their broadly similar interpretations of the myth, and let the doctrine of his divinity disappear with its mythical incarnational form of expression, they part company with the text and its form (as Bornkamm insists the preacher *must*!) and come suspiciously close to the *imitatio* motif against which Käsemann protests too much. Certainly the risen Lord Jesus is the crucified one, and any denial of that in Gnostic myth or docetic christology means losing the Christian gospel. But the hymn reaches its climax in the exalted Lord receiving universal worship, not in the humiliation of the crucified one. Käsemann's strongest argument against the ethical interpretation was its failure to do justice to vv. 9–11, and yet in his determination to keep discipleship down to earth his own interpretation makes the lordship of Christ relative to our obedience, as the hymn does not.

Käsemann is not entirely comfortable with Bultmann's interpretation of the mythological language of the New Testament, and looks for an alternative criterion for demythologizing within the kerygma itself. But he agrees with Bultmann about the need to interpret the myth in a way that will eliminate this inappropriate language. The context of their hostility to myth, made more explicit by Bornkamm, is the question how to *preach* on this text. But that is not the only, nor even the primary question guiding theological interpretation. A more basic question concerns the identity and truth of Christianity, and that means asking about the contribution of this passage to the christology of the New Testament. One way of posing this question is by asking about its relationship to the later dogmatic formulation, *vere Deus vere homo*. The humanity of Jesus is not in dispute, and the doctrine of his divinity is open to a diversity of theological explications. Most of them involve taking mythological language more seriously than Bultmann, Bornkamm, and Käsemann (even) finally do. It is fair to ask whether their hostility to myth, understandable in the context of preaching, is either necessary or compatible with adequate theological interpretations of the hymn.

An alternative approach would be to acknowledge the character of this religious language and resist either literalism or the attempt to make it into doctrine, but nevertheless to retain it as part of the language of prayer and praise and to consider its doctrinal implications. It would remain necessary to explain what this mythological language of preexistence and incarnation is getting at, and here the deeper reflections of the Fourth Evangelist can help.

There the mythical scheme of descent and ascent is used to help articulate the fundamental revelational conception of that gospel, that in having to do with Jesus we have to do with God.[29] That very loose interpretation of what Christians mean by their doctrine of the divinity of Christ seems broadly true to all the New Testament witnesses and seems to have been discovered in the experience of early Christian worship.[30] To understand the Philippians Christ-hymn along these lines is not to remove the myth by way of interpretation. Such language can stand in worship, where its christological truth-claim is related to the authenticity of the religious practice and experience it expresses and evokes, prior to ontological conceptualization by philosophical theology. Christians confess Christ crucified and exalted into their symbolic world, vindicated by God. Their discipleship is lived out on earth, where Christ took the form of a servant and was obedient unto death. But the hymn does not restrict our attention to the cross, as though *crux sola nostra theologia* were strictly meant. It requires us to follow the drama of our redemption into the heavens and to join in the universal worship of Jesus as exalted Lord. The hope and confidence that are generated by what God has done in Christ are part and parcel of the Christian confession and essential to Christian discourse.

This goal of the hymn in the glory of God the Father does not permit us to pass over the reality of the cross, but only insists that this is not the last word, and that what the epistle to the Hebrews calls "the joy that was set before him" (12:2) provides the context for Christian understanding of the cross of shame. There is no soteriological theory in this hymn, and no merit in smuggling one in by concocting an imaginary history of religions background. The story of the incarnate and exalted Lord implies a message and a way of salvation that in retrospect might be articulated in all manner of theory. The cross of Jesus is fact, and for faith what matters most is what God did next, not why God should have permitted or even required it.

The mythological framework of incarnation and ascent offers one way of reading the hymn that corresponds to some probable solutions to the individual exegetical problems it poses. The popular alternative of avoiding that myth, with all its resonance in Christian imagination and subsequent underpinning in classical christology, by turning instead to the story of Adam to illuminate the hymn is arguably less persuasive at the exegetical level and less fruitful religiously and theologically. But that is not to brand the Adam reading as illegitimate. This text is open to a variety of readings. Exegesis may blow the whistle and declare a proposal off-side, implausible, outrageous even. Or (as here) it may let the theological play continue.

The play of diverse theological interpretations may be illustrated by a more daring (or playful) example. The hymn does direct our attention to the ministry and cross of Jesus, even though it does not leave us there. One whose understanding of the gospel is decisively shaped by John or Hebrews will find no difficulty in joining Lohmeyer and fitting this hymn into those frames of reference. One whose understanding of the gospel is shaped rather by Mark might read it differently. The point at which Jesus in Mark's story is "in another form" is at the Transfiguration: μετεμορφώθη (9:8). But Jesus did not see the heavenly essence that was his by right as Son of God as something to be clung to. He went down into the plain and enacted the form of ministry that he taught his disciples (Mark 10:35–45; 14:36). Wherefore God highly exalted him. Mark gives no details but clearly presupposes the vindication of Jesus, and like Paul looks forward to his universal rule, which meanwhile his suffering disciples can acclaim. This is not to say that the Markan model is what the hymn writer had in mind, merely that it is possible to read it that way today.

Whether it is legitimate to read it that way today depends on our aims and claims. Such a reading may be called a Christian reading and a harmonizing one, and harmonizing rightly has a bad name among historical critics. But so long as one is not trying to prove anything doctrinally it is hard to see why orthodox Christian readers should not read the hymn in a way that corresponds to their belief structure. They can welcome the challenge of historical exegesis to traditional readings without supposing that the traditional framework is no longer tenable or illuminating. The christological dogma is not destroyed (as some of its supports are) by historical criticism, and it provides a more fruitful lens through which to read the New Testament theologically than some of the alternatives, especially the alternative of dispensing with theological frameworks of interpretation in the name of historical and exegetical purity (important as these are). Such a christological reading of the christological hymn would reflect its central interest in the ministry, death, and vindication of Jesus, but would shift the focus from its Johannine myth of preexistence and incarnation to a more Markan picture of the ministry, passion, and vindication of Jesus. Such a sidestepping of the question of preexistence might well seem illegitimate. But when we read or sing a religious text today, we are not bound to pick up all its details. This Christ hymn derives its religious power for a contemporary reader from the movement of its mythical drama, not from its belief in preexistence. That merely serves the contrast-shaped drama. When or if modern theologians talk of preexistence doctrinally, they do so in the quite different context of considering what is implied by speaking of the divinity of Christ, namely, the eternal Logos or the doctrine of the Trinity. Such issues are not relevant to the exegesis of the hymn but have often influenced its theological interpretation. Anyone who is open to a generous plurality of interpretations, extending as broadly as a liberal Christian orthodoxy, is likely to welcome also Käsemann's more defensible proposal, however open it remains to criticism, argument, and appreciation.[31]

NOTES

1. E. Käsemann, "Kritische Analyse von Phil. 2, 5–11," *ZThK* 47 (1950): 313–60. Also in his *Exegetische Versuche und Besinnungen* 1 (Göttingen: Vandenhoeck & Ruprecht, 1960), 51–95. ET by Alice F. Carse, *Journal for Theology and Church* 5 (New York: Harper & Row, 1968), 45–88.
2. ET from R. Morgan, *The Nature of New Testament Theology* (London: SCM Press, 1973). Reprint forthcoming.
3. I owe this suggestion to Calvin J. Roetzel of Macalester College.
4. The term *Sachexegese* is used in Bultmann's essay "Das Problem einer theologischen Exegese des N.T." (1925), for example. This essay neatly coordinates the words *Sachexegese* and *Sachkritik*. See *Anfänge der dialektischen Theologie* 2, ed. J. Moltmann (Munich: Kaiser, 1967), 53f.
5. E.g., R. Bultmann, *Faith and Understanding* 1 (London: SCM Press, 1969), 86, 93, 280.
6. Or so I argue in "Can the Critical Study of Scripture Provide a Doctrinal Norm?" in *JR* 76, no. 2 (1996): 206–32.
7. So R. P. Martin, *Carmen Christi* (Cambridge: Cambridge University Press, 1967), 90; (Rev. ed. Grand Rapids: Eerdmans, 1983); (3d ed. *The Hymn of Christ,* Downers Grove, Ill./Leicester: InterVarsity, Tyndale Press, 1997).

8. See E. Käsemann, in *ZNW* 43 (1950/1), 150–54.

9. E.g., J. D. G. Dunn, *Christology in the Making* (London: SCM Press, 1980), 114–25.

10. See K.-J. Kuschel, *Born before All Time? The Dispute over Christ's Origin.* (London: SCM Press, 1992).

11. On Paul's use of the hymn see Stephen E. Fowl, *The Story of Christ in the Ethics of Paul: An Analysis of the Function of the Hymnic Material in the Pauline Corpus* (Sheffield: JSOT Press, 1990).

12. O. Hofius, *Der Christushymnus Philipper 2:6–11* (Tübingen: Mohr [Siebeck], 1976), 3–17.

13. R. Bultmann, *DLZ* 51 (1930): 774–80.

14. K. Barth, *Erklärung des Philipperbriefes* (Zurich, 1928 [⁶1947]; (ET *The Epistle to the Philippians,* London: SCM Press, 1962).

15. In his excellent analysis of Käsemann's Pauline interpretation, David Way, *The Lordship of Christ* (Oxford: Oxford University Press 1991), 49, notes that Käsemann does not here distinguish sharply between tradition and interpretation.

16. *Christus der Herr* (Göttingen, 1908).

17. K. Barth, Preface to the second edition of *The Epistle to the Romans* (ET Oxford: Oxford University Press, 1933), 4.

18. See the recent commentaries of G. F. Hawthorne (Waco, Tex.: Word, 1983) and P. T. O'Brien (NIGTC, 1991) for emphatically ethical interpretations.

19. F. W. Beare (London: A. and C. Black, 1959) and R. P. Martin (op. cit.) were positive, but V. Taylor does not mention this essay in his lengthy discussion of Philippians 2 in *The Person of Christ in New Testament Teaching* (London: Macmillan, 1959), 62–79.

20. Käsemann's footnotes 27 and 28 refer to *TWNT* 4:750ff. and quote 758 (ET 4:750).

21. A. Oepke, in *TWNT* 3:661 (ET 3:661).

22. Käsemann here refers to 1 Cor. 1:26ff.; 2 Cor. 4:7ff.; 13:4 (also 7:6; 11:7; Phil. 4:12; Matt. 18:4; 23:12; Luke 1:52; Phil. 3:21; 1 Peter 5:6) to support his thesis.

23. Cf. Wrede's protest against an older style of New Testament theology: it "makes doctrine out of what in itself is not doctrine, and fails to bring out what it really is" (op. cit., 75).

24. See note 6, and "St John's Gospel, the Incarnation and Christian Orthodoxy," in *The Essentials of Christian Community,* ed. D. F. Ford and D. Stamps (Edinburgh: T. & T. Clark, 1996), 146–59.

25. D. Georgi, "Der vorpaulinische Hymnus, Phil. 2:6–11," in *Zeit und Geschichte* (Tübingen: Mohr [Siebeck], 1964), 263–93.

26. O. Hofius, *Christushymnus,* 118–40, disputes this and makes a strong case for finding the background of the hymn in scripture (cf. the quotation of Isa. 45:23).

27. E.g., G. Bornkamm in *Early Christian Experience* (London: SCM Press, 1969), 121, who regards Käsemann's as "the best theological exegesis" of this text.

28. It is possible to agree with R. B. Hays, *The Faith of Jesus Christ* (Chico, Calif.: Scholars Press, 1983) about the narrative substructure of Pauline theology without accepting his view of πίστις Ἰησοῦ as a subjective genitive.

29. My argument is spelled out in the articles referred to in notes 6 and 24.

30. Following the hint provided by Pliny in his letter to Trajan (*Epp.* X.96–97), discussed by R. P. Martin, 1–9, and also the thesis of W. Bousset, *Kyrios Christos* (²1921, ET Nashville: Abingdon Press, 1970).

31. The great theological teacher died on February 17, 1998, having responded to this essay a few weeks earlier. It is dedicated to his memory in continuing appreciation.

4.
Christ, Adam, and Preexistence

JAMES D. G. DUNN

I

Philippians 2:6–11 is arguably the most important testimony to the speed with which earliest christology developed.[1] This importance has invested the task of interpreting the hymn with unusual interest and has given disagreements in interpretation a particular edge. Of recent interpretations (or readings), one of the most fruitful but also most controversial has been in terms of Adam christology.[2] In previous studies of the hymn[3] I also have been very much impressed by the fact that the hymn as a whole seems to take the form of what may most simply be called "Adam christology." That is, in my view, it is structured both to reflect God's intention in creating humankind (Adam), and to contrast the traditional understanding of Adam's failure. In this way the hymn serves its purpose of illustrating and commending a habit of mind "which (was) also in Christ Jesus" (2:5).[4] As Adam was the "bad," degenerative pattern of humanity, Christ in contrast was the "good," redemptive pattern.

Such christology seems to have been quite widespread in the earliest churches. We may note especially the use of Ps. 8:6, describing God's intention in creating humankind, to complement Ps. 110:1 in describing the exalted Christ's lordship over all things. The "subjection of all things under his feet" (Ps. 8:6) in effect completed God's original purpose in giving newly created humankind dominion over the rest of creation.[5] The exalted Christ has fulfilled the function originally intended for humankind (Adam).[6] Elsewhere it is the *contrast* between Adam and Christ which is most to the fore. So particularly in the two most overt Adam/Christ parallels/contrasts: the disobedience of Adam set over against the obedience of Christ (Rom. 5:19), Adam and death set over against Christ and life (1 Cor. 15:21–22).

Does such a christology lie behind, or even on the face of Philippians 2:6–11? And if so, what significance does that fact have for our understanding of the hymn? In particular, does the parallel/contrast begin with Christ in preexistence or with Christ as a second Adam, that is, in mythical or meta-history?[7] Before we can take up these questions two methodological observations are in order.

II

First, the case for seeing Philippians 2:6–11 as an expression of Adam christology is not immediately obvious. No mention is made of Adam. The case depends on the recognition of allusions to Adam and to the pattern of Adam christology as more clearly evidenced elsewhere. In other words, *it depends on an awareness of how allusion functions.*

The fact of the matter is that too much of the debate on the exegesis of this passage has displayed rather crass artistic or literary insensitivity. Allusions by their nature are not explicit. Poets or literary critics who had to spell out every allusion and echo would undermine their art, and deprive their more perceptive readers of the moment of illumination, the thrill of recognition. Their artistic skills would be reduced to the level of high school examination "cribs." For example, in music it is fairly clear in the last movement of Brahms first symphony, with its echo of Beethoven's ninth, that Brahms is laying claim to be the latter's successor. Whereas Dvorak's ninth, "from the new world," contains echoes of American folk tunes, without actually quoting any. In literature, it would generally be recognized that the work of poets like John Milton and T. S. Eliot are full of allusions.[8] And one cannot begin adequately to appreciate the compositions of a hymn writer like Charles Wesley without being aware of the fact that they are shot through with scriptural allusions. Scholars and students will hardly need reminding that at the back of the usual New Testament Greek texts there is a whole catalog of allusions to the (Jewish) scriptures, which far exceed the number of explicit quotations.

So with Paul, and not least with regard to his use of Adam motifs elsewhere.[9] In particular, allusions to Adam and the Genesis account of creation and of "man's first disobedience"[10] are generally recognized in Rom. 1:18–25; 7:7–13; and 8:20.[11] So too the pattern of redemptive "recapitulation" (Irenaeus) is evident in a sequence of passages—both in the thought of Christ's identification with the human condition, under sin and under the law, in order to redeem that condition,[12] and in the thought of the exalted Christ as the pattern of a new humanity, with the divine image renewed and the divine glory restored.[13] It is too little appreciated just how comprehensive a motif Adam christology formed within Paul's gospel. Adam seems to be a figure who lay behind a great deal of Paul's theologizing. And the bulk of Paul's Adam theologizing seems to be allusive rather than explicit. It should occasion no surprise, therefore, if Paul understood or constructed the Philippian hymn to embody a similar allusion.

Second, how should the presence and recognition of such allusion in Philippians 2:6–11 influence the interpretation of the hymn as a whole? Here again much of the debate has failed to reckon with the subtle way in which allusion works. To make the recognition of allusions and their significance depend on precision of meaning in individual terms would run counter to the art of allusion. On the contrary, it is often the imprecision of the meaning of a term, or multifaceted imagery of a metaphor, that enables the interconnection or imaginative jump[14] that is the stuff of allusion. The importance of the point justifies its reiteration: exegesis of particular terms, which insists on only one referential meaning for each term and denies all the other possible meanings, will often be wrong exegesis because it unjustifiably narrows meaning (to either-or exegesis) and rules out associations that the author may have intended to evoke precisely by using a sequence of such evocative terms. It need hardly be pointed out that such hermeneutical considerations have particular relevance when the passage is a poem or a hymn.[15] The relevance of these reflections in this case should become clear as we proceed.

III

In assessing Philippians 2:6–11 it is not too difficult to identify several points of contact with the Adam tradition and Adam christology as we have already seen it.[16]

Philippians 2:6–11	Adam theology
[6]who, being in the form of God,	"In the image of God" (Gen. 1:27)
did not reckon to be equal with God	"You will be like God" (Gen. 3:5)
as something to be grasped,	They took and ate (Gen. 3:6)
[7]but emptied himself,	Subject/enslaved to corruption
took the form of a slave,	and sin (cf. Wis. Sol. 2:23–24;
and became in the very likeness of humankind.	Rom. 8:3, 18–21; 1 Cor. 15:42, 47–49; Gal. 4:3–4; Heb. 2:7a, 9a, 15)
And being found in likeness as a human being,	
[8]he humbled himself	Subject to death (cf. Gen. 2:17;
and became obedient unto death,	3:22–24; Rom. 5:12–21;
the death of the cross.	7:7–11; 1 Cor. 15:21–22)
[9]Wherefore, God has exalted him to the heights	Exalted and glorified (cf. Ps. 8:5b–6; 1 Cor. 15:27, 45; Heb.
And bestowed on him the name Which is over every name,	2:7b–8, 9b)
[10]that at the name of Jesus	
every knee should bow,	
in heaven and on the earth and under the earth,	
[11]and every tongue confess	
that Jesus Christ is Lord	
to the glory of God the father.	

In the space available it is unnecessary to lay out the points of comparison in greater detail. Apart from anything else, it is important to gain a feel for the "shape" of the structure as a whole. It is the fact that the allusions are sustained across that basic shape (descent and ascent) that as much as anything else suggests that the hymn was written (and was intended to be read) through the grid of Adam theology. It is the Adamic *significance* of Christ that the hymn seeks to express.

Nevertheless, the exposition of Philippians 2:6–11 in terms of Adam christology has been subjected to vigorous critique.[17] Four points in particular can be brought against it.

First, the hymn uses the term "form (*morphē*)" rather than the term used in Gen. 1:27, "image (*eikōn*)." In a discussion of allusion, however, such an argument carries less weight. We know that the two terms were used as near synonyms.[18] And it would appear that the writer preferred "form of God" because it made the appropriate parallel and contrast with "form of slave."[19] Such a double function of a term is precisely what one might expect in poetic mode.[20]

Second, a strong case has been made that the much discussed term in 2:6c, *harpagmos* ("something to be grasped"), has the extra precision of denoting something to be grasped in retention, rather than something to be grasped at.[21] But to press for one meaning to the exclusion of the other is, once again, an either-or exegesis that ill befits either the words' range of usage, or the poetic style of the present passage, or indeed the lengthy debate on its meaning. In fact, the evidence of the claim that the sense "retaining" inheres in the word itself is highly questionable.[22] *Harpagmos* is better taken with less precision as "act of robbery,"[23] or as equivalent to the English gerund usage, "seizing, grasping"—hence here, "as a matter of seizing, something to be grasped." Since the object of this action, "the being like God," (literally), is a clearer echo of Gen. 3:5,[24] the contrast with Adam's attempt to be like God[25] would hardly be missed by those who were familiar with Paul's Adam theology.[26]

The third objection to recognition of an Adam allusion is in effect that the hymn seems to split the failure of Adam and its outcome into two phases. First, the refusal to grasp equality with God (2:6) has as its converse the act of "emptying" (in contrast to "grasping"),[27] "taking the form of a slave" (in contrast to "being in the form of God"), and becoming like humankind (possibly an allusive contrast to the serpent's temptation, "You shall be like God") (2:7). But then the further act of "obedience to death" (2:8) is presumably set in contrast to the "disobedience" that brought sin and death (as in Rom. 5:19). This interesting two-phase feature, however, simply echoes the two phases of Adam's dying: "death" as expulsion from the garden and from access to the tree of life;[28] and death as Adam's final, physical dying (Gen. 5:5). The same two-phasedness is echoed in Rom 8:3 and Gal. 4:4–5. Here too, then, the Adam analogy is simply being stretched out to cover the whole life of Jesus, rather than only his death (as in Rom. 5:15–19), or also resurrection (as in 1 Cor. 15:21–22).

A fourth objection is that the latter half of the hymn ill fits an Adam christology, given the high exaltation envisaged in 2:9–11.[29] But this neglects the obvious parallel between Phil. 2:10–11 and 1 Cor. 15:24–28, the latter in direct continuity with the Adam-Christ contrast in 15:21–22, and itself embodying a clear allusion to Ps. 8:6 (15:27). It also ignores the fact that Jewish reflection on Adam was already embracing the thought of Adam's ascension to heaven and glorification.[30]

In short, the case for hearing a deliberate allusion to and contrast with Adam in Phil. 2:6–11 remains strong. Given the number and sequence of allusions[31] it could indeed be said that the Philippian hymn is, after Heb. 2:5–9, the fullest expression of Adam christology in the New Testament.

IV

Where does that leave the issue of the preexistent Christ? Here it needs to be stated again that the issue is in fact independent of finding an Adam christology in the Philippians passage.[32] Given the two-stage contrast with Adam just noted, an obvious understanding of the first stage would be from preexistence to existence (2:6–7) and from existence to death (2:8). All the more obvious, indeed, given the aorist tenses and language of 2:7.[33] "Emptied himself and took the form of a slave" (2:7ab) could possibly be understood as some act of self-abasement during Jesus' life.[34] But "became in the very likeness of humankind" (2:7c) is more naturally read as a reference to birth ("was born in the very likeness of humankind").[35]

An alternative possibility may be that the first stage envisaged is the mythic stage of meta-history or prehistory, in which Adam himself makes the transition from *adam* = humankind, to *adam* = the progenitor of Seth and other children (Gen. 5:1–5).[36] Or again, we noted above the two phases implied in the Genesis account of Adam's dying. Adam's grasping disobedience had a two-stage outcome: he was banished from the presence of God (and the tree of life) (3:22–24)— the first death (2:17); and he was thereafter subject to corruption and physical death (5:5). Is it possible, then, that the hymn's intention was to reflect that two-stage outworking of Adam's transgression? In each case, the Adam-Christ, by his own choice, freely embraced the outcome that Adam's grasping and disobedience brought upon humankind. He freely embraced the lot of humankind, as slave to sin and death, which was the consequence of Adam's grasping.[37] And he freely accepted the death that was the consequence of Adam's disobedience. In consequence he was superexalted (reversing both of the preceding two phases) to the status and role originally intended for humankind (Ps. 8:6).[38]

It is precisely the function of allusive poetry to set in motion such a sequence of reflections and parallels. But the fact remains that it has also set in motion the thought of Christ's preexistence. And a commentator could hardly draw out the one while disallowing the other. The problem would then remain of filling out that thought of preexistence. Is Christ Jesus then to be envisaged as making an Adamic choice at some time (!) in eternity? A choice in effect to become man? That is the almost inevitable corollary.[39] The only qualification that needs to be made is once again that this is an extended metaphor. In the parallel case of Wisdom christology, it is not simply Christ, God's Son, who was being spoken of in the Wisdom christology, but Christ as Wisdom.[40] So here it is not simply Christ Jesus as such of whom the hymn speaks, but Christ Jesus in the role of Adam, the Adam that God intended. Wisdom's preexistence allowed amazing language to be used of Christ.[41] So also Adam's prehistory allowed similarly amazing language to be used of

Christ. The mistake would be to collapse the metaphor into a straightforward state-ment of historical fact.[42] To dispense with the metaphor would be to lose sight of what it expresses. The metaphor *is* the message.

Whatever the actual (range of) imagery, however, the basic message of the hymn is clear enough. As a continuation of the appeal of 2:1–4, Christ is presented as one who did not stand on status but emptied himself, as one whose whole life speaks of serving and not grasping, as one whose way to exaltation was only through death. Even if it were judged not to be an expression of Adam christology, it would still be a powerful way of saying that in Christ, his death and resurrec-tion, God's original design for humanity finally achieved concrete shape and ful-fillment.

NOTES

This chapter reproduces some material from section 11.4 of my *Theology of Paul the Apostle* (Grand Rapids: Eerdmans, 1998).

1. E.g., M. Hengel, *The Son of God* (London: SCM Press, 1976), 1–2, regards the Philip-pian hymn as primary evidence that the most significant developments in christology had already taken place within the first twenty years of Christianity's beginnings. The single most significant "development" was, of course, the resurrection itself; see par-ticularly P. Pokorný, *The Genesis of Christology: Foundations for a Theology of the New Testament* (Edinburgh: T. & T. Clark, 1987).

2. C. H. Talbert, "The Problem of Pre-existence in Philippians 2:6–11," *JBL* 86 (1967): 141–53; G. E. Ladd, *A Theology of the New Testament* (London: Lutterworth, 1974), 420–22; M. D. Hooker, "Philippians 2:6–11," in *From Adam to Christ: Essays on Paul* (Cambridge: Cambridge University Press, 1990) 88–100; G. Howard, "Phil. 2:6–11 and the Human Christ," *CBQ* 40 (1978): 368–87; J. Murphy-O'Connor, "Christologi-cal Anthropology in Phil. 2:6–11," *RB* 83 (1976): 25–50; H. Wansbrough in NJB; J. Macquarrie, *Jesus Christ in Modern Thought* (London: SCM Press, 1990), 56–59; C. K. Barrett, *Paul: An Introduction to his Thought* (London: Chapman, 1994), 107–9; earlier bibliography in R. P. Martin, *Carmen Christi: Philippians 2:5–11 in Recent In-terpretation and in the Setting of Early Christian Worship,* SNTSMS 4 (Cambridge: Cambridge University Press, 1967, rev. 1983, 1997), 161–64.

3. See particularly my *Christology in the Making* (London: SCM Press, [2]1989), xii–xix, 114–21.

4. For this translation see Martin, *Carmen Christi,* 84–88; C. F. D. Moule, "Further Re-flexions on Phil. 2:5–11," in W. W. Gasque and R. P. Martin, eds., *Apostolic History and the Gospel: Biblical and Historical Essays,* F. F. Bruce FS, 265–66 (Exeter: Pa-ternoster, 1970), 264–76; P. T. O'Brien, *Philippians,* NIGTC (Grand Rapids: Eerd-mans, 1991), 205; G. F. Hawthorne, *Philippians,* WBC (Waco, Tex.: Word, 1983), 79–81; G. D. Fee, *Philippians,* NICNT (Grand Rapids: Eerdmans, 1995), 200–201; S. E. Fowl, *The Story of Christ in the Ethics of Paul: An Analysis of the Function of the Hymnic Material in the Pauline Corpus,* JSNTS 36 (Sheffield: Sheffield Academic Press, 1990), 89–101, while following the alternative rendering ("within the realm of Christ"), proceeds to argue that "2:6–11 functions as an exemplar within Paul's argu-ment" (92). See also L. W. Hurtado, "Jesus as Lordly Example in Philippians 2:5–11," in P. Richardson and J. C. Hurd, *From Jesus to Paul,* F. W. Beare FS (Waterloo, Ont.: Wilfrid Laurier University Press, 1984), 113–26 (esp. 120–25).

5. Psalm 8:6–8 obviously refers to Gen. 1:28 and 2:19–20.

6. See particularly 1 Cor. 15:25–27; Eph. 1:20–22; Heb. 1:13–2:8; note also the modification of Ps. 110:1b by incorporation of the phrasing of Ps. 8:6 into Phil. 3:21.

7. We should observe that such a transition, from mythical or metahistory to actual history is present in Genesis 1—5. It is clearest in 4:24–5:5, in the transition from *adam* = "humankind" to *adam* = the individual Adam. Earlier, LXX marks the transition by translating *adam* as *anthropos* up to 2:18, but thereafter (and including 2:16) as *Adam*. It should perhaps be added that "myth" or "metahistorical" does not mean "unhistorical."

8. R. Hays, *Echoes of Scripture in the Letters of Paul* (New Haven, Conn.: Yale University, 1989), 18–21, refers particularly to J. Hollander, *The Figure of Echo: A Mode of Allusion in Milton and After* (Berkeley: University of California Press, 1981). My postgraduate student Stephen Wright referred me particularly to H. Bloom, *A Map of Misreading* (New York: Oxford University Press, 1975).

9. In other places I have drawn attention to the importance of allusion in assessing the degree to which Paul drew upon Jesus tradition in his ethical teaching; particularly "Jesus Tradition in Paul," in *Studying the Historical Jesus: Evaluation of the State of Current Research*, ed. B. Chilton and C. A. Evans (Leiden: Brill, 1994), 155–78.

10. An allusion to Milton, *Paradise Lost* 1:1:1; but in thus identifying it I have weakened its effect as an allusion.

11. A glance at the principal Romans commentaries will indicate that the allusions in Romans 1 are more disputed, whereas those in Romans 7 and 8 are widely recognized.

12. Particularly Rom. 8:3; Gal. 4:4–5; and Rom. 15:8.

13. "Image"—Rom. 8:29; 1 Cor. 15:49; 2 Cor. 3:18; 4:4; Col. 3:10. "Glory"—Rom. 5:2; 8:18, 21; 1 Cor. 2:7; 15:43; 2 Cor. 3:18; 4:17; Phil. 3:21; Col. 1:27; 3:4; 1 Thess. 2:12.

14. The technical term is "trope."

15. L. D. Hurst's critique in (below, chapter 5) of my earlier position is a good example of failure to appreciate how allusion works, equivalent to the old confusion between parable and allegory. I refer particularly to his misrepresentation of my earlier exposition: "The view that once the Adam parallel is admitted *it must dominate the hymn so completely that every detail must be paralleled by the experience of Adam is questionable*" (p. 88—my emphasis). Other examples of failure to ask how allusion "works" will punctuate subsequent footnotes.

16. I have yet to see any alternative framework of thought into which the hymn "fits" at so many points (*pace* M. Rissi, "Der Christushymnus in Phil. 2:6–11," *ANRW* 2.25.4 [1987]: 3314–26 [here 3318 n18]). The discussion here makes no attempt to cover all the ground covered in my *Christology* 114–21, plus xviii–xix (2d ed.), but focuses on the issues that responses to these earlier statements provoked.

17. The most thorough of recent critiques has been by C. A. Wanamaker, "Philippians 2:6–11: Son of God or Adamic Christology?" *NTS* 33 (1987): 179–93.

18. Martin, *Carmen*, 102–19; S. Kim, *The Origin of Paul's Gospel*, WUNT 2:4 (Tübingen: Mohr [Siebeck], 1981), 200–204. As O'Brien observes, "most exegetes recognize that the semantic fields of the two terms overlap considerably" (*Philippians*, 263). What more could one look for in making an effective allusion?

19. That any explanation of "form of God" must make reasonable sense of this contrast is rightly emphasized by J. Habermann, *Präexistenzaussagen im Neuen Testament* (Frankfurt: Peter Lang, 1990), 110, 113–16; and Wanamaker, "Philippians 2:6–11," 181–83. But they both use "either-or" exegesis, in particular ignoring the fact that Gal.

4:4–5 and Rom. 8:3 can also be seen as expressing an Adam "interchange" theme (to use M. D. Hooker's term).

20. Cf. O. Cullmann, *The Christology of the New Testament* (London: SCM Press, 1959): "Without the background of Paul's doctrine of the two Adams, either these words can scarcely be understood, or we become lost in tangential theological speculations foreign to early Christianity" (177).

21. In recent scholarship note particularly Habermann, *Präexistenzaussagen,* 118–27; N. T. Wright, "Jesus Christ is Lord: Philippians 2:5–11," in *The Climax of the Covenant: Christ and the Law in Pauline Theology* (Edinburgh: T. & T. Clark, 1991), 77–83. For the earlier debate, see Martin, *Carmen Christi,* 134–53.

22. J. C. O'Neill, "Hoover on *Harpagmos* Reviewed, with a Modest Proposal Concerning Philippians 2:6," *HTR* 81 (1988): 445–9. For example, in the two disputed cases from Eusebius, *HE* 5:2:2–4 and 8:12:1–2 (in the first of which Phil. 2:6 is explicitly cited), the critical point is surely that death was not something already possessed by the would-be martyrs, but something they eagerly grasped at (*pace* Wright, *Climax,* 85).

23. See LSJ; BAGD.

24. The Hebrew *kĕ'lōhîm* (Gen. 3:5) could be translated by *isa theō* (Phil. 2:6) equally as well as well as by *hōs theoi* (Gen. 3:5 LXX). The Hebrew *kĕ* ("like") is translated by *isa* on a number of occasions in LXX (Job 5:14; 10:10; 13:28, etc.; Isa. 51:23; cf. Deut. 13:6; Wisd. Sol. 7:3). As usual, the article with the infinitive indicates something either previously mentioned, or otherwise well known. The earlier discussion of the Adam motif suggests that the Adamic temptation "to be like God" was well enough known in Jewish and early Christian circles. "It is hard to doubt that *to be on equality with God* was intended to evoke the story of Adam. It recalls much too clearly the temptation to which Adam fell" (Barrett, *Paul,* 108).

25. That Adam christology works by antithetic parallel is evident from Rom. 5:15–19.

26. The ambiguity of the relation between "form of God" and "being like God" closely echoes the ambiguity of the relation between "image of God" in Gen. 1:27 and "like God" in 3:5, as indeed also the ambiguity of the function of the tree of life in the garden prior to Adam's expulsion (did Adam have and lose eternal life, or was it to be constantly gained/retained/nourished?—cf. Gen. 2:16 and 3:22).

27. Cf. particularly Moule, "Further Reflexions," 272. The prominence given to the verb *ekenōsen* ("emptied himself") is another example of the danger of treating the hymn as a dogmatic statement ("what did he empty himself of?"; see Hawthorne, *Philippians,* 85, for the traditional range of answers). The function of the term is more to characterize than to define. Note Fee's helpful comment (*Philippians,* 210–11): "this is metaphor, pure and simple" (210).

28. Gen. 2:17—"in the day that you eat of it you shall die."

29. L. J. Kreitzer, *Jesus and God in Paul's Eschatology,* JSNTS 19 (Sheffield: Sheffield Academic Press, 1987), 224n72: vv. 9–11 "breaks the mould of any Adamic motif"; B. Witherington, *Jesus the Sage: The Pilgrimage of Wisdom* (Minneapolis: Fortress Press/Edinburgh: T. & T. Clark, 1994), 259.

30. *Life of Adam and Eve; Apocalypse of Moses* 37; *Testament of Abraham* A 11; cf. the subsequent exaltation of Adam in rabbinic literature (R. Scroggs, *The Last Adam* [Oxford: Blackwell, 1966], chapter 3).

31. Wright speaks of multiple intertextual echoes (*Climax,* 58).

32. In critiques of my earlier treatment of this them, it has been insufficiently observed that this point had already been made (*Christology,* 119–20). Cf. K. J. Kuschel, *Born be-*

fore All Time? The Dispute over Christ's Origin (London: SCM Press; New York: Crossroad, 1992), 262–63; Wright, *Climax,* 91–92, 95–97.

33. So most interpreters; e.g., A. T. Hanson, *The Image of the Invisible God* (London: SCM Press, 1982), 65; I. H. Marshall, "Incarnational Christology in the New Testament," in *Jesus the Saviour: Studies in New Testament Theology* (London: SPCK, 1990), 165–80 (here 170); Habermann, *Präexistenzaussagen* 147; O'Brien, *Philippians,* 223–27, 267; Fee, *Philippians,* 203n41 (both the latter with bibliography); Witherington, *Sage,* 261; G. O'Collins, *Christology: A Biblical, Historical and Systematic Study of Jesus* (Oxford: Oxford University Press, 1995), 35–36.

34. As an allusion to the Servant (J. Jeremias, "Zu Phil. 2:7: HEAUTON EKENOSEN," *NovT* 6 [1963]: 182–88; M. Rissi, "Christushymnus") or suffering righteous (E. Schweizer, *Erniedrigung und Erhöhung bei Jesus und seinen Nachfolgern* [Zurich: Zwingli, 21962], 93–99; followed by Martin, *Carmen Christi* 191–96, and Fowl, *Story* 73–75) the thought would already embrace that of Jesus' death (see, e.g. Rissi, *ANRW* 2.25.4 [1987] 3319–21, O'Brien, *Philippians,* 220–24).

35. So NRSV—"being born in human likeness"; NIV—"being made in human likeness." But also NJB—"becoming as human beings are"; REB—"bearing the human likeness." The parallel with Rom. 8:3 is particularly noticeable ("in the very likeness of"). In his critique of my earlier study Witherington, *Sage,* 263, ignores the significance of both Rom. 8:3 ("of sinful flesh") and Gal. 4:4 ("under the law").

36. See above, note 7.

37. Cf. Hooker: "At this point the one who is truly what man is meant to be—in the form and likeness of God—becomes what other men *are,* because they are in Adam" ("Philippians 2:6–11," 98–99).

38. To make the further claim that the hyperexaltation of 2:9 was a resumption of the divine mode of existence already enjoyed in 2:6 ("the pre-existent was already *Kyrios'*— R. H. Fuller, *The Foundations of New Testament Christology* [London: Lutterworth, 1965], 230) ignores not only the Adam motif (cf. Ps. 8:5–6), but also the consistent emphasis that *kyrios* was bestowed on Jesus at the exaltation (Phil. 2:9–11!) and the more likely implication of the verb, *hyperypsoō* (cf. O'Brien, *Philippians,* 236).

39. See particularly Wright's exposition (*Climax,* 90–98).

40. See further my *Christology,* 176–96 and xvii–xxii; Kuschel, *Born before All Time?* 274–76, 300–301, 305.

41. Some have found the key also to Phil. 2:6–11 in Wisdom theology (D. Georgi, "Der vorpaulinische Hymnus Phil. 2:6–11," in *Zeit und Geschichte,* R. Bultmann FS, ed. E. Dinkler [Tübingen: Mohr (Siebeck), 1964], 263–93; followed by Kuschel, *Born,* 255–66, and Witherington, *Sage,* 261–63). But a Wisdom allusion is far harder to hear in this case than in the creation language of 1 Cor. 8:6 and Col. 1:15–17. And as with most of the search for a pre-Christian Gnostic redeemer myth, the quest here has also proved fruitless (see, e.g., Hengel, *Son,* 25–41; my *Christology,* chapter 4; E. Schweizer, "Paul's Christology and Gnosticism," in *Paul and Paulinism,* C. K. Barrett FS, ed. M. D. Hooker and S. G. Wilson [London: SPCK, 1982], 115–23; Kuschel, *Born,* 248–50; O'Brien, *Philippians,* 193–94; *pace* particularly E. Käsemann, "A Critical Analysis of Philippians 2:5–11," *JTC* 5 [1968]: 45–88); preoccupation with Käsemann's thesis diminishes the value of J. T. Sanders, *The New Testament Christological Hymns: Their Historical Religious Background,* SNTSMS 15 (Cambridge: Cambridge University Press, 1971) and R. G. Hamerton-Kelly, *Pre-existence, Wisdom and the Son of Man: A Study of the Idea of Pre-existence in the New Testament,* SNTSMS 21 (Cambridge: Cambridge University Press, 1973).

42. Too many seem content to conclude "preexistence" without asking what that would have meant to Paul and his generation (e.g., Marshall, "Incarnational Christology"; Habermann, *Präexistenzaussagen;* Witherington, *Sage,* 270). It is to the credit of earlier studies (F. B. Craddock, *The Pre-existence of Christ in the New Testament* [Nashville: Abingdon Press, 1968]; Hamerton-Kelly) that they recognized an issue here (real or ideal preexistence, etc.). Cf. Hengel, *Son of God,* 72: "The problem of "pre-existence" necessarily grew out of the combination of Jewish ideas of history, time and creation with the certainty that God had disclosed himself fully in his Messiah Jesus of Nazareth. . . . Only in this way was the *unsurpassibility and finality of God's revelation* in Jesus of Nazareth expressed in a last, conclusive way."

5.

Christ, Adam, and Preexistence Revisited[1]

LINCOLN D. HURST

Philippians 2:6–11 continues to be one of the most disputed passages in the history of New Testament interpretation.[2] Much recent discussion has centered on its alleged "hymnic" structure,[3] whether or not the hymn is "pre-Pauline,"[4] and what ancient myth or figure served as its basis.[5] These questions are both vexing and crucial, but here I shall concern myself with an issue that may emerge as the most debated of all: does the passage refer to the action of a preexistent being who "empties himself" and "becomes" man, or does it refer from start to finish to the action of a human being, Jesus of Nazareth?

Since Lightfoot[6] and Lohmeyer[7] scholarly opinion has been somewhat agreed that the referent of the language is the preexistent Christ who, existing in the form of God, does not cling to his status but becomes human, suffers death, and is finally exalted by God. This position has been challenged by, among others, J. Murphy-O'Connor,[8] J. A. T. Robinson,[9] and J. D. G. Dunn,[10] all of whom argue in one way or another that it is the human Jesus who is the subject of all these actions. It is agreed by virtually all on both sides of the question that the "hymn" employs an Adam-Christ parallel,[11] and that the basis of the contrast is the action of Adam in "snatching" at equality with God, as opposed to an opposite action by Christ. The central issue to be decided is whether the act of Adam is contrasted with the act of the *heavenly* Christ or with that of the *human* Jesus. According to the Lightfoot understanding, the balance of the logic requires that "Adam, who grasped at a dignity to which he had not right, should be contrasted with Christ, who renounced a status to which he had every right."[12]

Philippians 2:5–11 has been used, along with 2 Cor. 8:9, to argue that Paul, as distinguished from the Fourth Gospel and the author of Hebrews, crossed the line from speaking of a preexistent *purpose* to speaking of a preexistent *person,* since the figure in the form of God exercises personal choice.[13] The arguments for the "preexistent" interpretation are presented thoroughly by R. P. Martin[14] and others[15] and need no restating here. Dunn, however, has mounted an impressive case for the exclusively "anthropological" approach, as it will be called here. Since his argument is the most thorough and widely circulated presentation of this position, I shall focus on it for the most part, with the contributions of others brought in as they are relevant.

Dunn argues that: (1) The verb "existing" (*hyparchōn*) in the phrase "existing in the form of God" (2:6a) does not necessarily denote timeless existence, but can simply mean "being." (2) "The form of God" (*morphē theou*) is a synonym for "the image of God" (*eikōn theou*) of Gen. 1:26f., that is, it denotes the state of Adam (and humankind).[16] (3) The "snatching" (*harpagmos*) at equality with God does not denote something that the figure already possesses (as in the normal trinitarian interpretation of the passage), but it refers to the action of Adam, who "snatched" at a condition which he did not possess, but to which he aspired. (4) Christ, as second Adam, reverses Adam's act and refuses to snatch at an equality to which he, as a human being, likewise had no right,[17] and willingly embraces the form of a servant—which Adam had to embrace unwillingly. (5) The verb *ginomai* in v. 7 does not mean "be born," but refers to Christ's "becoming" like humankind, that is, under the curse of sin. (6) "Taking the form of a servant," "coming to be like[18] men," and "being found in fashion[19] as man" (2:7–8) are all synonyms for Christ's identification with sinful humanity. (7) These acts are not to be traced to any particular point in the experience of Jesus: they were characteristic of his entire life.

Both the "incarnational" (Martin) and "thoroughgoingly anthropological" (Dunn) approaches have their difficulties. Murphy-O'Connor and Dunn have cataloged the problems of the "incarnational" interpretation. Except for (possibly) 2 Cor. 8:9,[20] such a teaching would be unprecedented in Paul and the rest of the New Testament[21] in attributing choice to the preexistent Christ. Also, once it is recognized that a preexistent *man* is ruled out due to insuperable objections,[22] the question of the *mode* of Christ's preexistence becomes problematic, particularly when it appears that his final state is more exalted than his preexistent state.[23] Yet, as Murphy-O'Connor illustrates,[24] everything turns on the presuppositions with which one begins. The position of Dunn and others is not without its problems, and these may turn out to be more crippling than those above. The main difficulties may be enumerated as follows:[25]

1. Dunn argues that a parallelism exists between *morphē theou* in 2:6 and *morphē doulou* in 2:7, and that one of the reasons that *morphē* was chosen over *eikōn* was that "it made the second half of the contrast clearer: he actually became a slave, not just *like* a slave."[26] But why, if the parallelism is taken seriously, should this not apply as well to the *first half* of the contrast, that is, he actually was divine, not just "like" God? It does appear here that Dunn is having it both ways.

2. That in Philo the *logos* can also be God's "image"[27] makes it possible, even if *morphē* is taken to be synonymous with *eikōn,* for Christ to be the *pretemporal* image of God, hence a preexistent being. In this case Phil. 2:6–11 would turn on a contrast of action by the two images: Christ, the pretemporal image, and Adam, the temporal (i.e., human) image.

3. Dunn states that *schēmati hōs anthrōpos* acts as a bridge to the next section in that it "resumes where the first movement of thought had reached" and "recapitulates the thought of the whole section."[28] Thus, as with the other two phrases, *schēmati hōs anthrōpos* refers to the human race's *fallen* condition. Yet "being found in fashion as man" seems too general for this usage, and it could simply

refer to the state of being human as opposed to the state of being divine. A limitation of the nuance to humankind in its *fallen* condition appears too narrow, particularly since that has already been covered in 2:7b ("form of a servant") and possibly by 2:7c ("born"—or "becoming"—"in the likeness of men"). Dunn's suggestion[29] that *hōs anthrōpos* is a subtle reference to Gen. 3:5 LXX ("you shall be as gods") is possible, but it could just as readily reflect the Hebrew of Ps. 8:5,[30] in which the human race is "a little lower than God."[31] This would provide a source of the term *anthrōpos* itself in a context of *a lower status than that of God*[32] (a context, incidentally, in which the status does not depend upon sinfulness).[33] Dunn[34] says that the contrast between God and man is usually framed in the form "God" and "men" (plural). Part of the contrast in Jewish thought is precisely between the holiness of the *one* God and the corruptibility and sin of *all* men.

Dunn looks to Rom. 2:29; 1 Cor. 1:25; Gal. 1:10, and so forth, as parallels. This makes the addition of the uncharacteristically singular *anthrōpos* in 2:8a all the more surprising, and, as an expansion of the preceding plural form, it would cast some doubt upon Dunn's argument that what is in view in v. 8a is a likeness to humankind in its sinful, fallen condition, "lacking the glory in which and for which Adam was created."[35] Murphy-O'Connor is probably closer to the mark in seeing *hōs anthrōpos* as pointing to "the divine intention as manifested in the first human creature." 2:7 would thus speak of Christ's identification with the human race in its fallen state, while 2:8a is a much more general and all-embracing assertion: "beginning to be like (sinful) men, being found in human form." The combination and order of the clauses implies a more comprehensive assertion than simply Christ's identification with humankind in his sinfulness; it appears to involve the human race as it empirically is *and* as it is in God's purpose.[36]

4. If the referent of the entire hymn is taken to be the man Jesus, what may be required is a state *before* he "took the form of a servant" during which he existed, as human, in the form of God. Dunn is not quite clear as to whether in his view the "form of God," since it is a synonym for *eikōn* (humankind), continues for Jesus after the form of the servant is assumed, or whether it is lost.[37] The logic of the hymn appears to require the latter, but in this case one may have to envisage a period in the experience of Jesus during which, as in the form of God, he did not exist in the form of a servant. This is difficult. Dunn[38] has foreseen the objection and attempts to undermine it by saying that

> to press this question is . . . to misunderstand what the hymn is trying to do. It does not seek to narrate a particular event or temptation as such, but simply describes in Adam language the character of Christ's whole life—just as Rom. 7:7–11 describes in Adam language the plight of everyman . . . his whole life constituted his willing acceptance of the sinner's lot (cf. 2 Cor. 5:21).

But this itself encounters problems: (a) It appears to require a Christ who, perpetually in the form of God, chooses continually to take on the form of a servant. Thus the clear-cut nature of the exchange is blurred. The Philippian hymn gives the impression of speaking of three[39] sequential stages (just as in the case of Adam there were two clear-cut stages): form of God, form of servant, exaltation. In Dunn's reconstruction the first two stages appear to "overlap." (b) The parallel with Romans 7 is initially impressive. Yet it breaks down at closer view, for when Paul says in Rom. 7:9 that "I died" (*apethanon,* aorist), it is clear that he is talking in a way which is best not taken literally. That at some point in his experience Paul died is, of course, possible (cf. Acts 14:19?), but the more natural meaning is a figurative one—death as a continuing experience or "way of life." The language is inherently safeguarded from literalistic misinterpretation. There is, on the other hand, nothing in the statement that Christ exchanged a glorious form for an ignoble one that requires the normal meaning of the words to be rejected in favor of a continuing experience or way of life.

5. What is the background of the *doulos?* Is it the servant of Isaiah 42—53, or is it the "slave" to corruption (Rom. 8:18–21) and elemental powers (Gal. 4:3ff.)?[40] Dunn[41] opts for the latter. Yet in Galatians Christ's assumption of the form of a slave cannot be the result of any *human* choice. Dunn attempts to ease this problem by asserting that the main point of Gal. 4:4 is not *birth,* since "born of a woman" was common Jewish idiom for "being human": the verb *ginomai* in the phrase *genomenon hypo nomon* thus means, simply, "who *had been* under the law."[42] This assertion is itself debatable, but, even if granted, it does nothing to vitiate the fact that in Galatians the point at which one comes under the powers is not something which can be *chosen*—it is the natural result of birth as a Jew under the law. Galatians 4:3 is usually taken as parallel in thought to Rom. 8:3, which also uses the "sending" formula,[43] except that in this case the wording is even closer to what Dunn thinks is the meaning of *en homoiōmati anthrōpon* in Phil. 2:7: Christ is sent *en homoiōmati sarkos hamartias.* The similarity of all three passages suggests that in Paul Christ's identification with human beings, whether through servitude to the powers (Galatians) or in likeness to sinful flesh (Romans), *begins automatically with the birth into Judaism.* There is nothing voluntary or praiseworthy here: any volitional element would have to be placed logically prior to the assumption of those states. Dunn's argument would be stronger if he had not been forced to tie Phil. 2:7 so closely to the bondage of Galatians and Romans. Had he been able to argue instead for the servant who voluntarily allows himself to be abased and wounded for others, there would be more of a case for the suggestion that in Philippians it is a human figure who voluntarily allows himself to be disgraced.

6. Dunn's suggestion that the self-emptying and assumption of the new form does not constitute a clear-cut point in time, but characterizes Christ's "whole life," is at first unlikely because of the aorists: "emptied," "having taken," "having become." Yet grammatically these verbs could be either constative (past action viewed in its *entirety*—e.g., *ebaptise tous anthrōpous*) or ingressive (past action viewed in its initiation—e.g., *di' hymas eptōcheusen,* 2 Cor. 8:9). If *ekenōsen* in Phil. 2:7 were viewed as constative, Dunn's case would carry a certain conviction. But this is highly unlikely. Most scholars (including Dunn) note the close parallel in form and content between Phil. 2:5ff. and 2 Cor. 8:9. Both passages speak of a state in the present (*hyparchōn, ōn*) which leads to the assumption, in the aorist, of a subsequent state. Dunn himself refers the aorist of 2 Cor. 8:9 to a definite point in the career of Jesus where one state is clearly exchanged for another: richness

becomes poverty. Dunn makes this point the cross,[44] while others refer it to the incarnation. What needs to be noted is the unlikelihood of the aorist in 2 Cor. 8:9 being *constative:* "becoming poor" is naturally taken, not as a series of past actions viewed in their entirety (constituting a "way of life"), but as a *definite point* where a new state (poverty) begins. Dunn's assertion that in Philippians 2 the aorist has *no* specific point in view, while in 2 Corinthians it does, appears somewhat arbitrary. One is thus left with the initial question: when, if the choice to assume the form of a slave is postulated to have taken place in Jesus' human lifetime, this could have taken place.

7. Dunn's suggestion that in Philippians 2 Christ undoes Adam's wrong *as a human being*[45] is not the only possible way of reading the Adam imagery. If the point of the passage is to present an ethical example of humility rather than to teach soteriology, the implied contrast could, as stated above, be between the heavenly Christ who, being in divine form, did not consider an equality that he possessed something to retain, but willingly assumed humankind's predestined (Ps. 8:5) state as "a little lower than God"; Adam, on the other hand, aspired to an equality (*hōs theoi*) to which he had no right, and unwittingly was made lower (a *doulos*) than his previous state. The preexistent Christ of Philippians 2 could therefore be said to assume a new state vis-à-vis (a) the powers (*doulos,* 2:7b), (b) human beings (*anthrōpōn,* 2:7c), and (c) God (*anthrōpos,* 2:8a). The thought would be paraphrased:

> who being in the form of God, did not reckon being *equal with* God a thing to be grasped, but assuming the form of a slave in the manner of all sinful human beings, and being found in fashion as human [now *lower than* God, Ps. 8:5], he humbled himself yet further, even to death, yes, death on a cross.

The view that once the Adam parallel is admitted it must dominate the hymn so completely that every detail must be paralleled by the experience of Adam[46] is questionable. That the emptying takes place as a human being is not conclusive, nor is there enough evidence that what is in focus in the hymn is *the undoing of Adam's sin.* All would admit that the purpose to which the hymn is put is paraenetic; its point is ethical—to imitate the attitude of Christ, not to develop Christ's second Adam role. Nowhere in Phil. 2:5–11 is Christ said, by his act, to *represent* human beings. The point of his act is its value as an example of supreme humility which others are to imitate.

8. Dunn's appeal[47] to allusion is not ultimately convincing. It is doubtful that it will do for his case what he seems to think it will, and those who have objected to the overall thesis may not be as innocent of the dynamics of literary allusion as is suggested.[48]

9. For me a crucial question raised by Dunn remains this: granted that "Adam seems to be a figure who lay behind a great deal of Paul's theologizing, and [that] the bulk of Paul's Adam theologizing seems to be allusive rather than explicit,"[49] would this *per se* rule out the possibility that Paul is alluding to a previous oral teaching, delivered during one of his stays with the Philippian church, at which time he contrasted the actions of the preexistent Christ with those of the human Adam? Why cannot the allusiveness extend just as well to the actions of a preexistent

Christ? Dunn's appeal to analogy creates at best a possibility rather than a certainty, and the case for allusion must be decided on other grounds, in the larger context of the overall stresses and balances of the hymn. Indeed, Dunn himself puts the question nicely: ". . . does the parallel/contrast begin with Christ in preexistence or with Christ as a second Adam, that is, in mythical or meta-history?"[50] Unfortunately, an appeal to allusion itself hardly settles this all-important question.

10. In order to establish his point Dunn now seems to be emphasizing the imprecision of the meaning of a term and the multifaced imagery of a metaphor. Here he reiterates the dangers warned against years ago by James Barr's "word-concept fallacy." Words do not contain within themselves a inherent meaning, apart from the context (in this case the Adam-Christ contrast) in which those words are used.[51] There are few who would disagree with this today. Therefore, at least for now, it may be best to regard the *harpagmos* debate as temporarily moot. Strong points have been made on both sides; while I continue to find the Moule/Wright[52] arguments compelling in regard to the parallels adduced, Dunn's counterargument (particularly with regard to the use of the Eusebius citations)[53] should provide some caution. The *harpagmos* question needs to be settled ultimately on other grounds.

But having said this, it appears that Dunn may have shifted ground somewhat since *Christology in the Making.* There he argues for a very precise, "either-or" meaning of the term *morphē:* It was chosen over *eikōn* because "it made the second half of the contrast clearer: he actually became a slave, not just *like* a slave." But why more precise, if, as he now claims, terms in the hymn are to be taken as vague, allusive and *im*precise?

11. Dunn's arguments above regarding the "meta-historical Adam" vs. the "historical Adam" may strike some as a bit too strained and abstruse to be convincing. Most of his language here will verge on being incomprehesible to the modern reader. One can only guess what its impact might have been on the ancient reader, including Paul!

12. A final question lingers with regard to the context of the hymn in Paul's ethics. Paul's whole appeal is based on the idea that Christ's action in emptying himself is praiseworthy. But what is there praiseworthy about not aspiring to a status to which one has no right in the first place? Can we believe that "God has given him a name above every name, that at the name of Jesus every knee should bow" because, unlike Adam, he simply refused to think more highly of himself than he ought? Or, putting it at a deeper, theological level, would simply reversing the deed of Adam entitle Jesus to the kind of elevation over all others with which the hymn reaches its climax? In Paul's ethical teaching one of the principles to which he returns again and again is the principle that Christians have rights, but they must be willing to surrender those rights if they clash with a greater principle, love. The Corinthians have the right to eat meat, but only if it does not result in the destruction of the weaker brother (1 Corinthians 8—10); women are equal with men in the church of Christ, but that equality must not be flaunted at the church's expense (1 Corinthians 11—14). Even Paul himself, in the opening verses of Philippians 2, reminds his readers that he has the right to go and be with Christ, but that he is pre-

pared to lay down that right for their sake; to continue "in the flesh" would be better for them.[54] Thus within the context of Paul's ethics it would seem to make more sense to say that the Christ of the hymn *already possessed* the right to be treated as equal with God, but freely surrendered that right for the sake of a greater principle—God's purpose of love in the incarnation. The voluntary laying down of rights already possessed, in other words, is central to Paul's ethical appeal elsewhere, and there is no reason to abandon this principle in our understanding of the hymn of Philippians 2.

Professor Dunn's *Christology in the Making* remains the best sustained treatment of New Testament christology since that of W. Bousset. His primary agenda is one I share—to attempt to understand what the first Christians thought, without the intrusion of later doctrinal perspectives and interests.[55] Such a goal is both admirable and necessary, and to a large degree Dunn succeeds where so many others have failed. But this makes the inclusion of a potentially unpersuasive thesis at the heart of his study all the more serious. One may agree strongly with one of the other pillars of Dunn's argument, that the comparison/contrast with Adam gives us the best reading of the hymn, without accepting his unnecessary corollary that the Adam-Christ parallel therefore demands that we abandon the idea of Christ's personal preexistence and equality with God in the hymn. That idea has stood well the test of time, and will continue to do so in the foreseeable future.

NOTES

1. This is a revised and expanded version of an article which first appeared in *NTS* 32 (1986): 449ff.
2. Cf. the authoritative survey of the history of the interpretation of the passage in R. P. Martin, *Carmen Christi* (Cambridge: Cambridge University Press, 1967; rev. 1983, 1997).
3. The history of religions school (and German opinion in general) has tended toward the view that the verses are non-Pauline in terms of authorship and thought, while British opinion on the whole has tended toward the view that, if the verses are not by Paul himself, they are by someone who was close to Paul (cf. F. W. Beare, *A Commentary on the Epistle to the Philippians* [New York: Harper & Bros., 1959], 30). J. M. Furness, "Behind the Philippians Hymn," *ExpTim* 79 (1967–68): 178, who compares Philippians 2 with other Pauline passages (such as 1 Corinthians 13 and 15), sees it as a "spontaneous expression of the writer's christological faith and the fine, poetic language as a natural consequence of the heightened feeling of this section of the epistle." J. G. Gibbs, "The Relation between Creation and Redemption according to Phil. II 5–11," *NovT* 12 (1970): 273, stresses the unity of the hymn with its context: "Clearly Paul did not begin in his letter with cosmic or metaphysical speculations which then were loosely related to Jesus of Nazareth." We shall assume in this study that the verses, whether by Paul or not, represent what Paul wished to say at that point in his argument.
4. This phrase, as commonly used, is notoriously vague. Does it refer to something which was written before Paul's lifetime, before his conversion, or before his writing of the letter? It is, of course, extremely difficult to distinguish those places where Paul draws upon a tradition which antedates him (or was framed independently of him) from those

places where he draws upon a tradition which he helped to frame. One criterion should be whether that tradition is attested more widely than in Paul's writings.

5. Furness, 178ff., has cataloged the various parallels which have been drawn: Alexander, Heracles, Nero, Caligula, Lucifer, Adam, and the servant. Contra H. Chadwick, "St. Paul and Philo of Alexandria," *BJRL* 48 (1965–66): 301, the nearest analogy to Philippians 2 is not Plutarch's description of Alexander's behavior in Asia, nor are the parallels with Heracles and the two Roman emperors close enough. The ideas surrounding Lucifer depend too much upon nonbiblical tradition. E. Käsemann, "A Critical Analysis of Phil. 2:5–11, *Journal of Theology and the Church* 5 (1969): 45–88, argues for an "anthropos myth" as enshrined in the Hermetic tract *Poimandres* (cf. also R. H. Fuller, *The Foundations of New Testament Christology* [London: Lutterworth, 1965], 76f.) and Philo. But it is now felt by many that Philo and Poimandres, texts which were thought to speak of the descent of a heavenly man, actually speak of the origin of a heavenly man, who in all likelihood is Adam (humankind in general) (cf., e.g., A. E. J. Rawlinson, *The New Testament Doctrine of the Christ* [London: Longmans, 1926], 125ff.; C. H. Dodd, *The Bible and the Greeks,* 2d ed. [London: Hodder, 1954], 145ff.; and G. B. Caird, *Paul's Letters from Prison* [Oxford: Oxford University Press, 1976], 103f.). The only two valid possibilities which remain are Adam and the servant.

6. Cf. J. B. Lightfoot, *St. Paul's Epistle to the Philippians* (London: Macmillan, 1927), 109–15.

7. Cf. E. Lohmeyer, *Kyrios Jesus: Eine Untersuchung zu Phil. 2,5–11* (Heidelberg: C. Winter, 1928).

8. "Christological Anthropology in Phil. 2:6–11," *RB* 83 (1976): 25–50.

9. *The Human Face of God* (London: SCM Press, 1973), 162ff.

10. *Unity and Diversity in the New Testament* (London: SCM Press, 1977; 2d ed. 1990), 134–36; *Christology in the Making* (London: SCM Press, 1980; 2d ed. 1989).

11. Cf. O. Cullmann, *The Christology of the New Testament* (London: SCM Press, 1963) 181; Murphy-O'Connor, passim; W. D. Davies, *Paul and Rabbinic Judaism* (London: SPCK, 1948), 41f.; M. D. Hooker, "Philippians 2:6–11," in *Jesus and Paulus: Festschrift für W. G. Kummel,* ed. E. E. Ellis and E. Grässer (Göttingen: Vandenhoeck & Ruprecht, 1975), 160–64; C. K. Barrett, *From First Adam to Last* (London: Black, 1962), 69–72; Robinson, *Human Face of God,* 163; and Dunn, *Christology in the Making,* 114ff.

12. Caird, *Paul's Letters from Prison,* 121.

13. Caird, "The Development of the Doctrine of Christ in the New Testament," in *Christ for Us Today,* ed. N. Pittenger (London: SCM Press, 1968), 79ff.; cf. also G. B. Caird and L. D. Hurst, *New Testament Theology* (Oxford: Clarendon, 1984), 340ff.

14. Cf. Martin, *Carmen Christi,* 99ff., passim.

15. In addition to the list of authors cited in *Carmen Christi,* cf. those writers cited in Martin's *Philippians* (New Century Bible, Grand Rapids: Eerdmans, 1976), 109ff., and Dunn, *Christology,* 310ff.

16. For the equivalence of *morphē* to *eikōn,* cf. Martin, "Μορφή in Philippians ii 6–11," *ExpTim* 70 (1958–59): 183, and *Carmen Christi,* 102–19. Until Lohmeyer the phrase "form of God" in v. 6 was seen as a reference to Adam. Cullmann, 178, while recognizing the Adam reference, interprets it as the Heavenly Man.

17. While Dunn is in general agreement with Murphy-O'Connor, they differ at this point. For Murphy-O'Connor, 2.6b speaks of something already possessed by Christ. However, he defines this not as "equality" but as the state of being "like God." He bases this on the allegedly weaker force of the adverb *isa* as opposed to the adjective *isos,* which

would denote equality. But this distinction cannot be pressed. The very parallel he cites (following P. Grelot) for this use of *isa, Odyssey* XV, 520 ("our people already honors him as if—*isa*—he were God"), would allow 2.6 to read "although he was in the form of God, he did not consider being [honored] as God [virtual equality] a thing to be grasped." Murphy-O'Connor's limitation of being "as God" to the notion of incorruptibility (free access to the tree of life) is, of course, possible, but it does not appear to be as convincing as is Dunn's argument for a more thoroughgoing equality.

18. *Homoiōma* in v. 7 is taken by most, including Dunn, to indicate similarity yet difference: "like sinful men." C. H. Talbert, "The Problem of Pre-existence in Philippians 2:6–11," *JBL* 86 (1967): 150f., however, suggests that *en homoiōmati anthrōpōn* reflects the designation of Seth in Gen. 5:3 as "in his (Adam's) own likeness (*demuth*)," i.e., it speaks of Christ simply as "son of Adam." This would provide an entirely different nuance from Rom. 8:3: *homoiōma* would not in any way distinguish Christ from the human race; it would mean a complete identity. In this case *en homoiōmati anthrōpōn* would have no bearing per se on the notion of human sinfulness, but would refer simply to the normal process of birth.

19. As in the case of *homoiōma,* the use of *schēma* in 2.7c is usually seen as indicating a nuance of difference: For Beare (q.v.) it means "something more within the human frame." Martin, *Carmen Christi,* 207, however, denies *schēma* any notion of differentiation from normal humanity: it means, simply, that "his *schēma* was such that those who saw Him gained the impression that He was a man . . . for it was by His *schēma* that this was registered."

20. The point at which Christ's "richness" becomes "poverty" is somewhat ambiguous (see below).

21. Contra Fuller, 236n10, for whom "the pre-existence-incarnation christology is so widespread that it can hardly be called specifically Pauline."

22. Cf. the powerful arguments of Caird, *Paul's Letters,* 103f. The preexistence of Christ as a man cannot be argued from 1 Cor. 15:47–49, where he is referred to as "the man from heaven" (in contrast to Adam, "the man of dust"), since Paul makes it clear that the heavenly man follows Adam rather than precedes him. Dunn rightly interprets the 1 Corinthians passage as referring to Christ as the man of the new creation, whose image Christians will bear when he returns from heaven (*Christology,* 107f., 308n41).

23. Talbert, 141.

24. Murphy-O'Connor (30–38) accuses Martin, Moule and others of reading the hymn in the light of a prejudgment toward preexistence, but is he not guilty of prejudice in the other direction when he claims that "since the hymn deals with Christ in his *concrete terrestrial condition,* one should begin with the working hypothesis that the author views Christ as man, and only if *this* hypothesis fails to explain the rest of the evidence should one envisage the hypothesis that he is a being of a higher order" (39, italics mine)? To *begin* with the assumption that the hymn deals with Christ only in his "concrete terrestrial condition" is clearly the result of a prior decision that "being like" God could only be true of humankind. But the pretemporal *Logos,* as God's *charaktēr* (for this usage in Philo, cf. R. Williamson, *Philo and the Epistle to the Hebrews* [Leiden: Brill, 1970], 428), could be said to be "like God."

25. For different accounts of the problems with the thoroughgoingly anthropological view, cf., e.g., Gordon D. Fee, *Paul's Letter to the Philippians,* NICNT (Grand Rapids: Eerdmans, 1995), 203ff.; Gerald F. Hawthorne, *Philippians,* Word Biblical Commentary 43 (Waco, Tex.: Word, 1983), 83ff.; and Moises Silva, *Philippians* (Grand Rapids: Baker, 1992), 115ff.

26. Dunn, *Christology,* 311n70 (italics mine). For the opposite view, cf. V. Taylor, *The Atonement in New Testament Teaching* (London: Epworth, 1945), 95f., who claims that *morphē doulou* means only "the form of a slave," due to Paul's built-in repugnance for the low condition of slaves.

27. Cf. above, note 24.

28. Dunn, *Christology,* 117.

29. Ibid., 118.

30. One need not follow Lohmeyer's belief, adopted by many (cf. Martin, 209n4), that underlying *hōs anthrōpos* in v. 8a is the *huios anthrōpou* of Dan. 7:13. It is astonishing how much attention has centered on Dan. 7:13 (cf. Martin, 208ff.), the wording of which does not fit. The simple step of going a stage back in Hebrew reflection to Psalm 8 (which we know to be a characteristically Pauline text—cf. 1 Cor. 15:25–7; Rom. 8:20; Col. 1:20; Phil. 2:10; and 3:21, etc.) is not mentioned as a possibility by virtually all commentators on Philippians. Cf. C. Spicq, *L'Epître aux Hébreux* (Paris: Gabalda, 1952), 1:163, who equates the "emptying" of Phil. 2:7 with being made "lower than angels" of Heb. 2:7f. While this of course does not reflect the Hebrew of Psalm 8, it may at least be a step in the right direction.

31. The Semitic features of the passage were well demonstrated by Lohmeyer, and, despite its Hellenistic images and concepts, it is generally assumed that the hymn could contain direct translation of the Hebrew Old Testament (cf. Murphy-O'Connor, 40).

32. It is often noted that "wherever Christ is designated anthropos in Paul's letters (cf. Rom. 5:12ff.; 1 Cor. 15:20–49), a contrast with Adam is intended" (Talbert, 149; cf. also Fuller, 236n19). If the background of 2.8a is Ps. 8.5, however, the contrast would be with God (cf. *isa theō,* which Dunn argues is equivalent to *hōs theoi* of Gen. 3:5 LXX) and the parallel with Adam (*hōs anthrōpos*).

33. Dunn, *Christology,* 318, does see in the hymn an allusion to Psalm 8, but not until 2.9ff.; i.e., it is only at the exaltation that Ps. 8:6 ("You put all things under his feet") is realized. This, however, does not mean that Paul could not have separated v. 5a of the psalm from v. 6 as denoting a prior stage (cf. 1 Cor. 15:25ff.).

34. Dunn, *Christology,* 311n68.

35. Page 117, following M. D. Hooker, "Interchange in Christ," *JTS* 22 (1971): 356f.

36. Murphy-O'Connor, 43. Dunn's (*Christology,* 117) appeal to Phil. 3:21, which speaks of "refashioning (*metaschēmatisei*) our body of lowliness," cannot anchor *schēma* in 2:8 to a notion of sinful humanity lacking the glory for which Adam was created in Ps. 8:4ff. The fact that *morphē* and its verbal form can be used for (a) Christ's prekenotic state (2.6) and (b) the subsequent glorified body (3.21) as well as the lowly state of a slave shows the fluidity with which such terms are used by Paul. Robinson, *Human Face of God,* 164f., appeals to the reversal of the words of the hymn in chapter 3; he suggests that "the state of being in the form of God is just as human as that of our present dishonour—in fact more truly and richly so" (cf. Phil 3:7–11, 20f., where Paul wishes to be "found" [*heurethō*] in him . . . being conformed [*symmorphizomenos*] to his death . . . who will refashion [*metaschēmatisei*] our body of lowliness [*sōma tēs tapeinōseōs*) to be conformed [*symmorphon*] to the body of his glory"). But what supplies the basis of the contrast in chapter 3 is undoubtedly "the form of a servant" as opposed to the resurrected form of glory. The first usage of *morphē* (*tou theou,* 2:6) is not involved, and it is not apparent what relevance chapter 3 has for it. Paul is not to be conformed to Christ's prior *morphē* (*theou*), but to that which comes after the *morphē doulou*—the exalted form. It is impossible to anchor terms such as *morphē* and *schēma* to a single nuance in chapters 3 and 4 of Philippians.

37. On the one hand, the statement that *morphē* was chosen over *eikōn* because there was no clear idea in either Jewish or earliest Christian thought that Adam had lost God's image (Dunn, *Christology,* 311n70) seems to imply that, for Dunn, the hymn writer wanted to stress that the image had been lost. On the other hand, his emphasis (ibid., 116) on the ambiguity in the Genesis narrative of what Adam lost and the supposed ambiguity carried over into the Philippian hymn, coupled with his generalizing approach to the kenosis as during Jesus' "whole life" (ibid., 120), makes any separation into clear-cut stages impossible.

38. Ibid., 120. Cf. also J. Harvey, "A New Look at the Christ Hymn in Philippians," *ExpTim* 76 (1964–65): 336: " . . . is this not what all of us—all, that is, except Jesus—seek to do, to become like God ourselves?"

39. Contra Fuller, *Foundations,* 207, who sees "five phases of existence" (preexistence, becoming incarnate, incarnate life, re-ascension, exalted state). The transitional stages are not necessary.

40. This is a much debated issue. Those arguing for the servant song background include L. Cerfaux, *Le Christ dans la Théologie de St. Paul* (1951; ET New York: Herder, 1962), 283ff.; H. Wheeler Robinson, *The Cross in the Old Testament* (Philadelphia: Westminster Press, 1955), 103ff.; Talbert, 152f.; Davies, 274, etc. There is something to be said for this view. But: (a) The absence elsewhere in Paul of servant imagery (cf. Caird, *Paul's Letters,* 102) would argue against it. (b) The verbal similarities presented by Cerfaux depend too much on Aquila's version of the LXX and the assumption that the hymn writer had an identical *Vorlage.* (c) Even if the *eidos* of Isa. 52:4 and 54:2 is synonymous with the *morphē* of the hymn, there is nothing in the servant songs to suggest that the servant ever existed in *eidos/morphē theou.* It is only by combining servant and Adam speculation that it becomes possible—but this is a multiplication of hypotheses. Using Occam's razor, all features of the Philippians passage can be explained from a background of Pauline-style thinking about Adam and his bondage (cf. Romans 1). (d) The subsequent lordship of Christ over the authorities in Phil. 2:10 would suggest, in the context of Pauline theology elsewhere, his previous *douleia* under them (so Fuller, 209, who speaks of his "thralldom to the powers of evil" in Phil. 2).

41. *Christology,* 115. He feels an allusion to the Hebrew of Isa. 53.12 is "just possible" (118), although a "more sustained allusion to the Servant of Isa. 53 is unlikely" (312n87).

42. Ibid., 40.

43. G. N. Stanton, "Incarnational Christology in the New Testament," in *Incarnation and Myth: The Debate Continued*, ed. M. Goulder (London: SCM Press, 1977), 153ff., states that the "sending of the Son" in Gal. 4:4 may be assumed, in the light of Paul's statements elsewhere, to imply preexistence. This, however, does not follow if the "sonship" for Paul is a human category drawn from Israel's experience. In neither Phil. 2:6–11 nor 2 Cor. 8:9 is Christ referred to as "Son."

44. For Dunn, *Christology,* 122, this new state begins at the point where "the richness of his communion with God . . . is [set] in sharp contrast with the poverty of his desolation on the cross" (122).

45. Ibid., 119. Dunn sees Philippians 2 as similar to Heb. 2:6–9 in that it depicts "the divine program for man being run through again in Jesus" (117). On p. 116 he runs the *hōs* in *schēmati heuretheis hōs anthrōpos* together with *etapeinōsen* so as to read, "as man he humbled himself," i.e., representation. But this is forced: *hōs* must be linked with what precedes ("being found as man"), not with what follows.

46. Ibid.: "Since the thought is dominated by the Adam/Christ parallel and contrast, the in-

dividual expressions must be understood within that context. The terms used in the hymn do not have any independent value; their sense is determined by their role within the Adam christology . . . " (italics his). Dunn's claim above (p. 80, n. 15) that I have here misrepresented him in such a way as to display something akin to a confusion of parable with allegory is a red herring which has nothing to do with my argument. It fails to distract one from the central point: no matter how the details of the hymn are understood, the Adam-Christ parallel stands without having to make the two figures thoroughly equivalent in terms of their prior status.

47. Cf. above, pp. 75, 78–79.
48. Cf., for instance, my edition of Caird and Hurst, *New Testament Theology,* which includes a lavish treatment of the allusiveness of Markan theology (pp. 31–34, 54, 314).
49. Cf. above, p. 75.
50. Cf. above, p. 74.
51. Cf. James Barr, *The Semantics of Biblical Language* (Oxford: Clarendon, 1961).
52. Cf. N. T. Wright, *The Climax of the Covenant* (Minneapolis: Fortress Press, 1991), 62ff.
53. Cf. above, p. 81, n. 22.
54. Cf. Wright, *Climax of the Covenant,* 88, who also points to Phil. 3:4ff., where "Paul describes the glories of his position as a Jew and tells how, for the sake of gaining Christ, he had turned his back on them."
55. Unlike the majority of Dunn's critics on the question of Philippians 2 (cf. the many he cites on pp. xxxiii–xxxiv of the second ed. of *Christology in the Making* [Grand Rapids: Eerdmans, 1989]), I have no doctrinal axe I am grinding in the matter. The truth or falsity of an idea does not stand or fall with any one passage, or even combination of passages. In another context—the christology of the epistle to the Hebrews—I have drawn similar conclusions to those which Dunn has drawn for Philippians 2. Cf. "The Christology of Hebrews 1 and 2," in *The Glory of Christ in the New Testament: Studies in Christology in Memory of George Bradford Caird,* ed. L. D. Hurst and N. T. Wright (Oxford: Clarendon Press, 1987), 151–64.

6

In the Form of God and Equal with God (Philippians 2:6)

GERALD F. HAWTHORNE

Since my Word Biblical Commentary volume on Philippians appeared in 1983, interest in Philippians 2:5–11 has continued. The fascination of scholars and students and preachers with these special verses remains unabated, no doubt because they make up one of the most beloved, one of the most beautiful, one of the most exalted, one of the most theologically and christologically significant texts of all the texts of the New Testament, if not indeed the most, and because there is still no sign that these verses have yet disclosed their full secrets or completely opened up their rich treasures.[1] This continuing fascination is easily observable by noting the number of commentaries that have been written in the intervening years as well as the many monographs and articles that address the whole or specific aspects of this "hymn."

It is now my not unwelcomed task to enter once again into the continuing stream of the "history of interpretation" of this magnificent "hymn" and in particular to isolate two highly important but difficult and much debated terms that appear immediately in its opening lines (2:6), namely, "in the form of God" (ἐν μορφῇ θεοῦ) and "equal with God" (ἴσα θεῷ) and to draw attention to the chief lines of discussion that have taken place concerning them from 1983 until the present. In order to do this, however, it will be necessary for me also to touch, if only glancingly, on the meaning of the participle, "being" (ὑπάρχων) and the extraordinarily troublesome expression, "he did not consider [something] *harpagmon*" (οὐχ ἁρπαγμὸν ἡγήσατο), both of which also appear in this initial strophe and are inextricably linked with the two expressions immediately under consideration:

ὃς ἐν μορφῇ θεοῦ ὑπάρχων
οὐχ ἁρπαγμὸν ἡγήσατο
τὸ εἶναι ἴσα θεῷ
("Who in form of God being
did not consider *harpagmon*
the being equal with God")

This "hymn" opens with the relative pronoun, "who" (ὅς), a characteristic element in other hymnlike confessions that appear in the New Testament (Col. 1:15; 1 Tim. 3:16; Heb. 1:3).[2] Its immediate antecedent is Christ Jesus (Χριστῷ Ἰησοῦ)–ὅς ἐν μορφῇ θεοῦ ὑπάρχων, "who in the form of God being." This pronoun thus links and identifies the historical Jesus of 2:5 with the section that immediately follows about the one existing "in the form of God," and "equal with God" (2:6).

The participle, "being/existing," that agrees with it grammatically is a circumstantial participle open to more than one interpretation, e.g. concessive ("although") or causative ("because"), about which more will be discussed later. It is formed not from the simple verb "to be" (εἰμί), a verb that is used over two thousand times in the New Testament, but from a much more rarely used (only sixty times) and perhaps stronger verb than εἰμί that at times conveys the idea of "to exist (really)."[3] Now of course, the question arises should one give to ὑπάρχων its full lexical meaning, or does the phrase "ὑπάρχειν ἐν" appear here simply as an idiom such as it seems to be in Luke 7:25 (ἰδοὺ οἱ ἐν ἱματισμῷ ἐνδόξῳ καὶ τρυφῇ ὑπάρχοντες ἐν τοῖς βασιλείοις εἰσίν) and should it thus be translated "in the sense that Christ was clothed with the divine form," as T. Nagata contends?[4]

To answer these questions I would point out that in a "hymn" like this where every word and tense (note the tense is present) is weighed, it seems only proper that ὑπάρχων be given its full meaning here. To be sure, though Moulton cautioned about overestimating the time value of the present participle, and warned that "grammar speaks to exegesis here [in Phil 2:6] with no decisive voice," yet in light of the context it is quite possible and indeed probable in my judgment and that of others, that "Paul used the participle rather than the finite verb because of Christ's always 'being' so." The language here "expresses as presupposition what the rest of the sentence assumes, namely that it was the preexistent One who 'emptied himself' at one point in our human history."[5] Whoever carefully reads the text must take note of the fact that the present participle ὑπάρχων stands in temporal contrast with the aorist participle λαβών in 2:7b, thus indicating that before this person described by ὑπάρχων took the form of a slave (2:7) he already existed in the form of God. Note that ὑπάρχων ("being/existing really") also stands in sharp contrast to the participle, γενόμενος ("having been born/having been made in the likeness of human beings—ἐν ὁμοιώματι ἀνθρώπων γενόμενος, 2:7c), a fact that "only makes sense if 'being in the *morphē* of God' presupposes prior existence as God."[6]

IN THE FORM OF GOD

I turn now to a discussion of the first of the two principal expressions that constitute the heart of this chapter—in the form of God (2:6a). What did Paul mean when he wrote that Christ Jesus always existed ἐν μορφῇ θεοῦ?[7] If the number and variety of interpretations given to this expression have any meaning it must be because it is of crucial importance for understanding the whole of the Christ-hymn, of fundamental significance for determining the christology of the entire passage. The difficulty of this phrase is proverbial, stemming not so much from the fact that the word μορφή ("form") appears only three times in the New Testament—twice in our "hymn" and once in the longer ending of Mark (16:12)—nor from the paucity of its use in the Greek Bible,[8] nor from an ignorance of its meaning in

Greek literature as a whole, but from an inability to know with certainty what Paul meant when he used this word to say that Christ Jesus existed "in the form of God" (ἐν μορφῇ θεοῦ), and thus from a sense of helplessness or inadequacy as to how to translate it here in 2:6–7.

It is common knowledge that the word μορφή itself has a wide range of meaning that embraces such ideas as stature, form, condition, feature, countenance, external appearance, and the like. In many sacred and secular texts it referred also to a person's good looks, attractive appearance, or charming features.[9] Writers used it to describe the shape of statues or of appearances in visions similar to persons, or of messengers sent from heaven in the form of young men.[10] In the New Testament the root μορφ- combines to create such words as μεταμορφόω ("to transform," Rom. 12:2; 2 Cor. 3:18), μορφόω ("to form, shape," Gal. 4:19); μόρφωσις ("embodiment, outward form," Rom. 2:20; 2 Tim. 3:5), συμμορφίζω ("be conformed to, to take on the same form as," Phil. 3:10), and σύμμορφος ("having the same form, similar in form," Phil 3:21).

From Homer onwards μορφή referred to that "which could be perceived by the senses."[11] But more than this. "It could also point to the embodiment of the form since possession of the form implied participation in its nature or character."[12] Hence, other early classical writers, especially the Greek philosophers (e.g., Aristotle), thought of μορφή, though perhaps not as equivalent in meaning to the Greek word οὐσία ("being/essence"), yet bordering on it, a word that called attention to the essential attribute of a person or thing. Following Lightfoot,[13] who had adopted this Aristotelian meaning of μορφή, I too concluded that it was in this sense that Paul was using the word here in the "Christ-hymn":

> "Μορφή always signifies a form which truly and fully expresses the being which underlies it" (MM, 417). Thus when this word is applied to God, his μορφή must refer to his deepest being, to what he is in himself, to that "which cannot be reached by our understanding or sight, precisely because God is ἀόρατος ["invisible"]: in fact the word has meaning here only as referring to the reality of God's being" (Cerfaux, *Christ*, 305). Μορφὴ θεοῦ, then, may be correctly understood as the "essential nature and character of God" (Vincent).[14]

For this I was gently chided,[15] and no doubt rightly so, for it is unlikely that Paul intended to use μορφή in such a deeply philosophical sense when he wrote of the "form" of God. In any case, as Martin pointed out, the consensus of present-day scholarly opinion is against such an interpretation.[16]

E. Käsemann in his groundbreaking essay rejected the classical background as a means of understanding the meaning of μορφή in Philippians: "The conceptual language of the hellenistic period moves within an ideological framework quite different from that of the Classical Greek era." Rather, he pointed out that μορφή now in this new period means "a mode of being [*Daseinsweise*] in a specific direction such as, for example, being in divine substance and power."[17] But Käsemann, too, has been criticized for attaching too much significance to the preposition ἐν here in Phil. 2:6, claiming that for Paul it "designate[s] the realm in which one stands and by which one is determined, as in a field of force,"[18] and for depending too heavily for his interpretation of this text upon parallels drawn from Gnostic dualistic literature of a "heavenly man" (e.g., *Sib.Or.* 8.458; *Corp. Herm.* 1.13–14).[19]

E. Schweizer's explanation of μορφή as meaning "status, condition, position,"[20] is an interpretation that seems to have endured, that continues to give direction to scholars interpreting the "Christ-hymn,"[21] that Martin considers on balance to be an attractive view that has most in its favor since it offers an easy parallelism between μορφῇ θεοῦ and μορφῇ δούλου—"He who was in the beginning . . . at God's side . . . chose to . . . accept the human condition, 'in the form of a servant,'"[22] and that appears to have resisted criticism, namely that such an understanding of μορφή is absent from Greek literature.[23] Martin's quotation of Tobit 1:13 (NEB), in defense of Schweizer to show that his understanding of μορφή can indeed be found in the literature, is not fully convincing: "Since I was whole-heartedly mindful of my God, the Most High endowed me with a presence (μορφή) which won me . . . favor." Both the translation of this same text in R. H. Charles's *Apocrypha and Pseudepigrapha,* and the textual notes that appear there—"When I remember my God with all my soul, the Most High gave me grace and favour [χαρ. κ. μορφ. (חנא וחסדא)] in the sight of Shalmaneser and I used to buy for him all things for his use"—may simply mean that the God-given handsome appearance and gracious manner of Tobit were such that they commanded the king's attention and confidence.

The fact that the idea of "appearance or visible form" lies at the heart of the meaning of μορφή has caused earlier scholars to interpret "the form of God" in which Christ Jesus existed in terms of the "glory" (δόξα) of God,[24] that radiating brilliance of God by which the writers of the Old Testament and intertestamental literature often described him and his presence.[25] This understanding of μορφή still informs scholars today. S. E. Fowl,[26] for example, infers both from the fact that the visible form of God is expressed in terms of God's glory in the LXX, and also from the fact that Paul on several occasions uses this same word as the visible manifestation of God's majesty,[27] that it is only proper to understand μορφὴ θεοῦ as a reference to God's glory, his radiance and splendor in which/by which his majesty is made visible. "By locating Christ in this glory, it conveys the majesty and splendour of his pre-incarnate state," and corresponds to John 17:5.[28] But Fowl is cautious and is careful to note that this understanding of μορφή in terms of δόξα is not because the idea of "glory" is inherent in the word "form" itself, but is derived from the larger context of that which describes the visible presence of God. It is used here to reflect Christ's exalted position; it is not intended as a dogmatic statement about Christ's nature but is used to say something about Christ's status.[29]

C. A. Wanamaker, who develops Philippians 2:6–11 in terms of a "Son of God" christology,[30] nevertheless asks what the outward "form of God" (2:6) might be. He gives as the most probable answer, his "divine glory," noting that in the Old Testament "glory" (*kabod*) is one of the primary attributes of God by which he is known or makes himself known to humans. The "glory of the Lord" is connected with the saving acts of the Lord,[31] and in Ezekiel and parts of the Penteteuch it appears as a technical term to describe theophanies.[32] For Wanamaker Paul understood the link between the outward appearance of Christ and his possession of divine glory to be confirmed by Phil. 3:21. Here Paul seems to have believed that in the general resurrection the Christian would share the form of the outward appearance of the glorious or luminous body of Christ.[33]

As attractive as this view is, it is open to serious objections that should make one slow to adopt it as the correct view. First, as I noted in an earlier writing,[34] it is impossible to apply this meaning of μορφή as "glory" (δόξα) to the parallel phrase that also occurs in this "hymn"—μορφὴ δούλου (2:7). Second, and equally as telling, is the lack of linguistic evidence that is necessary to make it reasonable for one to claim so confidently that the meaning of μορφή can be seen as an equivalent of δόξα or that δόξα can be employed as the key for interpreting the phrase, "in the form of God" (ἐν μορφῇ θεοῦ).[35]

There are those scholars who seek to get at the meaning of ἐν μορφῇ θεοῦ of Phil. 2:6 via the κατ' εἰκόνα ἡμετέραν of Gen. 1:26, that is, those who affirm that the expression "form" (μορφὴ θεοῦ) of Philippians is to be understood as an equivalent expression to "image" (εἰκὼν θεοῦ) of Genesis, and who thus interpret the entire "hymn" in terms of an Adam-Christ/first Adam-last Adam contrast.[36] J. D. G. Dunn, having adopted this understanding of the Philippian text, has been its most articulate advocate and continued loyal supporter.[37] He argues that here in the "hymn" Paul contrasts Jesus with Adam. "'The frontispiece of ii. 6a plays no role . . . in portraying the 'glory' from which Christ came, nor does it allude to his pre-temporal, heavenly state."[38] He is the man Jesus, a human being, the last Adam, who like the first Adam, was also in God's image (εἰκών). But unlike the first Adam who grasped at being equal with God (cf. Gen. 3:5, 22), Christ, the last Adam, refused to do this, refused to reach out and take that which was not rightfully his, refused to attempt to make himself like God, "equal with God." Rather, he deliberately chose to take on himself the lot of fallen Adam, "sharing Adam's subjection to *sin* and death" (italics mine),[39] and waited on God to exalt him and to bestow honor upon him. Others continue to follow Dunn[40] without the same kind of intellectual rigor that he displays, unaware of or indifferent to the serious criticisms that have been leveled and continue to be leveled against his exegesis of Philippians 2[41] or his attempt at blunting these criticisms.[42]

Two areas of weakness in the exegesis of Philippians 2 offered by Dunn and others stand out to me from among the many. First is the seeming heavy dependence these scholars place on μορφή as being equivalent to εἰκών. If these two terms are found not to be interchangeable terms, then certainly their position, to say the least, needs to be reconsidered. Steenburg,[43] in his careful philological study has made it sufficiently clear in my judgment that it is "inappropriate to assume a strict equivalence of μορφή and εἰκών."[44] The second area of weakness, much more crucial, lies in the answer one must give to Dunn's own insightful question, which in essence is as follows: What added significance for a soteriology focused exclusively on the cross and resurrection is provided by reading back Christ's exalted status into preexistence?[45] C. F. D. Moule has adequately answered this question for me, but it is an answer that runs counter to Dunn's interpretation of the "Christ-hymn" and that of his colleagues. Moule writes:

It is a familiar fact that the usually accredited test of a realistic doctrine of Christ is whether it yields a realistic doctrine of salvation. Can an inspired person . . . achieve what Christians experience in Christ, when they find in him humanity recreated and the new age beginning to be present? If Christ is authentically experienced as not only a teacher but a Savior, one who rescues the human will from its self-centeredness and, when he is allowed to do it, human society from its warped condition, can it be that he is no more than a supremely inspired person? There is no doubt that mainstream Christianity always found in Jesus Christ a Savior and no less—a creator and not an instructor or example only.

Information and example may have a limited effectiveness on individuals, given a will and a capacity to respond. But what if this capacity is diminished and the will is warped and what if something more than individual appeal is needed—something as radical as a new creation? Remaking from within by God incarnate seems alone sufficient. This view has been radically questioned; but it is difficult to avoid its force."[46]

Where then does this leave us? Are we any closer to answering the question about the meaning of ἐν μορφῇ θεοῦ than we were a decade and more ago? Perhaps not. But new objections that have weakened long-held positions have been forthcoming, new support for traditional interpretations have been generated,[47] and a new awareness, or perhaps a more acute awareness, that the meaning of μορφή must depend not only on its lexical meaning, but on the context(s) in which it appears (context is king!). To sum up:

> μορφή refers to that "which truly and fully expresses the being which underlies it."[48] The phrase ἐν μορφῇ θεοῦ is best interpreted against the background of the glory of God, that shining light in which according to the OT and intertestamental literature, God was pictured [see above]. The expression does not refer simply to external appearance but pictures the preexistent Christ as clothed in the garments of divine majesty and splendour. He was in the form of God, sharing God's glory. ἐν μορφῇ θεοῦ thus corresponds with John 17:5 ("the glory I had with you before the world began") and reminds one of Heb. 1:3 ("the radiance of God's glory and the exact representation of his being").[49]

Furthermore, the meaning of this phrase, ἐν μορφῇ θεοῦ, is more fully clarified by the clause that immediately follows: "not ἁρπαγμόν did he consider to be equal with God," another of the famous cruxes of this "hymn."

EQUAL WITH GOD

I turn now to a discussion of the meaning of the second principal part of this chapter, the phrase ἴσα θεῷ ("equal with God"). But it is impossible to do this without first placing it in its setting, that is, in the clause in which it appears— οὐχ ἁρπαγμὸν ἡγήσατο τὸ εἶναι ἴσα θεῷ (2:6bc)—and coming to terms with perhaps the most difficult word in the whole of the New Testament to understand— ἁρπαγμόν. Some sense of its difficulty can be discerned by noting the different ways in which various versions translate it: "thought it not robbery to be equal with God" (KJV); "did not cling to his privileges as God's equal" (Phillips); "did not

η ξεο γιι

count equality with God a thing to be grasped" (RSV); "did not regard equality with God as something to be exploited" (NRSV); "did not grasp at equality with God" (Goodspeed); "did not consider equality with God something to be grasped" (NIV); "did not cling to his equality with God" (JB); "did not think to snatch at equality with God" (NEB); "did not demand and cling to his rights as God" (New Living Translation), and so on.

Every exegete of Philippians has had to come to terms with this difficult and rare[50] word, because one's understanding of the phrase "equal with God" depends to a large extent upon how one interprets it.[51] Recently enormous help in unraveling the meaning of ἁρπαγμός has come through the careful philological studies of C. F. D. Moule[52] and R. W. Hoover.[53] My own commentary leaned heavily on Moule's studied conclusion as to its meaning—not an act of aggression or robbery (*res rapta*),[54] not a prize or treasure possessed and clung to greedily (*res retinenda*),[55] not a prize or gain which one does not have but which one reaches out to get (*res rapienda*),[56] not an act of being caught up or snatched away, a kind of "rapture" (*raptus*, taken passively),[57] but an act of snatching in the abstract sense, i.e., "acquisitiveness" (*raptus*, taken actively).[58] Nevertheless, Professor Moule, in private conversation with me, graciously bowed to Hoover and admitted that Hoover's philological study had won the day and in his (Moule's) judgment was the final answer to the enigmatic ἁρπαγμός. Hoover argues that ἁρπαγμός is a word that must not be considered by itself but as part of an idiomatic expression with the verb ἡγήσατο. When employed as a predicate accusative with ἡγεῖσθαι—οὐχ ἁρπαγμὸν ἡγήσατο τὸ εἶναι ἴσα θεῷ—it is not only possible but entirely appropriate, as confirmed by comparable usage in other literature outside Philippians, to translate ἁρπαγμόν "as something to take advantage of," or more idiomatically, "as something to use for one's own advantage."[59] Hoover's work has been challenged recently by J. C. O'Neill,[60] but not conclusively so,[61] and thus has been adopted as the correct understanding of ἁρπαγμός by the majority of recent interpreters of Philippians 2:6.[62]

But what does ἴσα θεῷ ("equal with God") mean in the light of all this? Even though many scholars today accept Hoover's understanding of ἁρπαγμός as "something to take advantage of," not all draw the same conclusion from this that he does about the meaning of "equality with God." For Hoover, Christ Jesus, who was "in the form of God," was also "equal with God" but as such did not take advantage of this fact for his own personal gain, which is to say that "for . . . Hoover the . . . 'advantage-taking' does not aim at τὸ εἶναι ἴσα θεῷ: it begins from it."[63] To use his own words: "in every instance which I have examined this idiomatic expression [οὐχ ἁρπαγμὸν ἡγήσατο τί refers to something already present and at one's disposal. The question . . . is not whether one possesses something, but whether or not one chooses to exploit something."[64]

Martin, who agrees with Hoover regarding the meaning of ἁρπαγμός, at least in part, nevertheless contrary to Hoover's conclusions reiterates his own earlier understanding of ἴσα θεῷ, which seems to make a distinction between Christ Jesus being in the form of God, and his being equal with God: Philippians 2:6b "states what Christ might have done, i.e., seized equality with God; only in verse 7 does it say what he chose to do, i.e., give himself . . . To ask what it was precisely that lay in his power as an advantage [Hoover's understanding of ἁρπαγμός] . . . the answer must be: the enjoyment and use of 'equality with God' in its characteristic expression, namely, the title to lordship as a springboard from which he might, had he so decided, have aspired to be the universe's ruler. He had the opportunity to grasp what lay within his reach—since he shared God's throne as his 'form' . . . and by an act of self-assertiveness and pride he might have striven to be Lord in his own right."[65] If I understand Martin correctly, Christ Jesus was "in the form of God," but was not "equal with God," in the sense that he was not Lord of the universe, Ruler of the world, Cosmocrator. Refusing to grasp this on his own, humbling himself instead to become human and the Savior of all humanity by his obedience and death, the Father bestowed on him that very thing for which he did not reach: "equality with God," i.e., the name of "Lord," before which name all in heaven and earth and under the earth will bow.[66]

Recently C. A. Wanamaker in developing his Son of God christology for the "Christ-hymn" articulated a view similar to that of Professor Martin. Wanamaker does not think that his interpretation of Christ being "in the form of God" forces one to conclude that Christ possessed divine equality in his preexistence. Rather, just the opposite. As an obedient son gains equality of power, authority, dignity with his father when the father chooses to share his prerogatives with him, so it was with Christ Jesus. Instead of grasping for such equality he waited and served. Thus "Philippians 2:9–11 envisages Christ gaining equality with God in preeminence and function by virtue of the fact that God has appointed him vicegerent (cf. 1 Cor. 15:24–28). What Christ refused to grasp God has granted as a reward for his self-abasement and suffering. . . ."[67]

For those who propose to understand the entire "hymn" in terms of a first Adam-last Adam contrast, both of whom were human, both of whom make the crucial, fateful, "archetypal" (Dunn's word) choice—one a disastrous choice, the other salvific—ἴσα θεῷ cannot mean "equal with God" in the traditional sense. Rather, these scholars reading Philippians 2:6 in light of Genesis 1:26 and 3:5, 22, and noting that ἴσα was used as ὡς to translate the Hebrew ⊃ (Gen. 3:5) understand ἴσα here in the "hymn" as meaning "like": Christ Jesus, who, as the first Adam, was made in the "image of God" (εἰκὼν θεοῦ) did not, as did the first Adam, make the choice to grasp at the opportunity to be completely like God (ἴσα θεῷ), but freely chose instead to accept "man's lot followed out to death," and as a consequence was exalted "to the status of Lord over all."[68]

P. Trudinger in 1991, following the Danish philologist L. L. Hammerich,[69] who claimed that ἁρπαγμός meant "the act of being caught up or snatched away—a kind or rapture," nevertheless parts company with him in his interpretation of this word in the Philippian text. For Hammerich Jesus had no need to experience a mystical rapture to be at one with God [ἴσα θεῷ], because as preexistent Son of God such oneness with God was his by nature. Trudinger rejects this because he believes that Paul here is speaking of Jesus, a human being as Adam was. Thus he suggests an interpretation of ἁρπαγμός as "a rapture" or "the act of being caught up," which enables us all to identify with Jesus, and he with us. The passage centers on Jesus' self-giving in love on the cross. Jesus' suffering and death were his glory, the signs of God's approval on his life's mission. He suggests then "that Paul, in the Philippian passage under consideration, may be interpreted as saying that Jesus' being at-one-with-God [ἴσα θεῷ] is seen not in some act of elevation to a glorious throne 'up there' . . . but precisely in his complete self-giving in love on the cross."[70]

In my judgment the correct understanding of "equal with God" (2:6b) is that which takes it in the close conjunction with "in the form of God" (2:6a). For Paul to say that Christ existed ἐν μορφῇ θεοῦ was to say that outside his human nature Christ had no other manner of existing apart from existing "in the form of God," that is, apart from possessing the rank, status, position, condition, function of God—however one wishes to express this μορφὴ θεοῦ, without making Paul speak in ontological terms.[71] That this is the correct interpretation is corroborated by the expression τὸ εἶναι ἴσα θεῷ ("the being equal with God") which follows. The definite article τό of τὸ εἶναι confirms that this second expression is closely connected with the first, for the function of the definite article here is designed to point back to something previously mentioned.[72] Therefore one should expect that τὸ εἶναι ἴσα θεῷ would refer epexegetically to the ἐν μορφῇ θεοῦ ὑπάρχων that preceded it. This means then that "the being equal with God" is precisely another way of saying "in the form of God." Or better still, whatever meaning one might put forth as a possible meaning for the expression μορφὴ θεοῦ can only be properly understood in terms of ἴσα θεῷ, and vice versa—τὸ εἶναι ἴσα θεῷ can only be properly understood in terms of ἐν μορφῇ θεοῦ.[73]

Let us return for a moment to the participle, ὑπάρχων ("being/existing"). In spite of recent voices raised against him, C. F. D. Moule's understanding of this verbal form as causative and not concessive—"precisely because he was in the form of God and equal with God" rather than "although he was . . . "[74] seems to be the correct one. As a consequence the entire opening verse of the "hymn" hangs together as a unit, not so much a "hymn" about Christ or to Christ; rather it is a marvelous anthem of praise that in effect describes the true nature of God. Is it important that Christ was "in the form of God," "equal with God?" For the Philippians the answer is Yes. For all Christians the answer is Yes: Christ Jesus defines God for us. Philippians 2:6 anticipates John 1:18 by several decades. Christ Jesus himself in the form of God and equal with God exegetes God for the world, brings him out into the open for all to see and know. I am in full agreement with Wright's statement, which for me sums up the meaning of and the effects of these two statements that have been the focus of this chapter. It is worth quoting in full:

> The preexistent son regarded equality with God not as excusing him from the task of (redemptive) suffering and death, but actually as uniquely qualifying him for that vocation. It is here . . . that the real underlying soteriology of the "hymn" is to be found. As in Romans 5:6ff., the death of Jesus is understood as the appropriate revelation, in action, of the love of God himself (compare too 2 Corinthans 5:19). ἐκένωσεν [2:7a] does not refer to the loss of divine atttributes, but—in good Pauline fashion [e.g. Rom. 4:14; 1 Cor. 1:17; 2 Cor. 9:3]—to making something powerless, emptying it of apparent significance. The real humiliation of the incarnation and the cross is that one who was himself God, and who never dur-

ing the whole process stopped being God, could embrace such a vocation. The real theological emphasis of the hymn, therefore, is not simply a new view of Jesus. It is a new understanding of God. Against the age-old attempts of human beings to make God in their own (arrogant, self-glorifying) image, Calvary reveals the truth about what it meant to be God. Underneath this is the conclusion, all-important in present christological debate: incarnation and even crucifixion are to be seen as *appropriate* vehicles for the dynamic self-revelation of God."[75]

NOTES

1. L. E. Keck (*Paul and His Letters,* Proclamation Commentaries [Nashville: Abingdon Press, 1984], 45) remarks that no christological passage in Paul's letters has generated more discussion than this one.

2. E. Norden, *Agnostos Theos: Untersuchungen zur Formengeschichte religiöser Rede* (Darmstadt: Teubner, [4]1956), 383–87. It should be pointed out that Phil. 2:6–11 is not a hymn in the modern sense of that term, nor is it a hymn in the sense that it reflects the meter of Greek or Semitic poetry. Even R. P. Martin himself, who entitled his extremely valuable book, which has provided the best overview of the issues and the literature on this passage up to 1967/[2]1983/[3]1997, *Carmen Christi,* comments: "It is a singular fact that it was not until the beginning of the twentieth century that the unusual literary character of Philippians 2:5–11 was detected and classified" (1983, 24). This remark should make one pause before unthinkingly calling this text a hymn, especially since the early patristic commentators, whose knowledge of Greek was native rather than acquired, seemingly showed no awareness of its hymn-like qualities. To be sure, one cannot deny the rhetorical structure of Phil. 2:5–11, its stylistic balance and parallelism, its rhythmic cadences, its use of chiasm, antithesis and alliteration, its unusual vocabulary, its important theological terms—all of which makes this section different from the context in which it appears (see R. P. Martin, "Aspects of Worship in the New Testament Church," *Vox Evangelica* 2 [1963], esp. 16–21; Basevi and Chapa, "Philippians 2:6–11," 343; and Marrow, "A Christological Paraenesis," 62). See also Fowl, *Story,* 24, whose aim was not to develop a detailed stylistic analysis of Phil. 2:6–11, but "to show that [this passage] is a distinct unit within the epistle both because of its shift in focus from the Philippians to Christ, and because of its particular formal and stylistic characteristics, which could reasonably be called poetic." It is interesting to note that although most of the modern translations and the latest New Testament Greek Text (Nestle-Aland, 27th ed.) set off Phil. 2:6–11 in a hymn-like format, there are some translations that do not: the RSV (but not the NRSV), the NEB, and most recently the New Living Translation (NLT, 1996). Perhaps, then, if one retains the word hymn to describe this section of Philippians, one should put it in quotation marks, "hymn," to remind one that it is not, strictly speaking, a hymn but a passage, as some have suggested, that "represents Paul's own exalted prose (a view gradually regaining favor) rather than an early Christian hymn whose lines of fairly equal length Paul has disequalized with addition" (Gundry, "Style and Substance," 288; see also Fee, "Philippians 2:5–11," 29–46). Nevertheless, whether poetry, hymn, or exalted prose, its very structure adds to the difficulty of interpretation. As one of my former students wrote: "In reading poetry, [one] must work harder; but the rewards are often greater. Reading the compressed language of a lyric, if done well, forces [readers] to

slow down and contemplate the meaning of words in elaborate patterns" (C. W. Pol-
lard III, University of Virginia, in an essay sent to me for consideration).

3. BAGD, s.v. ὑπάρχω. This special force of this verb is well attested in the New Testament (Acts 16:3, 20, 37; 17:24; 1 Cor. 11:7, 18; Gal. 1:14; 2:14). It is of interest to note
that the plural participle of ὑπάρχω, τὰ ὑπάρχοντα (and its related forms), frequently
means "possessions" (cf. Luke 12:33, 44; 1 Cor. 13:3), pointing to the fact that the verb
does not simply mean "to be," but "to be (in possession of)." One should note, however,
that in Hellenistic Greek this verb is a widely used substitute for εἰμί (BDF 414.1) and
is sometimes used in that diminished sense in the New Testament (Luke 8:41; 23:50).

4. T. Nagata, "Philippians 2:5–11: A Case Study in the Contextual Shaping of Early
Christology" (Ph.D. diss., Princeton Theological Seminary) (Ann Arbor, Mich., 1981),
as cited by Martin, *Carmen Christi* (1983), xx.

5. Moulton-Howard-Turner, *Grammar of New Testament Greek,* 1.127.

6. See Fee for this, *Philippians,* 203; also Motyer, *Message of Philippians,* 112; contra
Silva, *Philippians,* 123, who thinks it "unnecessary to see any special significance in
the use of ὑπάρχω (as opposed to εἰμί) and Dunn, *Christology* (1996), 114, who
says that the belief that Phil. 2:6–11 refers to Christ's preexistent state and status is a
presupposition rather than a conclusion, a presupposition which again and again
proves decisive in determining how this hymn is to be understood. Dunn's approach,
it seems to me, also starts from a presupposition, though a different one—the presupposition that the idea of the preexistence of Christ was a gradual developing historical
phenomenon, coming to its climax only late in the first century in the Fourth Gospel.
But Hengel writes that "the letter of Paul to the Philippians was written in the middle
50s C.E. if from Ephesus or at the beginning of the 60s if from Rome, and that the composition of the hymn [2:6–11] was possibly much earlier." Then he remarks that "the
[Philippian] hymn is the oldest of the three hymns [Phil. 2:6–11; Heb. 1:3; John
1:1–18] and is the most well-balanced of them all. From this it may be inferred that
Christological thinking between 50 and 100 C.E. *was much more unified in its basic
structure* than NT research, in part at least, has maintained. Basically the later developments are already there in a nutshell in the [Philippian] hymn. This means, however,
with regard to the development of all the early church's Christology, that more happened in the first twenty years than in the entire centuries-long development of doctrine" ("Christological Titles," 443, italics his; see also 441).

7. I have no desire to enter here into the debate over whether or not Phil. 2:6–11 is a pre-
Pauline hymn composed by some unknown Christian or simply an example of Paul's
own exalted prose, so I fall back on M. D. Hooker's remarks that much is known about
Paul's thought and that as the passage is used by him, regardless of its provenance,
the apostle used it in a "Pauline" way ("Philippians 2:6–11," in *Jesus und Paulus,* ed.
E. E. Ellis and E. Grässer [Göttingen: Vandenhoeck & Ruprecht, 1976], 151–52; also
now in M. D. Hooker, *From Adam to Christ: Essays on Paul* [Cambridge: Cambridge
University Press, 1990], 88–100); I also refer to D. J. Moo's comment that "method-
ologically it is necessary at least to maintain that whatever Paul quotes, he himself af-
firms" (*Romans 1—8* [Chicago: Moody Press, 1991], 49).

8. In the LXX several times, only four of which are in the canonical OT: Judg. 8:18a; Job
4:16; Isa. 44:13; Dan. 3:19; 4:33; 5:6, 9, 10; 7:28; Tob. 1:13; Wis. 18:1; 4 Macc. 15:4;
[Isa. 52:14 (Aq); Deut. 4:12 (Sm)].

9. For example, see note 8 above; see also Plutarch, *De E apud Delphos,* 18: ". . . our
form (μορφή) and our thought never remain identical"; an inscription from Epidau-
rus (320 B.C.E.): νεανίσκον εὐπρεπῆ τὰμ μορφήν ("a young man good-looking
with respect to his appearance"). See C. Spicq, *Theological Lexicon of the New Testa-*

ment, trans. and ed. J. D. Ernest (Peabody, Mass.: Hendrickson, 1994), 2.520–25 for these references and others and for a good discussion of the meaning of μορφή and its comparison and contrast with other semantically related words.

10. BAGD, s.v. μορφή.

11. J. Behm, *TDNT* 4.745.

12. O'Brien, *Philippians,* 205.

13. J. B. Lightfoot, *St. Paul's Epistle to the Philippians* (London: Macmillan, 1894), 127–33.

14. Hawthorne, *Philippians,* 83–84.

15. Martin, *Carmen Christi* (1983), xix.

16. But see now Fee, *Philippians,* 204; O'Brien, *Philippians,* 207, who writes: "From the NT contexts where μορφή and its cognates appear . . . it is clear that the word group describes not simply external appearance or behaviour but also that which inwardly corresponds (or is expected to correspond) to the outward;" also Silva, *Philippians,* 116.

17. Käsemann, "A Critical Analysis of Philippians 2:5–11," *Journal for Theology and Church* 5 (1968): 45–88, esp. 59–61. (See R. Morgan's chapter in this volume.)

18. Käsemann, "Analysis," 61. Paul does use ἐν in such a way (cf. Rom. 6), but certainly not always; one would be hard pressed to see such a meaning for the parallel construction found in Phil. 2:7—ἐν ὁμοιώματι ἀνθρώπων γενόμενος. In an extremely important new analysis and evaluation of the structure of the "Christ-hymn," R. H. Gundry writes, "Pairing and chiasm favor the synonymy of the form of God with equality to God, and thus disfavor taking the ἐν before μορφῇ θεοῦ to diminish the meaning of '[the] form of God,' as though existence in God's form meant less than being God's form. This argument increases in strength if the τό before εἶναι is anaphoric, referring the being equal with God back to existence in his form, and if the ἐν before ὁμοιώματι ἀνθρώπων does not diminish the meaning of '[the] likeness of human beings,' as though being in human likeness meant less than *being* human" ("Style and Substance," 283–84).

19. Georgi, "Der vorpaulinische Hymnus Phil. 2, 6–11," in *Zeit und Geschichte: Festschrift für R. Bultmann,* ed. E. Dinkler (Tübingen: Mohr [Siebeck], 263–93; J. T. Sanders, *New Testament Christological Hymns: Their Historical and Religious Background,* SNTS Monographs 15 (Cambridge: Cambridge University Press, 1971), 66–69; W. Pannenberg, *Jesus, God and Man* (ET, London: SCM Press, 1968), 151–54; E. Yamauchi, *Pre-Christian Gnosticism* (Grand Rapids: Eerdmans, 1973).

20. E. Schweizer, *Erniedrigung und Erhöhung bei Jesus und seinen Nachfolgern* (Zurich: Zwingli, 1955).

21. U. B. Müller, *Philipper,* 95: "Aufgrund der Parallelität von V. 6a und 6b, aufgrund auch der besonderen Ausrichtung der Zustandsbeschreibung auf die zweite Zeile mit der finiten Verbformulierung wird man die Wendung von der 'Gottesgestalt' primär als Aussage über die Würdestellung Christi verstehen müssen."

22. R. P. Martin, *Philippians,* NCB (Grand Rapids: Eerdmans, 1976), 96; see also idem, *Carmen Christi* (1983), xx.

23. See the chorus of objection raised against it in Hawthorne, *Philippians,* 83; in addition see J. Jervell, *Imago Dei: Gen. 1.26f. in Spätjudentum in der Gnosis und in den paulinischen Briefen* (Göttingen: Vandenhoeck & Ruprecht, 1960), 230–31.

24. H. A. W. Meyer, *Critical and Exegetical Handbook to the Epistles to the Philippians and Colossians* (Edinburgh: T. & T. Clark, 1875), 80, who defined μορφή as the divine "glory," that "form of being corresponding to the essence." Similarly J. Weiss, *Earliest Christianity* (New York: Harper & Bros., 1959), 2.478, who claimed that "the divine form" that Jesus possessed before becoming human was nothing other than "the Doxa of God himself, the glory and radiation of his being, which appears almost as an

independent hypostasis of God and yet is connected intimately with God." See Martin, *Carmen Christi* (1983), 102–19, and O'Brien, *Philippians,* 208.

25. E.g., Ex. 16:10; 24:16; 33:17–19; 40:34–35; 1 Kings 8:11; Lev. 9:6, 23; Isa. 6:3; 60:1–2; Ezek. 1:28; 43:3; 44:4; 2 Macc. 2:8; 3 Macc. 4:18; *1 Enoch* 14:21; *T. Lev.* 3:4; *Asc. Isa.* 10:16.

26. Fowl, *Story,* 50–54.

27. Cf. Rom. 1:23; 1 Cor. 11:7; 2 Cor. 3:18; 4:6. See also Luke 2:9; Rev. 15:8; 21–23.

28. Fowl, *Story,* 54, citing J. Behm, *TDNT* 4.751.

29. Ibid.; here he seems to return to Schweizer's view (noted above) and to endorse it with modification and explanation of what "position" or "status" means.

30. Wanamaker, "Philippians," 179–83.

31. Deut. 5:24; Ps. 97:6; Isa. 40:5.

32. Ex. 24:17; Ezek. 1:26–28; 10:4; Jos., *Contra Apionem,* 2.190; Philo, *Vita Mosis,* 1.66.

33. Wanamaker, "Philippians," 186–87; cf. also 1 Cor. 15:43; Rom. 8:29–30. Wanamaker, however, does not hold to the thought that possession of the form of God implied participation in the nature of God, since Christ did not possess divine equality with this glory (δόξα), 185–87, esp. 185. Contrast Wong, "Pre-existence," 270–73, who argues that "an absolute separation between form and substance, between appearance and nature cannot be made . . . what is revealed outwardly is only a consequence of something inside."

34. Hawthorne, *Philippians,* 82.

35. Steenburg, "Case against Synonymy," 80–81.

36. This was earlier suggested by C. H. Talbert, "The Problem of Pre-existence in Phil. 2:6–11," *JBL* 86 (1967): 141–53; also J. A. T. Robinson, *The Human Face of God* (Philadelphia: Westminster Press, 1973); J. Murphy-O'Connor, "Christological Anthropology in Phil. II, 6–11," *RB* 83 (1976): 25–50; G. Howard, "Phil. 2:6–11 and the Human Christ," *CBQ* 40 (1978): 368–87; and Borsch, "Further Reflections," 130–44. Several other scholars also see an Adam-Christ contrast in Philippians 2, but are not prepared to say that this requires them to relinquish belief in the preexistence of Christ: A. J. Bandstra, "'Adam' and 'The Servant' in Philippians 2:5ff.," *CTJ* 1 (1966): 213–16; G. B. Caird, *Paul's Letters from Prison* (Oxford: Oxford University Press, 1976); O. Cullmann, *The Christology of the New Testament* (London: SCM Press, 1959); Wright, "*Harpagmos*"; M. D. Hooker, "Phil 2:6–11," in *Jesus und Paulus,* ed. E. E. Ellis (Göttingen: Vandenhoeck & Ruprecht, 1975), 151–64; J. L. Houlden, *Paul's Letters from Prison* (Baltimore, Md.: Penguin, 1970); H. A. Kent, Jr., "Philippians," in *Expositor's Bible Commentary,* ed. F. E. Gaebelein (Grand Rapids: Zondervan, 1978); Martin, *Carmen Christi* (1967/²1983); H. N. Ridderbos, *Paul: An Outline of His Theology* (Grand Rapids: Eerdmans, 1975); Silva, *Philippians.*

37. Dunn, *Christology* (1980), 114–21, a position from which he has not retreated (see above, chapter 4 pp. 74–79) in spite of the many criticisms leveled against his thesis. He writes, "In the case of Phil. 2:6–11 it still seems to me that of all the contexts or paradigms of thought within which the text may be read in the endeavour of historical exegesis . . . , the one which provides the most coherent and most complete . . . reading is the Adam christology" (*Christology,* [²1996], xviii–xix). See also his "Why Incarnation? A Review of Recent NT Scholarship," in *Crossing the Boundaries,* M. D. Goulder FS, ed. S. E. Porter (Leiden: E. J. Brill, 1994), 235–56.

38. Martin, *Carmen Christi* (1983), xxi, interpreting Dunn.

39. Dunn, "Pauline Christology," 99.

40. E.g., Marrow, who writes: "If we look at Philippians 2:6–11 as consisting of two parts, not three, if we recognize its Christology as referring to the earthly existence of Jesus and his exaltation, not to his preexistence, then the 'intention of the author' becomes

clear. Paul exhorts the Philippians: 'Do nothing from selfishness or conceit, but in humility count others better than yourselves . . . ' (Phil. 2:3–4) . . . Such is the inexorable logic of following a crucified Lord. The confession of his lordship is validated only by a lived obedience to the way of the cross" ("Obedience and Lordship," 382; idem, "Christological Paraenesis," 61–73).

41. See Fee, *Philippians,* 209–10; Fowl, *Story,* 51; T. F. Glasson, "Two Notes on the Philippian Hymn (ii.6–11)," *NTS* 21 (1974–75): 138; Gundry, "Style and Substance," 285–86; Hawthorne, *Philippians,* 82–83; Hurtado, "Pre-existence," 744–45; Hurst, "Re-enter," 449–57 (see above, chapter 5); R. P. Martin, "Some Reflexions on NT Hymns," in *Christ the Lord, Studies Presented to Donald Guthrie,* ed. H. H. Rowdon (Leicester and Downers Grove, Ill.: InterVarsity Press, 1982), 37–39, esp. 46–48; O'Brien, *Philippians,* 263–68 for the most useful overview and critique of Dunn's position; Steenburg, "Case Against," 77–85; F. Thielman, Philippians, 127–28; D. H. Wallace, "A Note on Morphé," *TZ* 22 (1966): 19–25; Wanamaker, "Philippians 2:5–11," 179–83; Wong, "Problem of Pre-existence," 267–82.

42. Dunn, *Christology* (^{2}1996) xviii–xxv, and notes.

43. Steenburg, "The Case Against," 77–85.

44. Ibid., 85.

45. Cf. Dunn, "Why Incarnation?" 247.

46. C. F. D. Moule, *The Holy Spirit* (Grand Rapids: Eerdmans, 1978), 59.

47. I think especially of the stimulating and creative article by Gundry, "Style and Substance," 271–93; and chapter 4 of Wright's, *Climax,* 82–98; and the thorough, detailed exegetical commentaries of Fee, *Philippians,* 204–29; and O'Brien, *Philippians,* 205–62; and O'Brien's Appendix C, 263–68.

48. MM, 417.

49. O'Brien, *Philippians,* 210–11.

50. Only here in the New Testament, never in the LXX and only rarely in Greek literature outside the Bible, (primarily in the writings of the church fathers where they quote or allude to Philippians 2).

51. See N. T. Wright's excellent, detailed and clearly presented summary of the numerous interpretations of ἁρπαγμός through the centuries coupled with his own conclusion about its meaning in "ἁρπαγμός and the Meaning of Philippians 2:5–11," *JTS* n.s. 37 (1986): 321–52, now in chapter 4 of his book, *The Climax of the Covenant: Christ and the Law in Pauline Theology* (Edinburgh: T. & T. Clark, 1991), esp. 62–82.

52. C. F. D. Moule, "Further Reflexions on Philippians 2:5–11," in *Apostolic History and the Gospel: Biblical and Historical Essays Presented to F. F. Bruce on His 60th Birthday,* ed. W. W. Gasque and R. P. Martin (Exeter: Paternoster, 1970), 264–76; idem, "The Manhood of Jesus in the New Testament," in *Christ, Faith and History: Cambridge Studies in Christology,* ed. S. W. Sykes and J. P. Clayton (Cambridge: Cambridge University Press, 1972), 95–110.

53. R. W. Hoover, "The Harpagmos Enigma: A Philological Solution," *HTR* 56 (1971): 95–119.

54. The early Latin Fathers; cf. the KJV.

55. J. B. Lightfoot, *St Paul's Epistles to the Philippians* (London: Macmillan, 1868); cf. J. B. Phillips; *New Living Translation.*

56. Cf. R. P. Martin, *Philippians,* NCB (Grand Rapids: Eerdmans, 1976), 96–98; idem, *Carmen Christi* (1983), xxiii, 147–48; cf. Goodspeed; possibly also the RSV and the NIV.

57. L. L. Hammerich, "An Ancient Misunderstanding (Phil. 2:6 'robbery')," *Historisk-filosofiske Meddeleser udgivet af Det Kangelige Danske Videnskabernes Selskab* 41[4] (Copenhagen: Munksgaard, 1966).

58. Hawthorne, *Philippians,* 85.

59. Hoover, "Harpagmos," 118.
60. J. C. O'Neill, "Hoover on Harpagmos Reviewed, with a Modest Proposal Concerning Philippians 2:6," *HTR* 81 (1988): 445–49. Cf. also Wong, "Philippians 2:6–11," 277.
61. O'Neill arguing against Hoover concludes that the translation "robbery," which is "near nonsense," nevertheless seems "to be the only choice left." So as a result he decides to emend the text claiming that pious scribes omitted the second negative (μή) and replaced it with τό. Thus the translation of 2:6 should be, "who being in the form of God thought it not robbery not to be (μὴ εἶναι) equal with God" (449)!
62. Fee, Fowl, Martin, Melick, O'Brien, Silva, Strimple, Wright, et al.
63. Wright, "ἁρπαγμός" 339; idem, *Climax,* 79.
64. Hoover, "Harpagmos," 118.
65. R. P. Martin, *Philippians,* 96–97; see also his *Carmen Christi* (1983), xxii–xxiii.
66. See Wright, *Climax,* 72–73 for a critique of this view.
67. Wanamaker, "Philippians 2:6–11," 190. See O'Brien, *Philippians,* 208n18, and Silva, *Philippians,* 116n34 for a critique of Wanamaker's view.
68. Dunn, *Christology* (1989), 114–15, xix: "The point of the hymn is the epochal significance of the Christ-event, as determinative for humankind as the 'event' of Adam's creation and fall, with the question of pre-existence rather more an irrelevance and distraction than a help to interpretation. It is because Christ by his life, death and resurrection has so completely reversed the catastrophe of Adam, has done so by the acceptance of death by choice rather than as punishment, and has thus completed the role of dominion over all things originally intended for Adam, that the paradigm is so inviting, and so 'fitting' in the first place." See also Marrow, "Obedience and Lordship," 381–82; idem, "Christological Paraenesis," 69–70.
69. See note 57 above.
70. Trudinger, "Making Sense," 12–13.
71. But see Silva, *Philippians,* 115–16: "It is possible to cite parallels . . . in which morphé is used to designate what is distinctively divine in contrast to what is distinctively human [Philo, *Embassy to Gaius* 110; LCL 10:55; Josephus, *Against Apion* 2.190–191; LCL 1:369]. It appears then that Ltf. [and Hawthorne] although misguided in seeing here a more or less philosophical meaning of 'essence,' was not off the track in detecting a contrast between 'the true divine nature of our Lord' and 'true human nature' (p. 133). And it moreover follows that the Philippians passage, although not written for the purpose of presenting an ontological description of Christ, is very much consonant with the Trinitarian formulas of the fourth-century church." Cf. also Fee, *Philippians,* 204–5; O'Brien, *Philippians,* 210–11.
72. BDF 399, 1; see also Gundry, "Style and Substance" 283–84; Wright, *Climax,* 83; in addition to agreeing with me Wright also cites other examples, e.g., 2 Cor. 7:11 and Rom. 7:18, where two infinitives with their articles refer to the immediately preceding discussion.
73. Wong, "Philippians 2:6–11," 274: ἴσα θεῷ "stands closely to the μορφὴ θεοῦ and thus can be regarded as the consequence of Christ's being in the form of God. If this is accepted, the following interpretation of v. 6b seems acceptable. Christ was not only in the form of God; he was also equal with God."
74. Gundry, "Style and Substance," 283; Silva, *Philippians* 112; but see Wong, "Philippians 2:6–11," 275.
75. Wright, *Climax* 83–84.

7.

"When He at Last Is First!"

Philippians 2:9–11 and the Exaltation of the Lord

LARRY J. KREITZER

The hymn of Philippians 2:6–11 is a veritable mother lode and continues to yield many riches for any interpreter who chooses to work what is in effect a very old and valuable site. Exegesis of the passage has a long and distinguished history; from the earliest days of the church the hymn has figured prominently in theological discussion, most notably within debates about the person and work of Jesus Christ, less often for its teaching about eschatological matters. A minority of interpreters today challenge the essential unity of 2:6–11, or dispute that the pericope originally was an early christological hymn that the apostle has included within the letter.[1] On these two matters, at least, we have arrived at something of a scholarly consensus, although there remain continuing discussions about the form and structure of the original hymn and the possible Pauline interpolations into it, as well as a debate as to whether the interpretation of the hymn is dependent upon a correct determination of its form.[2] Our task within this study is to examine the final stanza of the christological hymn, vv. 9–11, where the exaltation of Jesus Christ is proclaimed and the ultimate triumph of God's purposes within creation is declared. We shall survey some of the more recent attempts to interpret these verses and place them within the larger context of the epistle to the Philippians and indeed within Paul's thought as a whole. The study divides into five areas: (1) the place of the christological hymn within ongoing investigations into Paul's apocalyptic eschatology; (2) the importance of vv. 9–11 to Paul's overall argument in Philippians; (3) the implications of 2:9–11 for the idea of the preexistence of Christ; (4) the allusion to Isa. 45:23 in vv. 10–11 and Paul's adaptation of the Old Testament text; (5) the concluding declaration in 2:11c and its implications for our understanding the relationship between Jesus Christ and God.

1. Philippians 2:9–11 and Its Place within Paul's Apocalyptic Eschatology

Albert Schweitzer at the beginning of this century first alerted us to the eschatological perspective that was an integral part of Paul's worldview. Schweitzer had the audacity—and vision—to challenge the prevailing scholarly opinions of his day and attempt to offer an interpretation of Paul that gave due attention to the apostle's eschatological beliefs. So, too, did Ernst Käsemann in 1960 in his celebrated article on "The Beginnings of Christian Theology,"[3] launching what in effect was a mortal blow to the prevailing Bultmannian interpretation of Paul (not to say the New Testament at large). Bultmann had attempted to demythologize eschatology in favor of existentialism, which he felt was more palatable to the twentieth-century person and which allowed the reappropriation of the meaning of the apocalyptic formulations contained within the New Testament to take place. This, Käsemann argued, was to do violence to the New Testament writings, and he set out a powerful critique against such demythologizing policies. Thus, Schweitzer and Käsemann set into motion an interpretative movement which is still with us today, and which shows little sign of abating.[4] The manner and extent to which Paul's thinking was determined by "apocalyptic eschatology" has been variously assessed, but its essential role as a starting point of analysis seems unassailable. A number of important studies have been produced over the past twenty years or so which attempt to illustrate this feature of Pauline thought. One of the most interesting has been J. Christiaan Beker's *Paul the Apostle: The Triumph of God in Life and Thought* (1980); his book will serve as a convenient point for us to begin our discussion.[5]

Beker describes Paul as "an apocalyptic theologian with a theocentric outlook" (362); he decries any interpretation of Paul which downplays the apocalyptic-theocentric nature of the apostle's thought in favor of a more narrowly focused christocentricism. According to Beker, Paul's thinking does have a coherence within it, namely, that his gospel message concerns the apocalyptic interpretation of the Christ-event.[6] However, he insists that the flow is always in that direction; Paul does *not* proclaim a christological interpretation of apocalyptic thinking, for that would be not only a violation of his Jewish monotheistic roots, but an inappropriate collapsing of eschatology into christology. Beker's work has been generally well received and a number of other studies have followed it, building upon the foundations which he laid and adding to the discussion in the process.[7] With that said, the book is not without its critics, most notably over the way in which the central motif of Paul's apocalyptic thought is handled and the rather forced integration of Galatians within the argument.[8] In any event, what is remarkable in all of this discussion is the relatively minimalist position that Phil. 2:6–11 has within both Beker's work and those who follow in his step. Indeed, it comes as something of a surprise to discover that the christological hymn, or portions of it, is mentioned only twelve times by Beker within his magisterial book of nearly 400 pages, while the concluding stanza of the hymn, arguably one of the most important eschatological passages contained in Paul's letters, is mentioned only six times within the volume.[9] None of these instances offers much in the way of substantial discussion of the passage; generally they come in a list of textual references and are mere proof texts for a particular point. This is all the more surprising given the fact that the theocentric note with which the christological hymn concludes ("to the glory of God the Father") lends itself so well to Beker's central thesis, which he tirelessly proclaims as "the triumph of God" (a phrase which occurs *three* times in the titles and subtitles of Beker's books!).

The same comment could be made about many of the discussions of Paul's eschatological thought that follow Beker's lead.[10] Quite simply, it is as if the contribution that 2:9–11 might make to such a discussion has been met with something of a conspiracy of silence. Perhaps the lion's share of scholarly attention has been so preoccupied with the christological implications of the hymn, most importantly the debate about preexistence (see below), that the eschatological facet of the hymn has been neglected. This is to be lamented, for it yields a one-dimensional interpretation of the hymn as it stands within the letter. Any persuasive exegesis of the christological hymn must give due attention to the eschatological perspective that underlies vv. 9–11.

2. The Purpose of Philippians 2:9–11 in Paul's Overall Argument

Considerable scholarly disagreement remains about the function of 2:6–11 within the larger purposes of Paul in his letter to the Philippians. A host of interlocking questions about the context and setting of 2:6–11 arises from a careful consideration of the letter, none of which can be answered simply. How does the christological hymn serve Paul's overall argument? It is generally agreed that the hymn contributes to Paul's ethical exhortation, but what precisely are the members of the church at Philippi being exhorted *to do?* How determinative is the exhortation contained in v. 5 for the passage as a whole? What is it that has occasioned Paul's writing to the Philippians in the first place? Such questions strike at the heart of any attempt to give the essentially eschatological vision presented in vv. 9–11 its proper place.

The longstanding debate over the so-called "ethical interpretation" of the hymn has been well documented and need not be rehearsed here.[11] Suffice it to say that a growing majority of interpreters agree that Paul does appeal to the example of the earthly Jesus (as expressed within the pre-Pauline hymn) and that he deliberately does so in order to elicit some action on the part of his audience. It may well be that traditional sayings of Jesus about humility and exaltation (such as that recorded in Matt. 23:12/Luke 14:11; 18:14), or even the tradition of Jesus acting as a servant to the twelve disciples at the Last Supper (as recorded in John 13:3–17),[12] are ultimately what lies behind the hymn. In any case, Paul wants the Philippians to act in humility and self-effacement and thereby follow the example of their Lord who was rewarded by God for his obedience.[13] But where does that leave us in interpreting vv. 9–11, an awkward paragraph which might be described as the Achilles' heel of the ethical interpretation of the hymn?[14] Jean-François Collange is certainly correct when he asserts that "any interpretation of one part of the hymn which fails to do justice to the other is misleading," and that leaves us with a problem.[15] The difficulty is that there is no immediately obvious connection between the exaltation theme contained in these verses and the exhortation based upon the ethical example of Jesus that clearly underlies vv. 6–8. It is difficult to incorporate the final stanza of the christological hymn within an interpretation of the passage that focuses solely on the ethical example of Jesus, an interpretation which, incidentally, seems demanded by the introductory declaration found in 2:5.[16] Clearly Paul invokes the hymn as a challenge to the Philippian church to end their discord and live more in accordance with the character of their Lord.[17] However, the concluding stanza of the hymn seems to be somewhat misdirected in this regard, and it is easy to view it as veering off on a tangent. Verses 9–11 of the hymn in this sense appear inappropriate to the task at hand. As Fred Craddock puts it, remarking on Paul's quotation of the hymn as part of his ethical exhortation to the church:

> It may be objected that . . . the quotation fails to make full use of this christological hymn; that is, Paul's answer would seem immeasurably larger than the problem which evoked it. After all, one does not roll out a cannon to shoot a rabbit.[18]

This should not overly concern us, however, since elsewhere Paul's thought takes similar flights of fancy and he occasionally does chase rabbits into nearby woods. We need not assume that every single twist and turn of the apostle's thought be unerringly relevant to the ultimate line of his argument. By all appearances, it is as if Paul has here taken the earlier christological hymn, a hymn that ultimately proclaims the exaltation of the Lord Jesus Christ by God the Father himself, and removes it from the christological frame in which it was originally set. He then inserts it into his own letter, placing it in a different frame, an ethical one, which is slightly smaller and which does not accommodate the full size of the hymn as a whole. The effect is that this ethical frame into which Paul places the christological hymn leaves the final stanza of vv. 9–11 hanging awkwardly outside this new enclosure. The disadvantage of this way of viewing vv. 9–11 is that they appear extraneous to the argument, a diversion, a red herring, so to speak. Understandably, to many such a way of viewing 2:9–11 seems an argument born out of desperation! Is there any way in which these verses can be interpreted as an integral part, not only of the hymn itself, but of Paul's line of argument within the letter proper? How can we determine the precise role that 2:9–11 has within the letter?

One of the new critical tools that has been applied to the Philippian hymn in recent years has the potential, at least in theory, to do precisely this. I speak of rhetorical criticism, the application of formal categories of classical Graeco-Roman rhetoric to a study of the Pauline letters (it should be remembered that the letters were intended to be *heard in public* rather than simply *read in private,* a fact that makes rhetorical criticism much more relevant than it might at first appear). Rhetorical criticism attempts to determine not only the kind of argument being pursued within a given letter, but also seeks to identify the formal steps of an argument and how the constituent rhetorical units contribute to the overall intention of the author. Three common means whereby a speaker/writer might try to persuade his audience are commonly noted: *pathos* (the appeal to emotion); *logos* (the appeal to reason); and *ethos* (the appeal to the moral character or reputation of the speaker and his argument). In addition, three traditional types of rhetoric are generally acknowleged: juridical speeches (which are intended to elicit a judgment); deliberative speeches (which are intended to effect a decision); and epideictic speeches (which are intended to promote agreement with or dissent from a particular stance).[19]

So how does Phil. 2:6–11 fare at the hands of this recently employed weapon in the scholarly armory? Four rhetorical assessments of Philippians are worth noting briefly; it is best to view them in chronological order, for they exhibit a progressive refinement of argument with regard to the role of 2:9–11. First, we note the work of Charles J. Robbins,[20] who looks at the rhetorical balance of the hymn as a whole and seeks to address the question of alleged Pauline interpolations into it. He argues that 2:6–11 is composed of twelve highly structured lines and that it fits conventional rhetorical style as it presently stands. In other words, what we have in our text is the original hymn: there are no Pauline interpolations. The removal of any of the alleged Pauline additions disrupts the cadence of the long-flowing clauses that are so characteristic of classical literature. Unfortunately, while Robbins's study may answer some questions about the authenticity of 8c or 11c within the structure of the hymn, he has nothing to say about the place of the hymn within the thought of the epistle as a whole, and eschatological matters are not discussed at all.

Second, we note the interpretation of Duane F. Watson,[21] who takes Philippians to be an example of deliberative rhetoric. He sees 2:5–11 as part of the letter's *probatio* (which runs from 2:1–3:21). In terms of form, the *probatio* is the section of a speech in which a speaker supports his case by citing examples which add an element of *ethos* to the argument. In effect, this is to assign 2:6–11 a role in the production, so to speak, but alas, it is not a terribly significant one. More to the point, there appears to be no distinctive place for 2:9–11 within the assessment; there is precious little offered here for our concern in establishing the eschatological dimension of the hymn.

However, Claudio Basevi and Juan Chapa,[22] our third example, differ in their assessment of the rhetorical function of the hymn, seeing it as occupying a central position in the letter as a whole. In their opinion the hymn is an *encomium* of Christ that sets forth the theological basis for everything else that is stated in the letter, a programmatic statement, as it were. They conclude their study with these words:

> Phil. 2.5–11 should be viewed as an encomium of Christ which demands a poetical form and has the function of a profession of faith. This lays the foundation for an exhortation to the afflicted community of Christians in Philippi. Knowing what Christ was and what he did, they would be encouraged to stay faithful to the gospel as well as united to Christ, to Paul and amongst themselves. (356)

This is surely a step forward, but what is disappointing about this particular rhetorical analysis is that, just as in the interpretations of Robbins and Watson, there is no explicit place given to vv. 9–11 of the hymn. To be fair, a powerful case is made for the centrality of 2:5–11 within the overall argument of Paul's letter, and there is much to commend their assessment of the various sections of the letter and their judgment that it is best viewed as an example of epideictic rhetoric. However, by focusing on *"what Christ was and what he did"* within the hymn they clearly concentrate on the first stanza, namely vv. 6–8. One wonders if the rhetorical force they suggest is operative here would be lost somewhat if the focus were shifted from what *Christ* did (stayed obedient even to the point of death on the cross—v. 8) to what *God the Father* did (exalted him to the highest level—vv. 9–11). In short, in this particular instance the rhetorical analysis promised much and delivered little, at least as far as helping us to see the contribution of 2:9–11 to the overall argument of the letter is concerned. The final stanza of the hymn might just as well not have been there at all, so little does it appear to offer in assisting Paul's aims in the epistle. A different way of examining vv. 9–11 is desperately needed, for none of the rhetorical analyses so far discussed seem to give the verses their due weight.

A much more promising rhetorical analysis of the hymn is that offered by L. Gregory Bloomquist,[23] who sees 2:6–11 as falling within the *exhortatio* of the main body of the epistle (known as the *argumentatio* and running from 1:18b–4:7). In this regard 2:1–11 stands alongside two other subsections of the *exhortatio,* namely 1:27–30 and 2:12–18, and all three share a common aim: the presentation of ethical examples as a basis for an exhortation to proper Christian conduct among the Philippians. While Bloomquist describes 2:6–11 as "a crucial nucleus within the letter" (160), the main point of his discussion is to suggest that Paul is deliberately styling himself as a fulfillment of Christ, particularly with regard to the suffering motif (which Bloomquist suggests runs through the letter like a scarlet thread). Paul wishes to stress that he suffers on behalf of the Philippians in the same way that Christ did when he was obedient to the divine mission placed upon him. That may be well and good, but once again 2:9–11 seems at this juncture to be given little direct attention within the discussion. About the closest one gets to it is the inference drawn from the linguistic and thematic parallels between 2:9–11 and 3:20–21 (which are set out by Bloomquist in a chart on his p. 165). In other words, the exaltation of Christ, which comes as a divine response to his obedience unto death, has its counterpart for Paul and the church at large in the eschatological picture painted in 3:20–21.[24] It is really in this connection that Bloomquist finally comes to address the role and function of 2:9–11, and even then it comes as something of an aside. It may well be that the fact that his study is primarily concerned with the suffering motif means that an interest in determining its theological counterpart, the exaltation motif, is inevitably going to be a secondary concern. In any event, we can rejoice that the theme of vindication does come out in the analysis, even if it is on the last couple of pages of the study. Bloomquist suggestively remarks that one of the functions of the suffering theme in Philippians as a whole is that "suffering points beyond itself to vindication." (196). He summarizes the role of the hymn in 2:6–11 with these words:

> The centrality of 2.6–11 and the presentation there of Christ as servant alert us to Paul's conviction that his life mirrors the experience of Christ, especially in terms of suffering. . . . (T)he main point of 2.6–11 is its underscoring the fact that vindication follows suffering. The experiences in Paul's life, reflecting as they do the Christ type, lead him to see that even as Christ as servant suffered and was vindicated, so he too, as well as the co-workers and the Philippians, will be vindicated or exalted. (195)

Bloomquist's analysis accords well with the provocative study by Stephen E. Fowl,[25] who also attempts to ground his interpretation of the function of the hymn within the concrete, historical situation in which the Philippian church found itself and to which Paul offered pastoral advice. Fowl here stresses that in all likelihood the Philippians were facing an unsympathetic, if not hostile, opposition and that Paul is forced by circumstances to address a church undergoing persecution from outside.[26] He takes as his starting point the study of the christological hymn put forward by Morna D. Hooker in 1975,[27] which argued that 2:6–11 not only supports Paul's argument in 1:27–2:4 but also relates to the point he is making about the future transformation of the believers in 3:20–21. In Hooker's opinion the hymn's theme of humility (contained in vv. 6–8) reinforces the exhortation made in 1:27–2:4, while the hymn's note of exaltation (contained in vv. 9–11) anticipates the discussion which later follows in 3:20–21. In effect, this means that 2:9–11 is taken by Hooker as having no real relevance to the theme of humility that the apostle had been pursuing up to that point in his argument, an assessment which Fowl rightly notes leads one to wonder why 2:9–11 was inserted into the text where it stands in the first place. This is an awkwardness in Hooker's interpretation that Fowl seeks to correct in his own study. His basic suggestion is that the whole of the hymn, both the theme of humility (vv. 6–8) and the theme of exaltation (vv. 9–11), are relevant to Paul's purposes not only in 1:27–2:4 but 3:20–21 also. He posits that in both passages Christ is being presented as an exemplar in which Paul sees a parallel to the Philippian situation and from which he is able to offer his advice to the congregation as to how they should proceed. Fowl summarizes the critical point in this way:

> We would argue that by viewing vv. 6–11 as an exemplar from which Paul draws an analogy to the Philippians' situation in order to justify the course of action he has urged in 1:27ff. we avoid the criticisms levelled against those who see 2:5–11 as proposing a model to be imitated. Further, in this view vv. 9–11 play a crucial part in the function of the passage. If God does not vindicate Christ's suffering and humiliation, there is no reason to expect the same God to save the Philippians if they remain steadfast in the face of opposition. (95)

A similar point is made with regard to the eschatological teaching contained in 3:20–21. Once again the idea of Christ serving as an exemplar is invoked by Paul, this time to correct a false understanding of eschatology on the part of Paul's opponents, notably the destiny of the believers. According to Fowl, an important corrective is thus injected by Paul as he seeks to correct the excesses of the opposition in Philippi:

> After urging imitation of his own example and the examples of those like him, Paul goes on to talk about the enemies of the cross of Christ. While this epithet surely applies to Paul's opponents in Philippi, it must also apply to a wider group as well. These enemies are unwilling to become like Christ in his death, which, as 2:8 emphasizes, was a death on the cross. Their theology can only accommodate the exalted Christ of 2:9–11. Paul, however, will not let them forget 2:6–8. (100)

While there are some features of Fowl's interpretation which might be called into question (his assumptions concerning the integrity of the epistle, or his reading of the opposition in Philippi as Judaizers, for example), there is every indication that this study represents an important new contribution to the study of the christological hymn in Phil. 2:5–11. Of special note is the fact that this interpretation does provide a plausible explanation of the function of 2:9–11 within the setting of the epistle as a whole. As even the briefest of explorations in the numerous recent commentaries on Philippians will demonstrate, this is not often the case. Any future study of 2:9–11 will have to reckon with the analysis that is here offered concerning the function of the hymn within the epistle in which it holds pride of place.

3. Philippians 2:9–11 and the Preexistence of Christ

Scholarly debate about whether or not the christological hymn in 2:6–11 teaches the preexistence of Christ continues unabated. A growing number of New Testament interpreters see vv. 6–8 of the hymn as an expression of Adamic christology (which stresses Christ's humanity as one made in the image of God), rather than the traditional view, which takes them to refer to the incarnation (stressing the divine kenosis and Christ's laying aside of deity in order to become man).[28] Nevertheless, despite the trend away from the traditional interpretation there are still a significant number of interpreters who believe that the christological hymn does contain the idea of Christ's preexistence within it, albeit not as unambiguously declared as we might like.[29] For the most part the christological debate revolves around vv. 6–8, and it is only in a secondary way that vv. 9–11 figure within the discussion. Occasionally vv. 9–11 are invoked as a structural counterpart to the incarnational movement implied in vv. 6–7; just as Christ came down from heaven and became incarnate, so he is returned to heaven in vindication following his death on the cross. Much depends on whether one feels 2:6–11 expresses the life of Jesus Christ in terms of two steps (incarnation-exaltation) or three steps (preexistence-incarnation-exaltation). Both interpretations are vigorously defended, and one is tempted to suggest that the matter is ultimately determined not by exegesis of the passage itself, so much as by the christological presuppositions of the exegete concerned.

The major contribution that vv. 9–11 have to make to this debate revolves around the meaning of ὑπερύψωσεν in 9a.[30] Does this verb suggest that the exaltation is *above* the station that Christ held previously, one that is *higher* than the one he had prior to his incarnation? If so, then one might argue that his preexistent state is the standard against which the exaltation is measured and infer that the hymn teaches a three-step christology (i.e., Christ is exalted to an *even higher station* than he held in his preexistence).[31] Most commentators now agree, however, that this reading of the verb lays too much stress upon its prefix (ὑπέρ); it thus fails to take into account the frequency with which superlatives function as comparatives within the New Testament, especially in Paul (a good parallel is Rom. 8:37). Admittedly, Paul is quite fond of using ὑπέρ constructions,[32] but this surely is an insufficient basis upon which to build a case for the preexistence of Christ in 2:9–11. The meaning of the verb, which is found only here in the New Testament, is correctly given by Barclay in his translation as "God *has given him the highest place*"; Gerald F. Hawthorne[33] offers a more conventional rendering: "God *exalted him to the highest place.*"

4. The Allusion to Isaiah 45:23 and
Paul's Adaptation of the Old Testament Text

It is frequently noted that in 2:9–11 we are presented with a sudden change of subject. In the opening two stanzas of the hymn (2:6–8) it has been Christ who was the focus of attention; it was he who was on center stage, so to speak. In the third stanza, however, it is God who becomes the principal actor; it is God who takes over the action of the christological drama.

A closer examination of the reworking of Isa. 45:23 in vv. 10–11 demonstrates that a theocentric passage has been christologically reinterpreted within the original hymn. We can assume that since Paul chooses to include this section of the hymn he agrees with the christological redirection expressed within it. The most important point for our consideration is that of the context of the passage in Isaiah; it is a declaration that the sovereignty of God will one day be acknowledged and proclaimed throughout the world. This affirmation of lordship is extensively reworked and made to apply to the exalted Christ, a reworking which is generally taken to indicate the investiture of God's power and authority, as embodied in his name (the Tetragrammaton!),[34] on the *Lord* Jesus Christ.[35] This central feature of the reworking of Isaiah 45 has been widely recognized and has been taken by many, including myself, to indicate the transferral of Old Testament language from God to Jesus Christ, a move that has important implications for a doctrine of the deity of Christ. Not all would go so far as this, however, and some would dispute that such a functional overlap between Jesus Christ and God necessarily means the *identification* of God and his messianic agent. For example, Neil Richardson denies outright transference and argues instead that in 2:10–11 we have an instance where "the universal Lordship of Jesus is the new expression of Jewish monotheism."[36] We could reply that Christ's lordship may well be an expression of Jewish monotheism, but it comes about precisely because he (Christ) is the human *embodiment* of that monotheistic God. One can only speculate about how long it would take for the distinction between worship and praise channeled through God's messianic agent and worship and praise of that agent as God incarnate to become so fine as to be impossible to discern; my own suspicion is that it was not very long at all and such an effacement is exactly what we see within this pre-Pauline hymn. Nevertheless, there are three other specific questions that arise from 2:10–11, which are worth noting briefly.

First, there is the question of the timing of the worship described. Does the "bowing of the knee" and the "confession of the tongue" take place in the future, at the parousia,[37] or is it something which is to be understood as a present reality, flowing out of the present exaltation of Christ to the heavens? Phrasing the question in such an either/or fashion is a false dichotomy; it is not present exaltation *or* future exaltation, but present *and* future exaltation which is in mind. In short, vv. 9–11 as a whole perfectly embody the now/not-yet eschatology so characteristic of Paul's epistles overall. The ἵνα clause with which the quotation opens does allow precisely such an interpretation, particularly when we remember that ἵνα can introduce either a purpose clause or a result clause. God's exaltation of Christ not only means that as a *result* he is worshiped as Lord within the life of the church on earth now, but the *purposes* of God will ultimately be brought to bear in all of creation, and Christ will be confessed as Lord in the future.[38] The future textual variant ἐξομολογήσεται is in this sense to be preferred to the aorist subjunctive ἐξομολογήσηται (the textual evidence between the two is fairly evenly distributed), although it should be remembered that aorist subjunctives often function as futures in the New Testament. In any case, the difference between Paul and the LXX on this point may be significant. The verb used in Isa. 45:23 is ὀμεῖται while the verb root in 2:10 is ἐξομολογέω; it could be argued that the shift is an indication of the liturgical nature of the hymn—that it served as a confession of faith.

Second, it is worth recalling H. Wheeler Robinson's suggestion that the servant songs of Isaiah may underlie the use of Isa. 45:23 in vv. 10–11, if for no other reason (beyond the fact that I eat lunch every day in the college dining hall with the stern portrait of this former Principal looking down at me, *daring* anyone to forget him!) than the fact that it allows a creative link to be forged with the first stanza of the hymn. Robinson put forward the idea that the servant-messiah motif is crucial for understanding Paul's thought in Philippians 2 (he assumes Pauline authorship for the hymn as a whole), and that this is clearly seen by the explicit reference to Christ's death on the cross (verse 8c). Moreover, Robinson goes on to argue, largely on the assumption that the suffering servant of Isaiah 53 is in the back of Paul's mind, that the focus of the kenosis described in 2:6–8 is not on Christ's incarnation, but rather on his crucifixion.[39] Robinson's key suggestion that ἑαυτὸν ἐκένωσεν in 2:7 is a translation of הֶעֱרָה לַמָּוֶת נַפְשׁוֹ from Isa. 53:12 has been taken up by others, notably Joachim Jeremias and C. H. Dodd, but it is not without its critics nowadays.[40]

Finally, we note the phrase "in heaven, on earth and under the earth (ἐπουρανίων καὶ ἐπιγείων καὶ καταχθονίων)" in 10c. This is an addition to the quotation from Isa. 45:23, although it is well in keeping with the universalistic vision of the Old Testament passage. Discussion continues as to whether these words were a part of the original hymn or were later added to it by Paul himself, but a decision about this one way or the other does not substantially affect the basic meaning of vv. 9–11. Some grammatical ambiguity exists, however, since the three nouns can either be masculine (denoting *persons*) or neuter (denoting *things,* i.e., impersonal beings or forces). Otfried Hofius disputes the common view that the three categories (in heaven, on earth, under the earth) refer to spiritual beings or the "powers and principalities" of the cosmos (as in Col. 2:15; Eph. 6:12). He suggests rather that "those in the heavens" refers to heavenly, angelic beings, "those on earth" refers to those who are living on earth when the future is consummated at the parousia, and "those under the earth" refers to people who have died and abide in Hades or Sheol.[41] The traditional creedal affirmation that Christ descended into hell may be of relevance here, given that such an idea is certainly contained in other early Christian writings (such as Matt. 12:40; 27:51–53; 1 Peter 3:19; 4:6; Ignatius's *Letter to the Magnesians* 9; Justin Martyr *Dialogue with Trypho* 32; Tertullian *On the Soul* 55; Irenaeus *Against Heresies* 3.20.4; 4.22.1; 4.33.1,12; 5.31.1; *Gospel of Peter* 10.39–42; and the *Gospel of Nicodemus*).[42] The idea of a descent to the underworld was much more widely known in the ancient Graeco-Roman world than is often appreciated,[43] and allusions to it appear elsewhere in the Pauline corpus. For example, there is good evidence to suggest that such a descent into the underworld is what lies behind the cryptic passage in Ephesians 4:9–10[44] (and perhaps even Romans 10:5–6?).

5. Philippians 2:11c and the Relationship between Jesus Christ and God

There have been several studies that suggest that the hymn arises directly out of, or at least reflects, the patterns of Jewish synagogue prayers and worship, including the use of Hallel hymns in Passover celebrations.[45] The description given by Pliny the Younger of Bithynian Christians antiphonally singing hymns to Christ as if to God may also be of relevance here.[46] This is about the closest description of how Phil. 2:6–11 may have been used in worship that we possess. How 11c would have figured within such an antiphonal arrangement is an open question, although the suggestion that both 8c and 11c were places within the singing where the two halves of the congregation joined their voices in unison is an attractive possibility.[47] In any event, it is best to see the phrase as a liturgical response based upon and proclaiming the lordship of Christ that the hymn declares. But what about the note of praise to God the Father with which this hymn of praise ends? It is at this particular juncture that the fine balance of christocentrism and theocentrism contained within the hymn is most readily seen.

The crucial point is that however exalted Christ is, even to the point of being raised to the highest place and being endowed with the very name of God himself, this is followed by a resounding proclamation that God the Father is the one who is worthy to receive the glory. We could say that the hymn ends on a note of subordination, with the Son stepping aside to allow God the Father to take his place as the focus of worship. The hymn thus proclaims that the wonders of what Christ has done in his obedience are more than matched by the wonders that God has done in his grace, and deliberately culminates in a line which makes that abundantly clear. At the end of the day everything has been accomplished "to the glory of God the Father."

The title I have chosen for this study ("'When He at Last Is First!': Philippians 2:9–11 and the Exaltation of the Lord") attempts to give voice to the delicately poised balance between Christ and God as expressed within the hymn, and is therefore dutifully ambiguous on two points. First, the title preserves the note of futuristic eschatology which, to my mind, seems foundational to Paul's thought. According to Paul there will come a time in the future ("at last!") when God's purposes will be brought to bear in the world and his(!) lordship will be universally acknowledged. Second, it rightly focuses on the "Exaltation of the Lord" as the main theme of this stanza within the overall hymn, but deliberately leaves open the question as to who is meant by "Lord." Is it Christ, or God? There is a sense in which the exaltation of Jesus Christ *is* the exaltation of God the Father; the one receives exaltation and the other bestows it, but both are involved and both are accorded due praise from the worshiping community for effecting the drama of redemption. The same sense of ambiguity pertains to the "he" in the title ("When

He at Last Is First"), which we could say fairly accurately summarizes Phil. 2:9–11. But just who is the "He" that is "First?" Again, it seems to me that there is a good case for taking it either way: Jesus Christ is First, preeminent over all, and because he is, this is to the glory of God the Father and gives birth to the truth that He himself is First. The hymn is Janus-like in this regard, proclaiming the lordship of both Jesus Christ and God the Father and ultimately confounding our attempts conclusively to file the concluding stanza away as an expression of either the apostle's christocentrism or his theocentrism. Perhaps this was one of the intentions of the hymn in the first place—to give voice to the realization that in Jesus Christ, the exalted Lord, the very presence of God the Father himself is encountered by a worshiping community.

NOTES

1. Notable recent exceptions to a pre-Pauline assessment of the hymn include: Seyoon Kim, *The Origin of Paul's Gospel* (Grand Rapids: Eerdmans, 1982), 147–49; I. Howard Marshall, *The Epistle to the Philippians,* Epworth Commentaries (London: Epworth Press, 1991), 47–48; D. A. Carson, Douglas J. Moo, and Leon Morris, *An Introduction to the New Testament* (Leicester: Apollos Books, 1992), 318–19; Moisés Silva, *Philippians,* BECNT (Grand Rapids: Baker, 1992); Gordon D. Fee, *Paul's Letter to the Philippians* (Grand Rapids: Eerdmans, 1995), 40–46. While admitting that the arguments are finely balanced, they all come down on the side of Pauline authorship of the hymn as a whole (Fee even questions whether 2:6–11 is a hymn at all).
2. Ernst Lohmeyer divided the hymn into six strophes each of which contained three lines, an assessment which has been widely accepted. I tend to agree with the structural analysis of the hymn offered by Joachim Jeremias, "Zu Phil ii 7: EAYTON EKENΩΣEN," *NovT* 9 (1963): 182–88. Jeremias divides the hymn into three strophes (vv. 6–7a, 7b–8, 9–11) each of which contains four lines; he takes "even death on a cross" (v. 8), "in heaven and on earth and under the earth" (v. 10), and "to the glory of God" (v. 11) to be Pauline interpolations into the original hymn. Joseph A. Fitzmyer, "The Aramaic Background of Phil 2:6–11," *CBQ* 50 (1988): 470–83, attempts a reconstruction of the original hymn as used by the Aramaic-speaking Palestinian church; in his estimation the only Pauline interpolation in the 18-line hymn is the reference to "even death on a cross" in v. 8 (he echoes Lohmeyer's analysis). The REB supports this suggestion regarding 8c, setting off the phrase with hyphens. For a recent study arguing that 8c was an integral part of the original hymn, see Otfried Hofius, *Der Christushymnus Philipper 2,6–11,* WUNT 17 (Tübingen: Mohr [Siebeck], 1976), 3–12. See above, p. 51.
3. E. Käsemann's article "The Beginnings of Christian Theology" (1960) was reprinted in his *New Testament Questions for Today* (Philadelphia: Fortress Press, 1969), 82–107. The same volume contains two other important articles related to the theme of apocalyptic literature, namely, "On the Subject of Primitive Christian Apocalyptic" (108–37) and "Paul and Early Catholicism" (236–51).
4. R. Barry Matlock, *Unveiling the Apocalyptic Paul: Paul's Interpreters and the Rhetoric of Criticism,* (JSNTSup 127 (Sheffield: Sheffield Academic Press, 1996), discusses the various scholarly attempts in this century to interpret Paul's apocalypticism. He offers a penetrating methodological critique of such endeavors. For an overview of

Paul's eschatological thought, see my article on "Eschatology" in *Dictionary of Paul and His Letters,* ed. Gerald F. Hawthorne, Ralph P. Martin, and Daniel G. Reid (Leicester and Downers Grove, Ill.: InterVarsity Press, 1993), 253–69.

5. Two other volumes followed this seminal work and were intended to communicate the substance of it to a more popular audience: J. Christiaan Beker, *Paul's Apocalyptic Gospel: The Coming Triumph of God* (Philadelphia: Fortress Press, 1982), and idem, *The Triumph of God: The Essence of Paul's Thought* (Philadelphia: Fortress Press, 1990).

6. For more from Beker on the question of Paul's coherence of thought, see "Paul's Theology: Consistent or Inconsistent?" *NTS* 34 (1988): 364–77; "Paul the Theologian: Major Motifs in Pauline Theology," *Interpretation* 43 (1989): 352–65; and "Recasting Pauline Theology: The Coherence-Contingency Scheme as Interpretive Model," in *Pauline Theology,* vol. 1: *Thessalonians, Philippians, Galatians, Philemon,* ed. Jouette M. Bassler (Minneapolis: Fortress Press, 1991), 15–24. It is perhaps worth noting that Beker's work comes at precisely the same time that many New Testament interpreters have been debating the theological inconsistencies (not to say contradictions) within Paul's thought, notably with respect to the continuing validity of the Jewish law for Christians. At the risk of oversimplification, one could speculate how it is that New Testament scholars appear to be able to live with such theological tensions more readily than systematic theologians do (keeping in mind, of course, as this observation is made that Beker is primarily a systematic theologian, while I am a New Testament scholar!).

7. See, e.g., Paul J. Achtemeier, "An Apocalyptic Shift in Early Christian Tradition: Reflections on Some Canonical Evidence," *CBQ* 45 (1983): 231–48; Leander E. Keck, "Paul and Apocalyptic Theology," *Interpretation* 38 (1984): 229–41; Barnabas Lindars, "The Sound of the Trumpet: Paul and Eschatology," *BJRL* 67 (1984–85): 766–82; Vincent P. Branick, "Apocalyptic Paul?" *CBQ* 47 (1985): 664–75; Richard N. Longenecker, "The Nature of Paul's Early Eschatology," *NTS* 31 (1985): 85–95; J. L. Martyn, "Apocalyptic Antinomies in Paul's Letter to the Galatians," *NTS* 31 (1985): 410–24; L. Joseph Kreitzer, *Jesus and God in Paul's Eschatology,* JSNTSup 19 (Sheffield: Sheffield Academic Press, 1987); Martinus C. de Boer, *The Defeat of Death: Apocalyptic Eschatology in 1 Corinthians 15 and Romans 5,* JSNTSup 22 (Sheffield: Sheffield Academic Press, 1989); Hendrikus W. Boers, "The Foundations of Paul's Thought: A Methodological Investigation—The Problem of the Coherent Centre of Paul's Thought," *Studia Theologica* 42 (1988): 55–68; Martinus C. de Boer, "Paul and Jewish Apocalyptic Eschatology," in *Apocalyptic and the New Testament: Essays in Honour of J. Louis Martyn,* ed. Joel Marcus and Marion L. Soards, JSNTSup 24 (Sheffield: Sheffield Academic Press, 1989), 169–90; Charles D. Myers, Jr., "The Persistence of Apocalyptic Thought in New Testament Theology," in *Biblical Theology: Problems and Perspectives: In Honor of J. Christiaan Beker,* ed. Steven J. Kraftchick, Charles D. Myers, Jr., and Ben C. Ollenburger (Nashville: Abingdon Press, 1995), 209–21.

8. Ralph P. Martin's review of Beker's work in *JBL* 101 (1982): 463–65; Joseph Plevnik, "The Center of Paul's Theology," *CBQ* 51 (1989): 461–78; and Matlock, 48–53, 247–50, 299–304, and 308–10.

9. One of the references to 2:9 is mistakenly given as 2:7 on page 168. Beker's follow-up book from 1982 does not contain any mention at all of Philippians 2:6–11.

10. This is true, for example, in the articles by Achtemeier, Lindars, Boers, de Boer, Longenecker, and Martyn cited in note 7 above. None of these contains so much as a cross-reference to Philippians 2:9–11 within its discussion of Paul's eschatology.

11. See G. N. Stanton, *Jesus of Nazareth in New Testament Preaching,* SNTSMS 27 (Cambridge: Cambridge University Press, 1974), 99–104, for a useful introduction to this matter. Stanton is responding to the seminal works by Ernst Käsemann, "A Critical Analysis of Philippians 2:5–11," *JTC* 5 (1968): 45–68, and Ralph P. Martin, *Carmen Christi: Philippians ii. 5–11 in Recent Interpretation and in the Setting of Early Christian Worship,* SNTSMS 4 (Cambridge: Cambridge University Press, 1967). Also worth noting on this matter is L. W. Hurtado, "Jesus as Lordly Example in Philippians 2:5–11," in *From Jesus to Paul: Studies in Honour of Francis Wright Beare,* ed. Peter Richardson and John C. Hurd (Waterloo, Ont.: Wilfrid Laurier University Press, 1984), 113–26, who offers some important observations as to the reasons why Käsemann adopted the position that he did on such matters. (See R. Morgan's essay chapter 3 of this book).

12. As suggested by Gerald F. Hawthorne, *Philippians,* WBC (Waco, Tex.: Word, 1983), 78–79.

13. Contra the interpretation of Karl Barth, *The Epistle to the Philippians* (London: SCM Press, 1962), 66. Barth is keen to avoid any suggestion of reward in vv. 9–11 because he fears it undermines the sovereign grace of God. However, rewards need not be payments, and they certainly can be graciously bestowed. Christ did not go to the cross in order to receive the reward of exaltation, but his going to the cross nevertheless results in his being so rewarded.

14. Thus Anthony T. Hanson, *The Living Utterances of God: The New Testament Exegesis of the Old* (London: Darton, Longman & Todd, 1984), 59, suggests that 2:9–11 represents a Pauline addition to the hymn. He does not say why Paul adds such a seemingly irrelevant paragraph at this point in the letter.

15. Jean-François Collange, *The Epistle of Saint Paul to the Philippians* (London: Epworth Press, 1979), 83.

16. Little wonder then that some interpreters continue to follow the lead of Ernst Käsemann and downplay the ethical interpretation in favor of one that concentrates on the position of the believers "in Christ," and therefore sees the declaration of Christ's lordship over all of creation (v. 9–11!) as the heart of the hymn. Lynn Allan Losie, "A Note on the Interpretation of Phil 2:5," *ExpTim* 90 (1978–79): 52–54, offers the intriguing suggestion that the whole of the christological hymn itself (rather than the ethical example of Jesus in vv. 6–8) is in mind when Paul writes "Set your mind on *this* . . . " However, the τοῦτο with which the verse commences would militate against this, pointing backward as it does to the exhortation given in 1:27–2:4.

17. We should not fail to notice that Paul does present other ethical examples for the Philippians to emulate in the course of the letter, notably Timothy and Epaphroditus (2:19–30), and himself (2:17; 3:15–17; 4:9). For a discussion of this, see Peter T. O'Brien, "The Gospel and Godly Models in Philippians," in *Worship, Theology and Ministry in the Early Church: Essays in Honor of Ralph P. Martin,* ed. Michael J. Wilkins and Terence Paige, JSNTSup 87 (Sheffield: Sheffield Academic Press, 1992), 273–84; William S. Kurz, "Kenotic Imitation of Paul and of Christ in Philippians 2 and 3," in *Discipleship in the New Testament,* ed. Fernando F. Segovia (Philadelphia: Fortress Press, 1985), 103–26; and the articles in this volume on *Imitatio Christi* (chapters 9 and 10). A. Boyd Luter and Michelle V. Lee, "Philippians as Chiasmus: Key to the Structure, Unity and Theme Questions," *NTS* 41 (1995): 89–101, suggest that 2:17–3:1a is the midpoint of the chiastic structure of the epistle. They see the presentation of Paul, Timothy, and Epaphroditus as models to be emulated by the church as fitting closely with the epistle's overall theme, which they identify as "partnership in the gospel."

18. Fred Craddock, *Philippians,* Interpretation (Atlanta: John Knox Press, 1985), 43.
19. It is not hard to see why rhetorical criticism has been a useful tool for those engaged in wrestling with the vexing problem of the unity and integrity of the letter to the Philippians. David E. Garland, "The Composition and Unity of Philippians," *NovT* 27 (1985): 141–73, provides a summary of scholarly investigation of this topic. Also, see L. Gregory Bloomquist, *The Function of Suffering in Philippians,* JSNTSup 78 (Sheffield: Sheffield Academic Press, 1993), 97–118.
20. Charles J. Robbins, "Rhetorical Structure of Philippians 2:6–11," *CBQ* 42 (1980): 73–82.
21. Duane F. Watson, "A Rhetorical Analysis of Philippians and its Implications for the Unity Question," *NTS* 30 (1988): 57–88.
22. Claudio Basevi and Juan Chapa, "Philippians 2:6–11: The Rhetorical Function of a Pauline 'Hymn,'" in *Rhetoric and the New Testament: Essays from the 1992 Heidelberg Conference,* ed. S. E. Porter and T. H. Olbricht, JSNTSup 90 (Sheffield: Sheffield Academic Press, 1993), 338–56.
23. Bloomquist, *The Function of Suffering in Philippians.*
24. Many commentators have noted the similarities between these two passages, a matter which has important repercussions for debate about the unity and integrity of the letter. W. J. Dalton, "The Integrity of Philippians," *Biblica* 60 (1979), remarking on the similarities of vocabulary and thought between the two passages, suggests that 3:20–21 builds upon the earlier hymn and represents "the application of Christology to the conditions of Christian existence" (98). For additional discussion on the relationship between 2:6–11 and 3:20–21, see John Reumann, "Philippians 3:20–21—A Hymnic Fragment?" *NTS* 30 (1983–84): 593–609; Darrell J. Doughty, "Citizens of Heaven: Philippians 3:2–21," *NTS* 41 (1995): 102–22.
25. Stephen E. Fowl, *The Story of Christ in the Ethics of Paul: An Analysis of the Function of the Hymnic Material in the Pauline Corpus,* JSNTSup 36 (Sheffield: Sheffield Academic Press, 1990).
26. Pheme Perkins, "Philippians: Theology for the Heavenly Politeuma," in *Pauline Thelogy Volume 1: Thessalonians, Philippians, Galatians, Philemon,* ed. Jouette M. Bassler (Minneapolis: Fortress Press, 1991), 89–104, reviews the current state of affairs on the question of opposition to Paul in Philippi. She sets out a plausible case for the difficulties Paul was facing in Philippi as arising from its position as a Roman city with a rich history and a mixed population. Although she takes Philippians to be comprised of at least three letters from Paul, there is, in her opinion, sufficient continuity between them to construct such a case. A similar line is taken by Edgar M. Krentz, "Military Language and Metaphors in Philippians," in *Origins and Method: Towards a New Understanding of Judaism and Christianity: Essays in Honour of John C. Hurd,* ed. Bradley H. McLean, JSNTSup 85 (1993): 105–27. Krentz argues that the references to πολιτεύεσθε in 1:27 and πολίτευμα in 3:20 suggest the Christians of Philippi were struggling against the ruler cult of the emperor Nero, which was flourishing in the city. This is an attractive possibility which may help explain the need for a confession of faith such as that provided in 2:10–11; however, other interpretations of πολιτεύεσθε and πολίτευμα are possible.
27. Reprinted in Morna D. Hooker, *From Adam to Christ: Essays on Paul* (Cambridge: Cambridge University Press, 1990), 88–102.
28. A classic formulation of this is J. D. G. Dunn's *Christology in the Making,* 2d ed. (London: SCM Press, 1989), 114–21.
29. See L. D. Hurst, "Re-Enter the Pre-Existent Christ in Philippians 2.5–11?" *NTS* 32

(1986): 449–57 (see now the expanded version in this volume, chapter 5); Teresia Yai-Chow Wong, "The Problem of Pre-Existence in Philippians 2.6–11," *ETL* 62 (1986): 267–82. Among recent commentaries, Peter T. O'Brien, *The Epistle to the Philippians,* NIGTC (Grand Rapids: Eerdmans, 1991), 263–68, and Gordon D. Fee, *Paul's Letter to the Philippians* (Grand Rapids: Eerdmans, 1995), 202–18, discuss the weaknesses of the Adamic interpretation.

30. The idea of exaltation may derive from Isa. 52:13 where God's servant "will be exalted and glorified" (ὑψωθήσεται καὶ δοξασθήσεται).

31. So Maurice Casey, *From Jewish Prophet to Gentile God: The Origins and Development of New Testament Christology* (Cambridge: James Clark & Co., 1991), 113–14.

32. Nineteen out of 28 instances of ὑπέρ compounds occurring in the New Testament are found in Paul. Gerhard Delling, "Zum steigernden Gebrauch von Komposita mit ὑπέρ bei Paulus," *NovT* 11 (1969): 127–53, discusses this.

33. Hawthorne, *Philippians,* 75.

34. I have previously called attention (*Jesus and God in Paul's Eschatology,* 108, 117, and 242–43) to the fact that the setting of the prophetic passage of Isaiah 45 is the period following the capture of Babylon by Cyrus. The suggestion that Cyrus (Κῦρος) could help set up a reference to the Lord (κύριος), combined with the fact that Cyrus was seen as a messianic figure (Isa. 45:1, 13!), remains an intriguing interpretative possibility, although not one taken up within recent commentaries.

35. Gordon D. Fee, *Paul's Letter,* 23, thinks that Paul is quoting the passage from memory.

36. Neil Richardson, *Paul's Language about God,* JSNTSup 99 (Sheffield: Sheffield Academic Press, 1994), 288.

37. The parousia of Christ is a prominent theme in Philippians (1:10; 2:16; 3:20–21, and 4:5).

38. As O'Brien, "Gospel," 238–39 argues.

39. H. Wheeler Robinson, *The Cross in the Old Testament* (London: SCM Press, 1955), 103–5.

40. On this, see Fowl, 61–64.

41. O. Hofius, 53–54. He does this largely on the basis of the reference to those in Sheol contained in Ps. 22:30 and the triadic arrangement found in such passages as Ps. 115:16–17 and Rev. 5:3. Ralph P. Martin, in the preface to the 1983 edition of his *Carmen Christi,* disagrees and describes such a suggestion as "eccentric" (xxvi). Fee, 224–25, agrees with Hofius on this point.

42. Jean Daniélou, *The Theology of Jewish Christianity* (London: Darton, Longman & Todd, 1964), 233–48, is a convenient place to see a number of texts that relate Christ's descent into hell.

43. Three well-known examples will suffice to illustrate the point: Aeneas's descent recorded in book 6 of Virgil's *Aeneid;* Orpheus's descent to recover his beloved Euridice recorded in book 10 of Ovid's *Metamorphoses;* and Hercules' descent into Hades to fetch the three-headed Cerberus recorded in book 2 of Apollodorus, *Bibliothetica.*

44. See my *Ephesians,* Epworth Commentaries (London: Epworth Press), 1997, where I suggest that the epistle to the Ephesians was originally written by a follower of Paul for the Christian congregation at Hierapolis in the Lycus Valley, partly on such an interpretation of Eph. 4:9–10. The point is that there was a so-called Plutonium (thought to be an entrance to the realm of the dead ruled by Pluto) situated just next to the temple of Apollo in the city. The site was something of a tourist attraction in the ancient world and is mentioned in several ancient sources, including Strabo, *Geography*

12.8.17 and 13.4.14. The digression in 4:9–10 appears to be a deliberate allusion to this geographical feature of the city, one which would have been well understood by the local inhabitants even if it remains somewhat obscure for us nearly 2,000 years later.

45. See Klaus Gamber, "Der Christus-Hymnus im Philipperbrief in liturgiegeschichtlicher Sicht," *Biblica* 51 (1970): 369–76; Hofius, 67–74; Martin Hengel, *Between Jesus and Paul* (London: SCM Press, 1983), 78–96; Ralph P. Martin, "Hymns, Hymn Fragments, Songs, Spiritual Songs," in Hawthorne, Martin, and Reid, 419–23.

46. *Letter to Trajan* 10.96.7, dated circa 112 c.e. The relevant portion of the Latin reads: "carmenque Christo quasi deo dicere secum invicem" ("chanting verses to Christ as if to God alternately among themselves").

47. Such a view presumes that these two phrases were part of the original hymn and not Pauline interpolations. See Collange, 8–9, 67–74, for an argument along these lines.

8.

The Worship of Jesus
in Philippians 2:9–11

RICHARD J. BAUCKHAM

Philippians 2:9–11 is the earliest extant text in which the worship of Jesus is depicted. As we shall see, it depicts Jesus receiving the worship uniquely due to the one God of Jewish monotheism. It therefore constitutes an important piece of evidence in the case for believing that Jesus was accorded divine worship from an early stage of the Christian movement and in a thoroughly Jewish Christian context of thought and practice. Recent scholarship[1] has increasingly recognized that the origin of the worship of Jesus cannot be attributed to pagan influence on Gentile Christians who had lost touch with Jewish monotheism, but in all probability occurred within the earliest Christian movement in Jewish Palestine. If Phil. 2:9–11 derives, as some argue, from a pre-Pauline hymn originally composed in Aramaic, then actually as a product of early Palestinian Jewish Christianity it evidences the worship of Jesus in early Palestinian Jewish Christianity. In this chapter, however, we shall not be concerned with the source-critical question. Rather we shall argue that Phil. 2:9–11 embodies a pattern of ideas relating the worship of Jesus to the exaltation of Jesus and to Jewish monotheistic faith which can also be found in a range of otherwise diverse early Christian texts and which most probably goes back to the earliest post-Easter christology. Thus, even if Paul himself composed Phil. 2:9–11, the understanding of the worship of Jesus that he expressed in these verses has nothing peculiarly or originally Pauline about it, but was widespread in the early Christian movement and derives from very early christological reflection.

Of course, Phil. 2:9–11 does not directly depict a Christian practice of worshiping Jesus. It depicts the worship of Jesus by every creature in the whole creation. But Christians who believed that the exalted Jesus deserves such acknowledgment of his lordship from all creatures must have accorded him just such acknowledgment of his lordship in their own worship. (If these verses come from a Christian hymn, then the singing of the hymn would itself be a form of worship of Jesus.) The passage must therefore relate to a Christian practice of worshiping Jesus. But its value as evidence for such a practice is much greater than a mere statement by Paul that Christians worshiped Jesus would be. It enables us to understand why Christians worshiped Jesus and what the theological and christological significance of the practice was. It is an important piece of evidence for the way early

Christians included Jesus in their Jewish monotheistic faith in the one God, thereby creating, not a deviation from Jewish monotheism, but a specifically Christian form of Jewish monotheism that can appropriately be called christological monotheism.

The worship of Jesus, as practiced by early Christians and as depicted in passages such as Phil. 2:9–11, must be an important focus in any attempt to understand the way early Christian christology related to Jewish monotheism. This is because monolatry—the exclusive worship of the one God—played a key role in Jewish monotheism. As I have put it myself in earlier publications:

> In the exclusive monotheism of the Jewish religious tradition, as distinct from some other kinds of monotheism, it was worship which was the real test of monotheistic faith in religious practice. . . . [I]n [Jewish] religious *practice* it was worship which signalled the distinction between God and every creature, however exalted. God must be worshiped; no creature may be worshiped.[2]

Jewish insistence on monolatrous worship is pervasive in Second Temple Judaism and apparent in scruples about any practice that could be construed as worship of humans or other beings regarded as gods by others. From all non-Jews who believed in or worshiped a high god but never supposed this to be incompatible with the worship also of lesser divinities, Jews were sharply distinguished by their monolatrous practice. This was a key part of their own highly self-conscious monotheism, and made most obvious in practice the absolute uniqueness they claimed for their God.[3]

However, it is important to be precise about the role of monolatry in defining Jewish monotheism. It cannot stand alone as a sufficient definition of the uniqueness of the God of Jewish monotheism.[4] This is because the exclusive worship of the God of Israel was precisely a recognition of and response to his unique identity.[5] For Second Temple Jews, it was because God was unique—in ways they were frequently willing to characterize—that he alone was worthy of worship. Most useful as ways of characterizing the unique identity of the one God and therefore found throughout Second Temple Jewish literature were the claims that the one God alone is Creator of all things and that the one God alone is sovereign over all things. By stating a unique relationship of the one God to all other reality, these claims draw an absolute distinction between the one God and all other reality. It is this absolute distinction that requires the exclusive worship of the one God and forbids the worship of any creature. For Jewish writers of this period, the reason beings other than the one God may not be worshiped—as they were by non-Jews—is that such beings are created by God, benefit humans only in a way that derives ultimately from God, and are ministers of God's will, not independent sources of good (e.g., Josephus, *Ant.* 1.155–156; *2 Enoch* 66:4–5 [J]; *Sib. Or.* 3:20–35). Worship in the Jewish tradition meant acknowledgment of the unique identity of God as the sole Creator and Ruler of all things.

It is in this context of the monotheistic significance of worship in the Jewish tradition that we can appreciate the full significance of three major aspects of the worship of Jesus in Philippians 2:9–11. *In the first place,* worship of Jesus by the whole creation is here associated with his exaltation to the position of divine sovereignty over the whole creation. Probably the most decisive step in the development of christology, a step taken at a very early stage, was the belief that Jesus had been exalted to sit with God on the throne in heaven from which God reigns over the whole creation.[6] In the context of Jewish monotheistic belief in the uniquely divine sovereignty over all things, this understanding of the exaltation of Jesus, most commonly expressed by allusion to Ps. 110:1,[7] had to mean that Jesus was included in the unique identity of the one God. For Jewish monotheism sovereignty over all things was definitive of *who God is*. It could not be seen as delegated to a being other than God. Angels might carry out God's will, as servants subject to his command in limited areas of his rule,[8] but God's universal sovereignty itself was intrinsic to the unique divine identity as sole Creator and Ruler of all. Hence Jesus' participation in or exercise of the divine sovereignty, symbolized by his sitting at the right hand of God on God's own throne, had to mean his inclusion in the divine identity itself. In that case, its corollary was the worship of Jesus, since worship is recognition of and response to the unique identity of the God who uniquely rules all creation. Jesus' inclusion in the unique identity of the one God who alone may be worshiped requires his inclusion in the monolatrous worship of this one God. Thus the suggestion that Jesus' exaltation was understood from an early stage as including him in the unique identity of the one God of Jewish monotheism is confirmed by passages, of which Phil. 2:9–11 is one, which depict the exalted Jesus receiving the worship of the whole creation.

There are three passages about the exaltation of Jesus in early Christian literature that both allude to Ps. 110:1 and also refer to the worship of Jesus by all the angelic powers of the heavens (Heb. 1:3–6; *Ascension of Isaiah* 10:14–15 and 11:23–32; *Apocryphon of James* 14:26–30). These quite independent passages attest a common theme that singles out the angels in order to make clear precisely Jesus' exaltation to the divine throne, high above all the angelic powers, from which, unlike any mere angelic minister of God, he exercises the divine rule over all things, even the angels. Three other passages (Polycarp, *Phil.* 2.1; Revelation 5; Phil. 2:9–11) include the angels in a depiction of the worship of Jesus by all creatures, heavenly and earthly. Only one of these alludes to Ps. 110:1:

> believing in the One who raised our Lord Jesus Christ from the dead
> and gave him glory and a throne at his right hand;
> to whom are subject all things heavenly and earthly;
> whom all that breathes worships;
> who is coming as the judge of the living and the dead.
>
> (Polycarp, *Phil.* 2.1)

This is clearly a traditional credal formula, quite independent of Phil. 2:9–11, with which it shares no terminology or biblical allusions. Philippians 2:9–11 itself refers to the exaltation of Jesus, not with allusion to Ps. 110:1, but with allusion to Isa. 52:13, a text elsewhere associated with Ps. 110:1 in reference to the exaltation of Jesus (Acts 2:23; 5:31).

The correspondence between Phil. 2:9–11 and Revelation 5 is particularly noteworthy. In both cases it is explicitly the crucified Christ (depicted symbolically as
the slaughtered Lamb in Revelation) who is exalted and worshiped. In Phil. 2:9–11
and Rev. 5:13 there are strikingly similar accounts of the worship of Christ by all
creation. Philippians 2:10–11 echoes Isa. 45:23 ("To me every knee shall bow,
every tongue shall swear"), but expands the "every knee . . . every tongue" of Isaiah, emphasizing the universality of the worship given to Christ with a formula en-
compassing the whole creation: "every knee shall bow, in heaven and on earth and
under the earth" (Phil. 2:10). Revelation 5, having portrayed the exalted Christ as
the Lamb in the midst of the divine throne in heaven (5:6; cf. 7:17), includes the
Lamb in the worship of God on his throne in heaven, and then expands the circle
of worship to include the whole creation:

> every creature in heaven and on earth and under the earth and in the sea, and all
> that is in them, singing, "To the one who is seated on the throne and to the Lamb
> be blessing and honor and glory and might forever and ever!" (Rev. 5:13)

It may not be accidental that these formulae for the whole cosmos have one of their
closest parallels in the second commandment of the Decalogue (Ex. 20:4; Deut.
5:8–9; echoed in *2 Enoch* 66:2–5; cf. also Neh. 9:6; Ps. 146:6; Rev. 10:6, which
lack "under the earth"): all those creatures whom it is forbidden to worship are depicted as themselves giving the worship due to God alone to Christ who shares his
throne. In any case, the emphasis on universality makes it clear that it is the
uniquely divine sovereignty over all creation that the exalted Jesus exercises and
that is therefore acknowledged in worship by the whole creation.

It is unlikely that Revelation 5 is dependent on Philippians. Together with
the other passages they attest a widespread—and therefore early—christological
schema, in which the exaltation of Jesus meant his participation in the unique divine sovereignty over all things, and therefore also its Jewish monotheistic corollary: the worship of Jesus by the whole creation in recognition of this divine
sovereignty.

The *second aspect* of Phil. 2:9–11 that we shall consider is that worship of Jesus by the whole creation is associated with the giving of the divine name to Jesus
at his exaltation. There can be no doubt that "the name that is above every name"
(v. 9) is YHWH: it is inconceivable that any Jewish writer could use this phrase for
a name other than God's own unique name.[9] Contrary to much comment on this
passage, the name itself is not "Lord" (κύριος: v. 11), which is not the divine name
or even a Greek translation of the name, but a conventional Greek reverential *substitute* for the name.[10] However, the fact that it was a substitute—evidently among
Greek-speaking Christians *the* substitute—for the Tetragrammaton is certainly relevant to the meaning of the passage. It connects the unique identity of God
(YHWH) closely with his sovereignty (κύριος) as a key identifying characteristic
of his uniqueness. Jesus is given the divine name because he participates in the divine sovereignty. Thus the confession "that Jesus Christ is Lord" (v. 11) is both a
surrogate for calling on him by his name, YHWH, and also a confession of his lordship.

In associating Jesus' exaltation to participation in the unique divine sovereignty with the bestowal of the unique name of God on Jesus, our passage again resembles another depiction of the exaltation of Jesus. According to Heb. 1:3–4, Jesus "sat down at the right hand of the Majesty on high, having become as much superior to angels as the name he has inherited is more excellent than theirs." Both passages associate the imagery of height—Jesus exalted to the divine throne in the height of heaven—with the unique superiority of the name he acquires. Only a divine name, superior to all other names (Phil. 2:9), can be superior to the names of angels (Heb. 1:4). This parallel itself makes it extremely likely that Hebrews, like Philippians, refers to the name YHWH. Most commentators think that the name in Hebrews must be "the Son," since it is this term that distinguishes the Son's status from that of angels in vv. 5–7. But this makes little sense of the expression "the name he has inherited." A son does not inherit the title "Son"; rather his being a son is the basis for his inheriting other things from his father. The meaning is that since Jesus, as the Son, inherited his Father's sovereignty over all things (v. 2), he also inherited his Father's name, which names the unique divine identity as sovereign over all things. The association of the unique divine name with the unique divine sovereignty is common to the depiction of the exaltation of Jesus in both Philippians and Hebrews, and probably therefore dates from very early christological reflection.

In Jewish monotheism the unique name of God, YHWH, names his unique identity. It is exclusive to the one God in a way that the sometimes ambiguous word "god" is not. Hence the bearing of this divine name by the exalted Jesus signifies unequivocally his inclusion in the unique divine identity, recognition of which is precisely what worship in the Jewish monotheistic tradition expresses.[11] As the one who exercises the unique divine sovereignty over all things, bears the unique divine name,[12] and thus is included in the unique identity of the one and only God, Jesus receives the worship of the whole creation.

The *third and final aspect* of Philippians 2:9–11 we must consider is that worship of Jesus by the whole creation expresses the *eschatological* monotheism of the Jewish tradition. Integral to Second Temple Jewish monotheism was the belief that, since YHWH is the sole Creator and Ruler of all things, he will come to be acknowledged as such by all his creation. In his eschatological action to save and to judge, he will vindicate and demonstrate his sole deity to the nations who presently deny it. By implementing fully his universal sovereignty, which at present appears to be contested by evil and by idolatry, YHWH will bring all he has created and rules to acknowledge his uniqueness as the only true God.

This eschatological monotheism was most powerfully expressed in the prophecies of Deutero-Isaiah, whose great monotheistic assertions were formative of Second Temple Jewish monotheism and constantly reechoed in its literature. YHWH's great act of eschatological salvation, the new exodus, will be accomplished in the sight of all the nations (Isa. 52:10), will manifest his glory to all flesh (40:5), and will bring all the nations to acknowledge him as the only God. This is especially the theme of Isaiah 45 (see especially vv. 5–6, 14), culminating in YHWH's invitation and solemn oath:

There is no other god besides me,
a righteous God and a Savior;
there is no one besides me.
Turn to me and be saved,
all the ends of the earth!
For I am God and there is no other.
By myself I have sworn,
from my mouth has gone forth in righteousness
a word that shall not return:
"To me every knee shall bow,
every tongue shall swear."

(Isa. 45:21b–23)

The repetition of the standard monotheistic formula[13] in the first, third, and fifth lines should be noted: the theme of the passage is emphatically the acknowledgment of the one and only God as the only God and the only Savior. The universal obeisance, prophesied with God's most solemn guarantee (v. 23), is therefore unequivocally a matter of monotheistic worship. As a result of his eschatological act of salvation, YHWH's sole deity is universally acknowledged.

It is Isa. 45:23 to which Phil. 2:10–11 plainly alludes ("so that . . . every knee should bend . . . and every tongue should confess"). This is agreed by almost all scholars, but its full significance is rarely appreciated. It shows the concern of the Philippians passage to be a typically Jewish monotheistic one and the worship of Jesus it depicts to be precisely a matter of the exclusive monotheistic worship of the Jewish religious tradition. The claim of Phil. 2:9–11 is that it is in the exaltation of Jesus, his identification with and as YHWH in YHWH's universal sovereignty, that the unique deity of the God of Israel comes to be acknowledged as such by all creation. YHWH's sole sovereignty and unique deity are recognized when the exalted Jesus exercises that sovereignty and bears the name YHWH. The eschatological monotheistic expectation of Deutero-Isaiah and Second Temple Judaism is fulfilled through the revelation of Jesus' inclusion in the unique divine identity. Eschatological monotheism proves to be christological monotheism.

Philippians 2:9–11 is therefore a christological version of Deutero-Isaianic eschatological monotheism. We may expand on this conclusion by way of four additional observations. First, we may note that in this as in the other respects already noticed the parallel with Revelation 5 is striking. There too worship is a matter of the eschatological acknowledgment of the divine sovereignty by all creation. The worship of the Lamb is the inclusion in the worship of God (5:13) of the one who has "conquered" (5:5), that is, has achieved the decisive victory in the establishment of God's eschatological kingdom in which he will reign with God on the divine throne (11:15; 22:3). Worship of God and the Lamb on the throne in Revelation 5 anticipates the worship in the New Jerusalem (22:3). Thus Revelation 5 also provides a christological version of eschatological monotheism.[14]

Second, it is noteworthy that both Philippians 2 and Revelation 5 take care to include Jesus in the worship of God, not to present him as an object of worship alternative to God his Father.[15] This is essential if the worship of Jesus is to be an expression of eschatological monotheism. In Phil. 2:9–11, kneeling at the name of Jesus and confessing him to be Lord are "to the glory of God the Father." In Revelation 5, the angelic worshipers who continually worship God (4:8–11) now worship the Lamb, along with myriads of angels (5:11–12), while the climax of the scene is the worship by every creature in the whole cosmos of both God and the Lamb (5:13). These are two ways of including Jesus in the cultic acknowledgment of the unique divine identity. The first does so no less than the second. It cannot mean that merely *honoring* Jesus is a way of *worshiping* God,[16] since this was precisely the way sophisticated pagans related polytheistic worship to recognition of a single supreme God. Jewish monotheists always rejected it (e.g., Philo, *Spec. leg.* 1.31). Jesus is not here honored as a servant of God. He is worshiped because he participates in the unique divine sovereignty and bears the name YHWH, which names the unique divine identity. Since he does so as the Son of his Father, sharing— not rivaling or usurping—his Father's sovereignty, worship of Jesus is also worship of his Father, but it is nonetheless really worship of Jesus.

Third, it is clear that Phil. 2:9–11 cannot be understood as an expression of an Adam christology. Jesus is not here exalted to the human dominion over other earthly creatures given to humans at creation (Gen. 1:28), but to the uniquely divine sovereignty which is acknowledged by all creation when God's sole deity as the one and only God is universally confessed.

James Dunn, who attempts to read the whole of the christological passage in Philippians 2 in terms of an Adam christology,[17] has cited as a parallel to Philippians 2:9–11 a passage from the *Life of Adam and Eve* in which God requires the angels to worship Adam.[18] In this passage (13–15) Satan refuses to worship Adam when the angels are commanded to do so. Adam is introduced to the angels by God as "our image and likeness" (13:3), and Michael commands the angels, "Worship the image of the Lord God, as the Lord God has instructed" (14:1). The devil refuses to worship because he "will not worship one inferior and subsequent to me" (14:3). It is clear that worship here is intended to indicate the angels' recognition of Adam's superiority to them, in that he is the image of God. It should be said that the scene is exceptional in the literature of Second Temple Judaism,[19] and, in view of the very uncertain history of the Adam literature, this passage (which does not appear in the Greek or Slavonic, but only in the Latin, Armenian, and Georgian versions of the Adam cycle) cannot be certainly regarded as a Jewish text of our period. But in any case the "worship" of Adam here can be distinguished from properly divine worship. The Latin uses *adorare,* but since the Armenian and Georgian versions both use words which mean "to bow down, to prostrate oneself"[20] we can be fairly sure that the Greek original used προσκυνεῖν. The word describes a gesture that in itself was not exclusive to divine worship (and, indeed, not employed in most Jewish worship). It could be an acceptable way of acknowledging a human superior (e.g., Gen. 18:2; 19:1; 23:7, 12; 33:2; 1 Sam. 28:14; 1 Kings 2:19; 2 Kings 2:15) or even an angelic superior (LAB 18:9, *adoravit eum in terra*). In Isaiah 45, where the universal acknowledgment of YHWH's lordship is expressed by the bowing of every knee (45:23), the Gentile captives who "bow down" to Israel are clearly not worshiping, since they say "God is with you alone, and there is no other; there is no god besides him" (45:14; cf. Rev. 3:9). The context in each case gives the gesture a different significance. The gesture of prostration became unacceptable to Jews in contexts which gave it idolatrous overtones, such as reverence for monarchs who claimed divinity (cf. *Add. Esth.* 13:12–14; Philo, *Leg. Gai.* 116; cf. Acts 10:25–26). But the context determined its meaning. It was worship of God where the context indicated that God's unique sovereignty was being acknowledged. In the context in the *Life of Adam and Eve* it is clear that the gesture is required of the angels because Adam is the image of God, which suggests both his superiority to them and his inferiority to God. Adam does not occupy the divine throne.

This example does show that not the gesture of prostration, but what is being recognized or acknowledged about the object of worship is the real issue. In Revelation, the gesture of prostration before the Lamb (5:8, 14) is worship because it takes place in the divine throneroom where all prostration must be to the unique divine sovereignty, and because it accompanies doxologies (a form reserved, in Jewish usage, to the worship of the one God) addressed to the Lamb and to God and the Lamb together (5:12, 13). Similarly Christ's enthronement at God's right hand and the subjection of all things heavenly and earthly to him make the worship of Christ by the whole creation in Polycarp's confessional formula (*Phil.* 2.1) clearly a matter of acknowledging the exalted Christ's participation in the unique divine sovereignty. It is arbitrary to distinguish these close parallels from the scene in Philippians 2:9–11 and to treat the latter as expressive of no more than an Adam christology. When one who bears the name YHWH receives the universal acknowledgment of his lordship portrayed in Isa. 45:23 as the eschatological achievement of YHWH's unique rule, it is strictly worship that is portrayed. It is not a matter of restoring human dominion over other creatures, but of establishing YHWH's own unique rule over all of creation.[21] This is made certain by the clear allusion to Isa. 45:23, by contrast with the absence of any convincing reference to Adam in these verses.[22]

Fourth, although this point cannot be fully developed here, it is worth pointing out that the whole of the christological passage in Phil. 2:6–11 can be understood as a christological reading of Deutero-Isaianic prophecy. The allusion to Isa. 45:23 in vv. 10–11 is all but universally agreed, though its full significance is by no means always appreciated. More debatable are allusions to Isaiah 52—53 in vv. 7–9,[23] but a good case can be made especially for allusions to Isa. 52:13 and 53:12, the summarizing verses at the beginning and the end of the suffering servant passage, in these verses of the Philippians passage ("poured himself out . . . to death. . . . Therefore also God exalted him to the highest place"). The basic conceptual structure of Phil. 2:6–9 is that *because* Christ humiliated himself to the point of death, *therefore* God has highly exalted him. This structure is given by Isa. 52:13, according to which it is because the servant poured himself out to death that God will allot him a portion with the great, that is, will highly exalt him (cf. 52:13). But since the terminology describing the servant's exaltation in Isa. 52:13 also describes the exalted position of God on his throne in Isa. 6:1 and 57:15,[24] Isa. 52:13

can easily be read (by means of the Jewish exegetical principle of *gezera shawa,* according to which passages with striking verbal resemblances serve to interpret each other) to mean that the suffering servant is exalted to share the divine throne in heaven, as early Christian interpretation also took Ps. 110:1 to mean.

What has not been noticed, even by those who agree that Phil. 2:7–9 has the suffering servant of Isaiah 52—53 in view, is the way the allusions to Isaiah 52—53 and to Isaiah 45 cohere. Early Christians, for whom Isaiah 40—66 was *the* scriptural account of the meaning of the events of Jesus Christ and his future, the influence of which can be traced throughout the New Testament, did not read the so-called servant passages in isolation from the overall themes of eschatological salvation and eschatological monotheism that dominate these chapters. The servant of the Lord is the one through whom God accomplishes the new exodus, the eschatological act of salvation, in the sight of the nations, thereby manifesting his glory and demonstrating his unique deity to the nations. Thus Phil. 2:6–11 reads Deutero-Isaiah to mean that the career of the servant of the Lord, his suffering, humiliation, death, and exaltation, is the way in which the sovereignty of the one true God comes to be acknowledged by all. God's unique rule receives universal acclaim when it is exercised by the one who humiliated himself in obedience to God to the point of death and was therefore exalted to the divine throne. God's sole deity receives universal worship when the crucified and exalted Jesus reveals the unique divine identity to which he himself belongs.

In conclusion, the worship of Jesus in Philippians 2 should be understood within the Jewish monotheistic tradition, in which worship is recognition of the unique identity of the one God as sole Creator and Ruler of all things, and in which this God's sole deity is expected to come to be acknowledged in worship by the whole creation. This eschatological monotheism took christological form in the earliest Christian reflection on the exaltation of Jesus, according to which Jesus had been exalted to the divine throne in heaven, exercising the unique sovereignty of God over all things and therefore included in the unique divine identity. In his eschatological exercise of divine rule and in his bearing of the unique divine name, therefore, Jesus is the one who receives the worship in which the whole of God's creation finally acknowledges God's unique deity. This pattern of thought is not peculiar to Philippians 2 but is shared with a variety of other passages in early Christian literature and must therefore go back to a very early stage of Jewish Christianity.

The role of the worship of Jesus in this pattern of thought is highly significant for the relationship between christology and Jewish monotheism. A thoroughly Jewish monotheistic concern is central here: that the one and only God will be acknowledged as such by the worship of God's whole creation. Within the context of Jewish monotheistic thought and practice, this monotheistic concern can be served by the worship of Jesus only if Jesus himself is seen as belonging to the unique divine identity. Unless Jesus is included in the unique divine identity, worship of Jesus by the whole creation would subvert Jewish monotheism. It would not be "to the glory of God the Father" but quite the opposite. Contrary to what much scholarly comment on New Testament christology assumes, early Jewish Christians did not preserve Jewish monotheism (and could not have preserved Jewish monotheism) by exalting Jesus to the divine throne as a mere agent of God. They preserved Jewish monotheism by including Jesus in the unique identity of the one God as Jewish monotheism understood this. Participating in God's unique sovereignty over all things and bearing the unique divine name, the exalted Jesus belongs to the unique divine identity, which is precisely what monotheistic worship recognizes. The worship of Jesus thus expresses the eschatological monotheism of the Jewish tradition in the christological form which Christian understanding of the exaltation of Jesus gave it.

NOTES

1. See R. T. France, "The Worship of Jesus: A Neglected Factor in Christological Debate?" in H. H. Rowdon, ed., *Christ the Lord,* D. Guthrie FS (Leicester: InterVarsity Press, 1982), 17–36; M. Hengel, "Hymns and Christology," in idem, *Between Jesus and Paul,* trans. J. Bowden (London: SCM Press, 1983), 78–96; L. W. Hurtado, *One God, One Lord* (Philadelphia: Fortress Press, 1988), chap. 5; R. Bauckham, "Jesus, Worship of," *ABD* 3: 812–19.

2. R. Bauckham, *The Climax of Prophecy: Studies on the Book of Revelation* (Edinburgh: T. & T. Clark, 1993), 118; this appeared earlier in idem, "The Worship of Jesus in Apocalyptic Christianity," *NTS* 27 (1980–81): 322–23; and is quoted by Hurtado, *One God,* 38; cf. also R. Bauckham, "Jesus, Worship of," 816 ("Judaism was unique among the religions of the Roman world in demanding the *exclusive* worship of its God. It is not too much to say that Jewish monotheism was defined by its adherence to the first and second commandments"); idem, *The Theology of the Book of Revelation* (Cambridge: Cambridge University Press, 1993), 58–59.

3. For the importance of monolatry for Jewish self-definition, see J. M. G. Barclay, *Jews in the Mediterranean Diaspora from Alexander to Trajan (323 BCE–117 CE)* (Edinburgh: T. & T. Clark, 1996), 429–34.

4. L. W. Hurtado, *One God;* idem, "What Do We Mean by 'First-Century Jewish Monotheism?'" *SBL Seminar Papers 1993,* 348–68, has, following my own work, rightly emphasized the importance of cultic practice in defining Jewish monotheism. But in my view he has tended to attribute to it too exclusive a role in this, not recognizing that, for Second Temple Judaism, exclusive worship of the one God was precisely recognition of that God's unique identity, which itself had to be characterized in other terms.

5. My understanding of the unique identity of God according to Second Temple Jewish monotheism and of the inclusion of Jesus in this unique divine identity in New Testament christology is developed in my 1996 Didsbury Lectures, to be published as *God Crucified: Monotheism and Christology in the New Testament* (Carlisle: Paternoster; Grand Rapids: Eerdmans, forthcoming), and will be further developed in a much larger study, provisionally entitled *Jesus and the Identity of God: Jewish Monotheism and New Testament Christology.*

6. See especially M. Hengel, "Sit at My Right Hand!" in idem, *Studies in Early Christology* (Edinburgh: T. & T. Clark, 1995), 119–225.

7. This is the verse of the Old Testament to which christological allusion is most often made in early Christian literature. See the list of quotations and allusions in D. H. Hay, *Glory at the Right Hand: Psalm 110 in Early Christianity,* SBLMS 18, (Nashville:

Abingdon Press, 1973), 45–46, and add *Epistle of the Apostles* 3; *Ascension of Isaiah* 10:14; 11:32.

8. The evidence of Second Temple Jewish literature does not support the view that it was common for Jewish writers to envisage a single principal angel (or exalted human) to whom *all* of God's rule over the whole creation was delegated by God, as, for example, Hurtado, *One God,* argues.

9. The phrase "the name of Jesus" (Phil. 2:10) has led some to suppose that "Jesus" must be "the name that is above every name" (v. 9). But the phrase "the name that is above every name" itself, together with the allusion to Isa. 45:23 in vv. 10–11 (see below), require that it is at the divine name YHWH that every knee shall bow. So it would seem that "the name of Jesus" is not the name Jesus, but the name YHWH that the exalted Jesus bears. But there is also a possibility that seems not to have been noticed. The name Jesus, like many Jewish names, contains the divine name. It means: "YHWH is salvation" (the full form of the name יְהוֹשֻׁעַ = יֵשׁוּעַ יְהוָה). The name is peculiarly appropriate to the context of the allusion to Isa. 45:23 in Phil. 2:10–11 (Isa. 45:21–22: "a righteous God and a Savior . . . Turn to me and be saved"). It could be that the name Jesus is regarded as a new kind of substitute for or even form of the divine name, so that Phil. 2:10–11 means: "at the name YHWH-is-Salvation every knee should bend, . . . and every tongue should confess that Jesus Christ is Lord (i.e., YHWH)."

10. J. A. Fitzmyer, "The Semitic Background of the New Testament Kyrios-Title," in idem, *A Wandering Aramean,* SBLMS 15 (Missoula, Mont.: Scholars Press, 1979), 115–42; A. Pietersma, "Kyrios or Tetragram: A Renewed Quest for the Original Septuagint," in *De Septuaginta* (Mississauga, Ont.: Benben Publications, 1984), 85–102.

11. The angel Yahoel in the *Apocalypse of Abraham,* who is authorized by God to employ the power of the divine name (10:3, 8), is not a true parallel to the exalted Jesus bearing the divine name. Yahoel is based on Ex. 23:21 (the angel in whom is God's name) and is the heavenly high priest, corresponding to the high priest in the Jerusalem temple who has the Tetragrammaton inscribed on his headdress and who alone pronounces the divine name in blessing. This complex of ideas is quite different from that in Philippians 2, where Jesus bears the divine name in connection with his exercise of God's eschatological rule over the whole creation.

12. For other New Testament texts that attribute the divine name to Jesus, see C. J. Davis, *The Name and Way of the Lord,* JSNTSup 129 (Sheffield: JSOT Press, 1996).

13. For this formula, see Deut. 4:35, 39; 32:39; 1 Sam. 2:2; 2 Sam. 7:22; Isa. 43:11; 44:6; 45:5, 6, 14, 18, 21, 22; 46:9; Hos. 13:4; Joel 2:27; Wisd. 12:13; Jdt. 8:20; 9:14; Bel 41; Sir. 24:24; 36:5; 4Q504 [4QDibHama] 5:9; 1Q35 1:6; Bar. 3:36; *2 Enoch* 33:8; 47:3; *Sib. Or.* 3:629, 760; 8:377; *Orphica* 16; Philo, *Leg. All.* 3.4, 82.

14. Revelation 5 does not have an explicit allusion to Deutero-Isaiah, comparable with that in Phil. 2:10–11, but elsewhere Revelation takes up the eschatological monotheism of Deutero-Isaiah explicitly, when it applies the monotheistic formula "the First and the Last" (Isa. 44:6; 48:12)—with the variations "the Alpha and the Omega" and "the Beginning and the End"—to Christ (Rev. 1:17; 2:8; 22:13) as well as to God (Rev. 1:8; 21:6). See Bauckham, *Theology,* 25–28, 54–58.

15. On Revelation, see Bauckham, *Theology,* 59–61; idem, *Climax,* 133–40.

16. Cf. J. D. G. Dunn, *The Partings of the Ways* (London: SCM Press, 1991), 194.

17. J. D. G. Dunn, *Christology in the Making* (London: SCM Press, 1980), 114–21.

18. Dunn, *Partings,* 194–95; others who take this passage as evidence that Jews could imagine—or even practice—the worship of Adam are A. Chester, "Jewish Messianic Expectations and Mediatorial Figures and Pauline Christology," in *Paulus und antike*

Judentum, ed. M. Hengel and U. Heckel, WUNT 58 (Tübingen: Mohr [Siebeck], 1991), 64; D. Steenberg, "The Worship of Adam and Christ as the Image of God," *JSNT* 39 (1990): 77–93.

19. It appears, however, in later Christian texts about Adam: J. E. Fossum, *The Name of God and the Angel of the Lord,* WUNT 36 (Tübingen: Mohr [Siebeck], 1985), 171–72.

20. G. A. Anderson and M. E. Stone, eds., *A Synopsis of the Books of Adam and Eve,* Early Judaism and Its Literature 5 (Atlanta: Scholars Press, 1994), 11–12.

21. This formula is never used for Adam's dominion, which is usually limited to the earth (e.g., *Jub.* 2:14; *2 Enoch* 31:3), though 4 Ezra 6:46, 54 includes the heavenly bodies (cf. *2 Bar.* 14:18–10), and Wisd. 10:2 makes Adam ruler of "all things" (following Ps. 8:6).

22. Wright, *The Climax of the Covenant* (Edinburgh: T. & T. Clark, 1991), 93–94, unsuccessfully attempts to have his cake and eat it, i.e., an Adam christology *and* a full recognition of the monotheistic significance of the allusion to Isa. 45:23. The two are incompatible.

23. Martin, *Carmen Christi,* rev. ed. (Grand Rapids: Eerdmans, 1983), 167–68, 182–90, 211–13, 240, 313–15; Wright, *Climax,* 60–62.

24. Isa. 52:13: "he shall be *exalted* (ירום) and *lifted up* (נשא) and shall be very high (גבה)." Isa 6:1: "I saw the Lord (אדני) sitting on a throne, *exalted* (רם) and *lofty* (נשא)." Isa. 57:15: "thus says the *exalted* (רם) and *lofty* (נשא) One."

9.

Christology and Ethics in Philippians 2:5–11

STEPHEN FOWL

1. INTRODUCTION

Almost fifty years have passed since the publication of Ernst Käsemann's "Kritische Analyse von Phil. 2,5–11."[1] Käsemann's primary aim was to undermine the "ethical idealist" interpretation of this passage characteristic of liberal Protestantism in the late nineteenth and early twentieth centuries. Despite its many strengths, Käsemann's argument was limited to opposing a very particular way of talking about the relationships between christology and ethics as regards this passage. Nevertheless, as Käsemann's views gained scholarly currency they seem to have worked to limit most types of considerations about the relationships between christology and ethics.[2] During this time, scholarly interest in this passage focused primarily on form-critical analyses that abstracted Phil. 2:5–11 from its context in the epistle. In addition, exegetical discussion of this text tended to reduce it to its presumed history of religions background.

Over the past twenty years there has been a shift away from these scholarly emphases. Form-critical and history of religions approaches to this text have been challenged in terms of both their methods and their results. In addition, while Käsemann's work seemed for a time to have ruled out interpretations of this passage that read it as an ethical story, there has been a renewed interest in discussing how this story functions ethically.[3]

To say that there is renewed interest in the relationships between the story of Christ narrated in 2:6–11 and the ethical concerns of the rest of the epistle, is not to say that there is agreement about the nature of these relationships. In the course of this essay I cannot hope to do justice to the scholarly discussions either of the story of Christ narrated in 2:6–11 or of the debates about how this story is related to other parts of the epistle. Instead, I will address some particularly significant developments and contributions to the discussion of this passage. First, I will try to lay out some issues raised by the recent scholarly interest in epistolary style and rhetoric. Second, I will make some brief remarks about current views on the interpretation of 2:6–11 including the christology reflected therein. Third, I will then take up points I first argued for in *The Story of Christ in the Ethics of Paul*.[4] While I still think that the story of Christ narrated in these verses functions as an exemplar that Paul "phronetically" applies to the common life of the Philippians, I now think that this phronetic application of 2:6–11 can be extended more broadly throughout the epistle, and I will try to show what this looks like. Finally, I want to address some issues from contemporary moral philosophy and theology concerning whether calls to imitate moral exemplars, such as we find in Philippians, necessarily entail the eradication of individual difference.

2. RHETORICAL FORM AND
THE MORAL DEMANDS OF PHILIPPIANS

Much recent work on Paul has been devoted to examining his epistles in the light of Graeco-Roman rhetorical and epistolary conventions. Most of this work has not directly focused on Philippians. Recently, however, Loveday Alexander—among others—has argued that Philippians is to be understood as a "family letter."[5] The aim of such letters was to provide news and reassurance about the state of the sender, to seek news and reassurance about the state of the recipients, and to strengthen the ties between the family members.[6] The great strength of Alexander's analysis is that she is able to give an account of Philippians that shows how the entire letter fits into a known conventional style. Thus this analysis provides a decisive counter to those who see the letter as a redacted collection of fragments.[7] A potential pitfall of too heavy a reliance on this formal analysis is that it will not pay sufficient attention to the moral and theological work Paul's accounts of his own situation and his expressed desires for the Philippians are meant to do. Unlike the standard family letter, at least one of the main points of "business" of Philippians is Paul's attempt to get the Philippians to view things—such as Paul's imprisonment, God's activity in Christ, and the experiences of Timothy and Epaphroditus—in such a way that they themselves will be capable of thinking and acting in particular ways. As Craig Wansink has recently argued:

> Family letters may focus primarily on the act of communication between members of the family. Phil. 1:12–26 may reflect "reassurance about the sender" and Phil. 1:27–2:18 may be a "request for reassurance about the recipients." At the same time, however, there is much more at stake in each of these sections: there is ethical reasoning; there is moral admonition; there is theological reflection. A stark formal analysis runs the risk not only of reducing each section of the letter to particular predictable elements, but also of failing to note ways in which the sections themselves are interrelated.[8]

While attention to formal conventions may be quite significant in resolving some interpretive debates in regard to Philippians, I do not think that such analyses will do much to advance discussions about the relationships between the christology of 2:6–11 and the moral demands Paul makes in the epistle. For this, we will need to turn first to a brief examination of 2:6–11 and then to the ways echoes of this passage resound throughout the text of the epistle.

3. THE PRESENTATION OF CHRIST IN 2:6–11

There is much already in this volume that deals with the various exegetical complexities of this passage. Further, I have already given an extensive account of these verses in *The Story of Christ in the Ethics of Paul*. Hence, I limit my comments to those verses and issues that are most crucial to my larger task and to material that has appeared subsequent to my previous arguments.

Virtually all discussions of this passage recognize a basic plot line that elaborates Christ's descent from some heavenly state to the earthly realm. His obedience leads to his death which, in turn, results in divine exaltation. Or, to put it more bluntly, what we have here is a down/up pattern with the change in direction occurring in the transition between vv. 8 and 9. Given this relatively straightforward pattern, one might find it surprising that this passage has generated so much interpretive disagreement over such a long period of time. The problem that generates most of this interpretive disagreement concerns how one identifies and describes Christ's initial state related in v. 6. What does it mean to say that Christ Jesus ἐν μορφῇ θεοῦ ὑπάρχων? What does it say about him to claim οὐχ ἁρπαγμὸν ἡγήσατο τὸ εἶναι ἴσα θεῷ? In a wide variety of literature the μορφή of God is taken to say something about the visible appearance of God.[9] Several scholars have moved from similar observations about μορφή to equate μορφή with εἰκών as a way of connecting claims about Christ who is in the μορφή of God with the account of Adam's creation κατ᾽ εἰκόνα θεοῦ in Gen. 1:26.[10] This connection, however, is illusory and cannot be supported on linguistic grounds.[11]

In the LXX the visible form of God is often described in terms of God's δόξα, God's glory and splendor, by which the majesty of God is made manifest to humanity.[12] There are also several occasions where Paul uses δόξα to refer to the visible manifestation of God's majesty (cf. Rom. 1:23; 1 Cor. 11:7; 2 Cor. 3:18; 4:6).[13]

It seems most adequate, then, to take the μορφή of God as a reference to the glory, radiance, and splendor by which God's majesty is made visible. By locating Christ in this glory, it conveys the majesty and splendor of his preincarnate state (cf. John 17:5). This first clause of v. 6, then, says something about Christ's exalted status or position.[14]

The following clause, οὐχ ἁρπαγμὸν ἡγήσατο τὸ εἶναι ἴσα θεῷ, further defines that exalted status. More importantly, however, it tells us Christ's disposition or attitude toward that status. In *The Story of Christ in the Ethics of Paul* I argued in favor of R. W. Hoover's view that ἁρπαγμός designates "something to take advantage of."[15] I also noted that N. T. Wright had also argued in favor of this view in an essay published in 1986.[16] Since then Wright has developed this argument even more thoroughly in a chapter of his book, *The Climax of the Covenant*.[17] Wright gives a comprehensive taxonomy of the various ways this phrase has been read, clearly laying out the strengths and weaknesses of each view. He is then able to marshal the evidence for the view that Phil. 2:6 claims that Christ did not view equality with God as something to be taken advantage of in a way that makes such an interpretation now the definitive word on this clause.

The sense of οὐχ ἁρπαγμὸν ἡγήσατο will then be that Christ, in contrast to what one might have expected . . . , refused to take advantage of his position. This is not . . . a matter of not adopting, in his incarnate existence, a life-style of divine splendour, whatever that might mean in practice. The emphasis of v. 7 shows that the refusal described by the phrase was a refusal to use for his own advantage the glory which he had from the beginning. The all-important difference in meaning between this view and the standard *retinenda* approaches is that *nothing described by either ἐν μορφῇ θεοῦ ὑπάρχων or by τὸ εἶναι ἴσα θεῷ is given up;* rather, it is reinterpreted, understood in a manner in striking contrast to what one might have expected.[18]

Given this starting point in v. 6, the rest of the basic "down up" story of vv. 7–11 takes on a very particular texture. The self-emptying described in v. 7 is not an account of Christ's stripping off of divine attributes. It becomes an elaboration of the view that Christ's equality with God was not something to be used for his own advantage. It claims that the vocation commensurate with this exalted position is demonstrated through incarnation and steadfast obedience leading to crucifixion. As Wright notes, "The real humiliation of the incarnation and the cross is that one who was himself God, and who never during the whole process stopped being God, could embrace such a vocation."[19] The exaltation related in vv. 9–11 then becomes God's vindication of Christ's obedience.[20] The exaltation serves as God's affirmation that Christ's dispositions and actions related in vv. 6–8 are the actions and dispositions appropriate to one who is equal to God. "It is the affirmation, by God the Father, that the incarnation and death of Jesus really was the revelation of divine love in action."[21]

Before moving on to discuss how this story of Christ is used to underwrite the moral demands of Philippians, I would like to make some brief comments about the christology of this passage. These comments concern the relationships between Phil. 2:6–11 and Paul's Adam christology.[22]

Wright vigorously asserts that Phil. 2:6–11 is an example of Paul's Adam christology. In doing this, however, he sharply distinguishes his views from J. D. G. Dunn's arguments about the role of Adam in this passage.[23] On Dunn's view, Phil. 2:6–11 offers an implicit contrast between Adam, who grasps at equality with God and fails, and Christ, who does not grasp (a *res rapienda* view of ἁρπαγμός), but is exalted by means of his obedient death. Adam's grasping fundamentally alienates humans from God. This alienation is rectified by Christ's activity related here in Philippians. Dunn's view has been substantially undermined from a variety of perspectives, and I will not rehearse those criticisms here.[24]

Wright distinguishes his views from Dunn's in several ways: In Wright's Adam christology, Adam, Israel, and Christ are closely connected. Adam perfectly displays God's intentions for humanity. Through Adam's disobedience that harmonious relationship between God and humans is damaged (though not destroyed). As part of God's dramatic restoration of the relationships characteristic of Eden, Israel is chosen to display God's intentions for humanity to the world: "Israel is God's true humanity. . . . Israel will be given the rights of Adam's true heir."[25] As Paul develops this view, Christ as the Messiah fulfills this role:

That which was purposed in Genesis 1 and 2, the wise rule of creation by obedient human beings, was lost in Genesis 3, when human rebellion jeopardised the divine intention, and the ground brought forth thorns and thistles. The Messiah, however, has now been installed as the one through whom God is doing what he intended to do, first through humanity and then through Israel. Paul's Adam-christology is basically an Israel-christology, and is predicated on the identification of Jesus as Messiah, in virtue of his resurrection.[26]

When it comes to reading Phil. 2:6–11, Wright is quite clear that Adam and Christ are contrasted, though not in a rigid parallelism. Hence, he is able to read v. 6, in accordance with the best linguistic evidence, as a reference to Christ's preexistence, thus avoiding Dunn's conclusion that the passage says nothing about Christ's preexistence because of its links to Adam.[27] As Wright sees it, Philippians 2:6–11 contrasts Adam with Christ in the following way:

> Christ's obedience is not simply the replacement of Adam's disobedience. It does not involve merely the substitution of one sort of humanity for another, but the solution of the problem now inherent in the first sort, namely, sin. The temptation of Christ was not to snatch at a forbidden equality with God, but to cling to his rights and thereby opt out of the task allotted to him, that he should undo the results of Adam's snatching.[28]

Wright goes on to claim that 2:9–11, with its clear reliance on language from Isa. 45:23, "credits Jesus with a rank and honour which is not only in one sense appropriate for the true Man, the Lord of the world, but it is also the rank and honour explicitly reserved, according to scripture, for Israel's God and him alone."[29] This shows clearly the further points at which Christ might be contrasted with Adam without there being a strict parallelism.

Throughout his chapter on Phil. 2:6–11, Wright not only argues that 2:6–11 should be read in the light of and as an example of Paul's Adam christology, but that this passage is closely linked to Rom. 5:12–21. It is here that I wish to raise some questions. My point is not to criticize Wright's Adam christology as a whole.[30] Nor do I want to argue that the views of Christ in Romans 5 and Philippians 2 are incompatible. I do, however, want to note some significant differences between these two passages that tend to be glossed over in Wright's account. The obvious point of contact between the two passages is their emphasis on Christ's obedience. In Romans 5, however, Christ's obedience is specifically contrasted with Adam's disobedience. The importance of this contrast in Romans 5 is to show how the damage caused by Adam's sin is reversed by Christ's obedience, thus redeeming humanity and demonstrating the righteousness of God. That is, the Adam/Christ contrast in Romans has soteriological importance. Philippians 2, however, makes no direct soteriological statement. Further, in Romans 5 Adam's trespass allows the regnant power of sin to enter the cosmos, bringing death with it. To the extent that Phil. 2:9–11 articulate the cosmic effects of Christ's obedience, they do so along different lines.

What is explicit in Romans 5 is the emphasis on the sin that enters the world through Adam and how Christ defeats the power of sin through his obedience. If this is presupposed, it is certainly not emphasized or made explicit in Phil. 2:6–11.

Instead, 2:6–11 initially focuses on the preexistent Christ's disposition toward his equality with God and subsequent obedience. Unlike Romans 5, Philippians 2 says something about the character of that obedience; it is obedience that extends as far as death, even crucifixion.[31] In Romans 5 one might claim that since Paul speaks about sin and death as powers (5:14, 21), Christ's death could be seen as a form of submission to these powers in order to bring about their ultimate defeat (cf. 6:2ff.). In this way Christ becomes obedient unto death. This is not what is stated in Phil. 2:8.[32] Christ's obedience is μέχρι θανάτου not θανάτῳ or εἰς θάνατον. Death is not portrayed as a personalized power to whom Christ is subject. Rather, death— death on a cross—is the extent to which Christ is obedient. The unstated, but presumed, one to whom Christ is obedient is God.[33] Finally, in Romans 5 Christ's obedience results in justification for humanity. In Phil. 2:9–11 Christ's obedience results in exaltation and, ultimately, glory for God—points that (as Wright indicates) have no real analog in Romans 5.[34]

Let me be clear here. My point is not to show that there are inconsistencies between the pictures of Christ presented in Romans 5 and Philippians 2. I have no question that these passages identify one and the same character. Further, I have no doubt one can fit these two passages into a coherent Pauline christology. My point is simply to note some very real differences of emphasis between these two passages. Romans 5 emphasizes Christ's obedience as part of a larger account of how God's saving activity in Christ counters the disobedience of Adam. The explicit aim here is to narrate and summarize the story of human disobedience that Paul begins in 1:18, showing how Christ's obedience works to restore God's intentions for the world first displayed in Eden, and then reiterated with the call of Abraham and the formation of the people of Israel. The upshot of this is to reveal the righteousness of God (1:16–17). Rather than fitting Christ's obedience into a narrative of salvation, Phil. 2:6–11 focuses on the quality of Christ's obedience as we follow Christ's descent from equality with God to the humiliation of the cross. Through its focus on God's exaltation of the obedient crucified one we are told something about the character of God. It is just these points—emphasized in Phil. 2:6–11 and not in Rom. 5:12–21—which are taken up by Paul and applied to the life of the Philippians in the rest of the epistle. Given these points, it is now time to turn to examine the ways the story of Christ narrated here in 2:6–11 shapes the moral demands Paul makes of the Philippians.

4. THE STORY OF CHRIST
IN THE ETHICS OF PHILIPPIANS

Wayne Meeks has argued that "this letter's most comprehensive purpose is the shaping of a Christian *phronēsis,* a practical moral reasoning that is 'conformed to [Christ's] death' in hope of his resurrection."[35] That is, Paul is trying to form in the Philippians the intellectual and moral abilities to be able to deploy their knowledge of the gospel in the concrete situations in which they find themselves, so that they will be able to live faithfully (or "walk worthily" 1:27). Within this scheme the story of Christ narrated in 2:6–11 functions as an exemplar, a concrete expression of a shared norm from which Paul and the Philippians can make analogical judgments about how they should live.[36] The bulk of the rest of this essay will be spent trying to display how some of the arguments in Philippians make this clear.

If, viewing the epistle as a "family letter," the epistle both seeks and offers assurance (and reassurance) about Paul and the Philippians, it is clearly assurance of a particular sort. Paul is imprisoned, and the Philippian community seems to have been facing both hostility from without and some level of divisiveness within. It is not clear to what extent the Philippians were being persecuted. They clearly have opponents (1:28), and Paul speaks of them being granted the privilege of suffering for the sake of Christ (1:29). Further, Paul's comments about how the Philippians are to live in the light of this situation could apply to a wide variety of situations of persecution. He begins the epistle by assuring the Philippians that God is indeed at work in them and will continue this work until the day of Christ (1:6, repeated in 2:13). If Paul's imprisonment and the persecution of the Philippians raised questions about the coherence or continuation of God's activity, Paul's comments in 1:3–18 would work to allay those concerns. Paul offers assurances about himself and reassures the Philippians by offering them assurances about God and God's desires and actions on their behalf (and on his behalf as well).

Paul's confidence about these matters is not simply wishful thinking. While Paul has yet to make specific reference to any particular account of God's activity in Christ, it is fair to say that Paul's convictions about the coherence and continuation of God's activity are grounded in his convictions about God's activity in Christ and God's prior activity in Paul's own life and in the life of the Philippian church. As God redeemed and exalted the obedient, humiliated Christ, so God will redeem the obedient, though suffering, Paul and the obedient, though suffering, Philippians if they remain faithful, "standing in one spirit, striving together with one accord for the sake of the gospel" (1:27). What underwrites Paul's confidence in the first chapter of the epistle is not simply a cheerfulness that convention demands. Rather, it is a manner of practical reasoning (note the use of φρονεῖν in 1:7) which begins from convictions about what God has done in Christ. Those convictions, in turn, help provide Paul with a particular point of view, from which Paul can consider his own situation and that of the Philippians as not merely hopeful, but as an example of God's "good work."

Paul moves on in 1:19–26 to reflect more systematically on his own situation. There has been some recent discussion of Paul's comments in 1:19–26 that shows their relevance for my purposes as well. This passage clearly has connections to what precedes. There is a close conceptual parallel between Paul's assurances in 1:12 that his circumstances have actually worked to advance the gospel, and Paul's conviction in 1:19 that, "through the Philippians' prayers and the help of the spirit of Jesus Christ," Paul's situation will result in his salvation. What is particularly interesting, however, is this passage's connection to what follows.

In 1:19–26 Paul articulates his own preference to die and to be with Christ (1:21, 23). He also notes, however, that it is "more necessary" for the Philippians that he "remain and continue" in the flesh (1:24). He even goes so far as to claim that he has some sort of choice in the matter, as is observed by Wansink: "In 1:22, Paul writes, 'which I shall choose I cannot tell.' In 1:21 and 23, he seems to show a clear preference for death. However, because it is 'more necessary' to remain alive on account of the Philippians (1:24), Paul then resolves the tension created in 1:22 and announces that he will 'remain and continue with you all.' "[37]

There are a variety of interesting questions arising from this passage. What sort of choice did Paul really have about his future? Did he contemplate suicide or a more passive form of voluntary death? Was it really in his hands to choose to remain in the flesh? All of these questions have been the subject of discussion over the past few years, but they are beyond the scope of this essay.[38] What is most important for a discussion of christology and ethics has to do with how Paul's claims here are connected to the demands he makes of the Philippians in 1:27–2:4. Here Paul urges the Philippians to unite in the face of opposition.[39] They must stand firm in one spirit and in one mind, striving together for the faith of the gospel (1:27). In chapter 2 Paul demands specific types of behavior to insure that steadfast unity will prevail. In 2:2 he commands the Philippians to be of the same mind (again using φρονεῖν). In addition, the Philippians are to have the same love, bound together in one soul. Through his use of φρονεῖν, Paul admonishes them to have a common orientation or pattern of thought. Paul continues in vv. 3–4 to note that nothing would be more destructive of the unity that Paul sees as essential for the salvation of the community than for the Philippians to maintain a spirit of partisanship and empty conceit. In contrast to these vices, Paul urges the Philippians to adopt the virtue of humility, considering the needs of others rather than their own.

In 1:19–26 the Philippians find a specific manifestation of looking after the needs of others rather than one's own. In this passage Paul makes it clear that, given the options of whether "to depart and be with Christ" or to remain in the flesh in service to the gospel (and the Philippians), he prefers to depart. In 1:22 he claims that it is unclear which of these two options he will choose. By 1:24–25, however, he has resolved the matter in favor of looking after what is more necessary for the Philippians rather than himself.[40]

Paul's reflections about his own life and death serve as a particular manifestation of the types of actions and dispositions he wants the Philippians to manifest in 1:27–2:4. Both Paul's reflections and the subsequent demands of 1:27–2:4, however, find exemplary expression in the story of Christ rendered in 2:6–11. Indeed, the force of 2:5 is to encourage the Philippians to let the picture of Christ presented in 2:6–11 guide their common life by means of drawing analogies between this story of Christ and the sorts of situations the Philippians face. To put the analogy crudely: If the Philippians will unite in a steadfast adherence to the gospel (which will entail the practice of the virtues in 2:2–4), even in the face of opposition, then God will save them in the same way God saved the obedient, humiliated, and suffering Christ in 2:6–11. Paul's admonition in v. 5 is a call to recognize this, a call to apply to their common life the precedent that is theirs by virtue of the fact that they are in Christ. To do this requires practical reasoning. As Wayne Meeks notes, 2:5 with its use of φρονεῖν might well be translated, "Base your practical reasoning on what you see in Christ Jesus."[41]

Paul's analogical extension of the story of Christ in 2:6–11 to the common life of the Philippian church is extended further in 2:12–18 by means of further admonitions to forsake factionalism (2:14) and encouragements to stand firm in the midst of hostile surroundings (2:15–16). Here we also get further assurances that God is at work in the lives of the Philippians (2:13). Again, the point here is not simply to calm the Philippians but to make strong assertions about the character of God, assertions that are underwritten by the story of what God has done in Christ. Paul seems to recognize that his own imprisonment and the opposition faced by the Philippians raise some questions about the coherence and even the presence of God's work in the world. Paul's point in 2:14–18 is that it is not suffering and opposition that threaten to render God's world incoherent, as much as the Philippians' possible failure to remain faithful.

Further, within this context, Paul's "news" about Timothy and Epaphroditus in 2:19–30 is not meant simply to reassure the Philippians, but to offer them further models of those who do not seek after their own interests but the interests of others.[42] Paul's practical reasoning based on 2:6–11, can provide him, and the Philippians, with the basis for commending the actions of Timothy and Epaphroditus and for admonishing Euodia and Syntyche in 4:2 to employ a common Christ-focused practical reasoning (again φρονεῖν).

In a much more systematic way than in 1:19–26, Paul offers an account of his own life in 3:2–16 as a manifestation of a form of practical reasoning based on the story of Christ in 2:6–11. As his account shows, one of the primary tasks of practical reasoning is learning how to view things in the right way. Once one does this, then one can draw the appropriate types of analogies and act in the appropriate ways. Throughout 3:2–16 Paul is seeking to combat those (presumably members of the Philippian church) whose *phronēsis* is set on earthly things (3:19).[43] In this light, Paul's account of his life in 3:2–16 is really account of how his perspective or point of view was transformed through his encounter with Christ. This transformation enables Christ-focused practical reasoning, which works to form a life that "knows the power of [Christ's] resurrection, is capable of sharing in his sufferings and becoming like him in his death" (3:10) since, as 2:6–11 make clear, this is the manner of life that God vindicates.[44]

In this light, the call to become fellow imitators of Paul, his associates, and those who live in a similar way (3:17) is primarily a call to understand what God has done in Christ in the way that Paul has understood, embodied, and articulated it. From this one can then walk as someone who is not an enemy of the cross of Christ. The imitation called for here is really a call to adopt Paul's manner of practical reasoning, a practical reasoning based on what they see in Christ Jesus (2:6–11).[45] The imitation called for here is not a wooden sort of identical repetition, but a "non-identical repetition"[46] based on analogy, examples of which are seen in 1:19–26; 1:27–2:4; 2:12–18; 2:19–30, and 3:2–16.

5. CHRISTOLOGY AND ETHICS:
SOME CONTEMPORARY CONCERNS

In a recent work, Elizabeth Castelli has examined Paul's discourse of imitation from the perspective of the work of the late French philosopher Michel Foucault.[47] She makes two interrelated points about imitation language in Paul. First, it works as part of a discourse of power, reinscribing and naturalizing certain configurations of power within the Pauline congregations.[48] Second, the logic of imitation moves to eliminate difference as one party moves toward becoming the same or identical with the imitated party: "The favored movement is from difference toward similarity—or, ideally, and absolutely, toward sameness. Sameness itself becomes a more highly valued quality, and it is a quality which automatically inheres in the model in the mimetic relationship of model-copy."[49] Castelli's work brings some of the crucial issues of contemporary philosophy and theology to bear on Paul's epistles. In the brief space left to me in this essay, I would like to address the relationship between sameness and difference in regard to my discussion of christology and ethics in Philippians.[50]

I have argued here that Paul seeks to form (or see formed) a particular type of practical reasoning in the Philippians. His explicit language about imitation in 3:17 and the implicit calls to "imitate" Christ, Paul, Timothy, and Epaphroditus all demand the exercise of practical reasoning. In fact, in regard to human action and belief, language about imitation cannot really operate without practical reasoning. This is because the sort of behavior called for can never be strictly identical with the model to be imitated. Practical reasoning is the activity of noting similarities *and differences* between an exemplar and the particular context in which one tries to live in a manner appropriate to that exemplar. What one strives for is nonidentical repetition based on analogies one draws between the exemplar and the context in which one finds oneself.

Even in Philippians Paul offers his own reflections about his choice of life over death as an example of putting the needs of others before one's own desires in 1:19–26. He also, however, presents Timothy's *and* Epaphroditus's actions as similar examples of this disposition distinct from Paul's example. One might even note the brief comments directed to Euodia and Syntyche as an example by means of antithesis of the dispositions and actions Paul desires for the Philippians. Of course, all of these different examples are directed by the story of Christ in 2:6–11. In short, the dispositions and actions Paul demands of the Philippians, under the example of God's activity in Christ, can be displayed in a variety of ways that conform to particular identities and contexts. There is both analogical continuity between these characters and individual and communal differentiation. Rather than a difference obliterating sameness, Paul's language of imitation in Philippians is designed to produce an ordered, harmonious diversity. Given this (admittedly underdeveloped) account, I would conclude by submitting that the real questions for discussing both Paul and contemporary Christian communities concern the manner in which diversity is conceived. Is it (should it be) ordered and harmonious (on analogy with the triune life of God) or perhaps should it be seen as a violent agon of disconnected individuals, each struggling with and policing the other?[51]

NOTES

1. E. Käsemann, "Kritische Analyse von Phil. 2,5–11," *ZTK* 47 (1950): 316–60.
2. Both the translation of this essay into English in *Journal for Theology and Church* 5 (1968): 45–88 and Ralph Martin's extensive discussion of Käsemann's position in *Carmen Christi* (Cambridge: Cambridge University Press, 1967) did a great deal to advance Käsemann's views (see above, chapter 3).
3. This way of stating the issue comes from Steven Kraftchick, "A Necessary Detour: Paul's Metaphorical Understanding of the Philippian Hymn," *Horizons in Biblical*

Theology 15 (1993): 9. Kraftchick cites the works of Hooker, Kurz, and my own discussion as examples of this shift.

4. S. E. Fowl, *The Story of Christ in the Ethics of Paul,* JSNTSup 36 (Sheffield: JSOT Press, 1990).

5. L. C. A. Alexander, "Hellenistic Letter Forms and the Structure of Philippians," *JSNT* 37 (1989): 87–101; reprinted in *The Pauline Writings: A Sheffield Reader,* ed. S. Porter and C. Evans (Sheffield: Sheffield Academic Press, 1995), 232–46. My citations will be from this reprinted version. In particular Alexander draws her examples of the "family letter" from texts in J. White, *Light from Ancient Letters* (Philadelphia: Fortress Press, 1986).

6. "For our purposes, the most significant structural feature of this letter and others like it is the lack of a clear 'body,' if by that we mean a business section framed by, and clearly separable from, the exchange of family greetings and news. Put another way, the whole point of these letters—their real 'business'—*is* this exchange of news between the sender and his family" (Alexander, 239).

7. "The centrality of 1.12 thus ties in with observations of a deep unity of thought between ch. 2 and ch. 3 which in turn confirms that the decision to dismember Philippians has been premature" (Alexander, 246).

8. See C. S. Wansink, *Chained in Christ* (Sheffield: Sheffield Academic Press, 1996), 106. Wansink himself sees Cicero's letter to his brother Quintus 1.3 as a family letter, which is much closer to Philippians than those cited by Alexander. I would concede that this is true for Wansink's interest in how Paul's imprisonment shapes his theology generally and how to read 1:18–26 more specifically. Even here, however, Cicero's letter does not aspire to do the sort of moral and theological formation that Philippians does.

9. This is not to oppose appearance to reality or essence. See my *The Story of Christ in the Ethics of Paul,* 49–55.

10. Some who do this are Martin (1983), 116; J. Murphy-O'Connor, "Christological Anthropology in Phil II,6–11," *RB* 83 (1976): 25ff.; George Howard, "Phil. 2:6–11 and the Human Christ," *CBQ* 40 (1978): 368ff., and M. Hooker (1990), 96–97.

11. See my *The Story of Christ in the Ethics of Paul,* 50–52. See also N. T. Wright, *The Climax of the Covenant* (Edinburgh: T. & T. Clark, 1991), 72, who comes to a similar judgment.

12. See Ex. 16:10; 24:16; 33:17ff.; 40:34f.; 1 Kings 8:11; Isa. 6:3; Ezek. 1:18; 43:3; 44:4; 2 Macc. 3:8. Also see 3 Macc. 4:18; *1 Enoch* 14:21; *T. Levi* 3:4; *Asc. Isa.* 10:16. See also A. M. Ramsey, *The Glory of God and the Transfiguration of Christ* (London: Longmans, Green, 1949), 15–18; L. H. Brockington, "The Septuagintal Background of the New Testament use of δόξα," in *Studies in the Gospels,* Festschrift for R. H. Lightfoot, ed. D. Nineham (Oxford: Blackwell, 1955), 1–8.

13. See also Luke 2:9; Rev. 15:8; 21:23; also Brockington, 7–8.

14. In this regard my conclusions are similar to those of E. Schweizer, *Erniedrigung und Erhöhung bei Jesus und seinen Nachfolgern* (Zurich: Zwingli, 1955), 54n234; also P. Bonnard, *L'Epître de Saint Paul aux Philippiens* (Neuchâtel: Delachaux & Niestlé, 1950), 42, but they are arrived at for different reasons.

15. R. W. Hoover, "The Harpagmos Enigma: A Philological Solution," *HTR* 64 (1971): 95–119.

16. N. T. Wright, "ἁρπαγμός and the Meaning of Phil. 2.5–11," *JTS* 37 (1986): 321–52.

17. All my discussion of Wright's views will be from this version of the argument.

18. Wright, *The Climax of the Covenant,* 83.

19. Ibid., 84.
20. See the exegetical discussion for this position in *The Story of Christ in the Ethics of Paul,* 64–69.
21. Wright, *The Climax of the Covenant,* 86.
22. One of the most significant essays dealing with the christology of this passage, but which lies outside the scope of this chapter, is David Yeago's "The New Testament and Nicene Dogma: A Contribution to the Recovery of Theological Exegesis," in *Theological Interpretation of Scripture,* ed. S. E. Fowl (Oxford: Blackwell, 1997), 87–100. Yeago's essay builds on the findings of Wright's work and decisively undermines the notion, all too common among biblical scholars, that there is a radical discontinuity between the New Testament and later trinitarian doctrines. He is able to show that "the Nicene *homoousion* is neither imposed *on* the New Testament texts, nor distantly deduced *from* the texts, but rather describes a pattern of judgments present *in* the texts, in the texture of scriptural discourse concerning Jesus, God and Israel" (87).
23. See J. D. G. Dunn, *Christology in the Making* (London: SCM, 1980), 101ff.
24. See my *The Story of Christ in the Ethics of Paul,* 69–73; Wright, *The Climax of the Covenant,* 91–94; Also John R. Levison, *Portraits of Adam in Early Judaism* (Sheffield: JSOT Press, 1988), 20–21.
25. Wright, 24.
26. Ibid., 29.
27. See Wright's point on p. 92, "The presence of Adam-christology, then, says nothing of itself against pre-existence. It may actually require it, and when we set such a christology alongside the meaning of v. 6 for which we have argued it coheres very well indeed."
28. Ibid., 91–92.
29. Ibid., 94.
30. Levison, 22–24, is critical of Wright's reconstruction of the role of Adam in postbiblical Judaism.
31. Sometimes Wright gives the impression that Romans 5 claims that Christ is obedient unto death (see, e.g., 57).
32. This is against Käsemann, 73–77. Wright, 92, also seems to hold this view, citing Lohmeyer's *Kyrios Jesus,* Sitzungsbericht der Heidelberger Akademie der Wissenschaften, Phil.-hist. Kl., Jahrgang 1927–28, 2d ed. (Heidelberg: Carl Winter, 1961).
33. See the discussion in *The Story of Christ in the Ethics of Paul,* 63.
34. My own view is that a text like Isa. 52:13–53:12 is probably a closer parallel to Phil. 2:6–11 than Rom. 5:12–21. See *The Story of Christ in the Ethics of Paul,* 72 ff., for the details. This so-called servant christology also fits into Wright's Israel christology. He simply emphasizes the Adamic aspects of this Israel christology to a greater degree in his discussion of Phil. 2:6–11.
35. See Wayne A. Meeks, "The Man from Heaven in Paul's Letter to the Philippians," in *The Future of Early Christianity: Essays in Honor of Helmut Koester* (Minneapolis: Fortress Press, 1991), 333. Meeks's essay, which appeared at the same time as *The Story of Christ in the Ethics of Paul,* makes the same sorts of arguments about Paul's moral reasoning. Note also that the verb φρονεῖν occurs 10 times in Philippians.
36. See my *The Story of Christ in the Ethics of Paul,* 92–96, 198–207, for an account of analogy as the way in which practical reasoning (*phronēsis*) operates. In that work I linked the notion of exemplar to the work of T. Kuhn. As I, too briefly, indicated there, and as Meeks's work also shows, this mode of reasoning is a fundamental part of Aristotle's ethics as well as Greco-Roman moral philosophy.

37. Wansink, *Chained in Christ,* 115. Wansink points to Cicero who, while in prison, wrote to his brother, Quintus, that he remained alive (presumably not taking his own life) out of consideration for Quintus as a clear parallel to this sort of reasoning. See Cicero, *Ad Quintum Fratrem* 1.3, and the discussion in Wansink, 107–11.

38. See A. Droge, "Mori Lucrum: Paul and Ancient Theories of Suicide," *NovT* 30 (1988): 263–86; also Droge and J. D. Tabor, *A Noble Death: Suicide and Martyrdom among Christians and Jews in Antiquity* (San Francisco: Harper & Row, 1992). Wansink, chapter 2, gives a fuller discussion of this passage in its wider epistolary context.

39. See my *The Story of Christ in the Ethics of Paul,* 85–92, for a fuller exegetical discussion of these verses.

40. See Wansink, 118, who notes: "Philippians 1:18b–29 has not often been linked to Paul's admonition to unity in 1:27–2:11. When it is assumed that Paul was unsure of whether he *preferred* to live or die, the apostle is robbed of personal initiative and is seen only as a passive figure. Paul, however, does not use verbs like βούλομαι or θέλω; he uses the verb αἱρήσομαι and, by doing so, presents himself as an example for his factious sisters and brothers thereby initiating the pattern of 'life for others' which subsequently runs throughout the epistle."

41. See Meeks, 332. For a fuller account of the exegetical complexities of 2:5 see my *The Story of Christ in the Ethics of Paul,* 79–92.

42. See Meeks, 334.

43. See ibid., 332. The contrast here is not between judgments that rely on *phronēsis* and those that do not. Rather the contrast is between the *phronēsis* appropriate to those whose commonwealth is in heaven and those whose *phronēsis* is directed by earthly concerns.

44. As I indicated in *The Story of Christ in the Ethics of Paul,* chapter 4, I disagree with Morna Hooker that there is a direct taking up of 2:6–11 in 3:2ff. There is some similar vocabulary, but I actually think these similarities can be misleading. Further, I think it is not likely that Paul models his autobiographical comments here on the pattern of 2:6–11, as Wright, 88, argues. Wright's notion is that Paul viewed his achievements in Judaism as something he might have used for his own advantage but did not. I agree that Paul does not renounce his Judaism. Rather, he reconceives it in the light of Christ, rejecting his earlier view. This does not strike me as analogous to Christ who has an exalted position which he does not take advantage of, but defines in terms of obedience. There is a further "disanalogy" in that there is nothing in Christ's preexistence which could be classified as "garbage" in the light of the cross. See the next essay, by Brian Dodd.

45. See the discussion of 2:5 above.

46. I take this phrase from a variety of different works by John Milbank. Most notably, "Can a Gift Be Given: Prolegomena to a Future Trinitarian Metaphysic," in *Rethinking Metaphysics,* ed. L. G. Jones and S. E. Fowl (Oxford: Blackwell, 1995), 119–61.

47. See Elizabeth Castelli, *Imitating Paul: A Discourse of Power,* Literary Currents in Biblical Interpretation (Louisville, Ky.: Westminster/John Knox Press, 1991).

48. "The thesis of this study is that the notion of mimesis functions in Paul's letters as a strategy of power. That is, it articulates and rationalizes as true and natural a particular set of power relations within the social formation of early Christian communities" (Castelli, 15).

49. See Castelli, 21.

50. I will leave for now the discussion of the ways in which Paul's discourse is implicated in patterns of power.

51. Those familiar with John Milbank's *Theology and Social Theory* (Oxford: Blackwell, 1990) will recognize the debt I owe to that work in formulating the issues in this way. See also Catherine Pickstock's *After Writing: On the Liturgical Consummation of Philosophy* (Oxford: Blackwell, 1998).

10.
The Story of Christ and the Imitation of Paul in Philippians 2—3

BRIAN J. DODD

The focus of the scholarly discussion of Phil. 2:5–11 has shifted in recent years, reflecting in many ways the shift in Pauline scholarship. Formerly, the emphasis was on the prehistory and form of this passage. Some recent studies have shifted attention to the literary function of this "hymn" as it is set in its Philippian context.[1] The questions being asked of the text are: How is the story of Christ being used in the ethical exhortation of its setting in Philippians? How does the employment of the example of Christ influence other hortatory concerns that Paul addresses in the letter? And now: How does Paul's use of his own personal example in Philippians 3 mirror and exemplify how the Philippians are to imitate Christ? This chapter addresses the last question.

Recently, it has been asserted again and again that Paul's composition of Philippians 3 demonstrates how his life mirrors, conforms to, and exemplifies Christ's example, which he outlines in Phil. 2:5–11. Many voices have joined this chorus.[2] It is the purpose of this study to challenge this notion, stated in two of its more simplistic forms: "Philippians 2—3 is centered on the pattern of imitation of both Christ and of Paul in their self-emptying of prerogatives";[3] and, "both the linguistic echoes and the general 'form' of the narrative seem intentionally designed to recall the Christ narrative in 2:6–11."[4] I will argue that it is unreasonable to suppose that the text reflects an implicit reverberation. I will use the space allotted here to demonstrate how Paul's purpose in Philippians 3 is not merely to counsel the self-emptying of prerogatives, and that his exhortation in the corrective of chapter 3 has little to do with echoing or recalling Phil. 2:5–11. It seems fairly clear that his purpose in chapter 3 is to ward off any move among the Philippians to accept the necessity of circumcision or other forms of "Judaizing." While it is true that Paul, like his portrayal of Christ's example, models self-abnegation in Philippians and elsewhere (e.g., 1 Cor. 9), it is reductionistic to condense the message of Philippians 3 to this: "Eschewing what might seem best to him and opting for what serves the needs of others he puts himself fully in accord with Jesus Christ (2:5–11)"[5]—this applies to what he says about his imprisonment in Phil. 1:21–26, but not to what he says about his former way of life in Judaism in Philippians 3. It is clear he did not give it up merely for the sake of his auditors, but so he could "gain Christ" (3:8).

1. THE LITERARY RELATIONSHIP
OF PHILIPPIANS 2 AND 3

One telltale sign for many interpreters that the hymn has influenced Paul's self-presentation in Philippians 3 is how both Christ and Paul "regard" their former positions. In the hymn, Christ did not "regard" or "consider" his former status as something to cling to, but as something to yield in obedience to God (2:6; ἡγήσατο). It is then noted how Paul eschews his Jewish credentials, "regarding" them and "everything else" now as "loss" in comparison with the knowledge of Christ Jesus as his master (3:7–8). The use of the word "regard" three times in these two verses convinces some interpreters that Paul here intends for his auditors to make an association between his mindset and Christ's, thus providing a one-two punch as examples for their emulation (explicitly, 2:3, 6). Indeed, Philippians 2—3 uses this verb six of the eight times it is found in the undisputed Pauline epistles (the other two being 2 Cor. 9:5; 1 Thess. 5:13).

There are indicators that this is a faulty leap to make. One of the occurrences of the verb in these chapters (2:25) appears to have no relevance at all to the hymn. Paul "considers it a necessity" to send Epaphroditus back to them. What possible connotation can we derive from this "echo" of the verb here? Does this not rather appear to be cordiality and etiquette of a personal letter? But there is a more serious objection to supposing the verb in chapter 3 is intended merely to mimic its use in the hymn. When we consider the related word group, "think" or "have in mind" (φρονεῖν in Philippians: 1:7; 2:2[2x]; 2:5; 3:15[2x]; 3:19; 4:2, 10[2x]), which is prevalent in the letter, the supposed echo of "regard" in chapter 3 is instead placed within the larger hortatory framework of Philippians. Paul appeals again and again to their thinking—their mindset, their moral reasoning—so that they will live out their obedience to Christ in esteem and compassionate concern for one another.[6] "Have this mindset" (τοῦτο φρονεῖτε ἐν ὑμῖν, 2:5) is the thrust of Paul's overall exhortation to those he wants to live as citizens of Christ's commonwealth on earth (1:27; 3:20). Paul's hortatory usage of Christ's pattern and his own example should be related to this broader epistolary design, rather than more narrowly linked up with one another as supposed intentional echoes.

Furthermore, the downward "reckoning" of Christ as he humbled himself by donning human form is not at all parallel to Paul's consideration of his former status within Judaism. Christ yields his former position, a privileged position. But Paul does not view his own former status as merely "something not to be taken advantage of."[7] On the contrary, his former position is considered "refuse" (3:8; σκύβαλα), hardly an allusion to how Christ regarded his divine position. Paul's self-exemplification is not of humility (as Wright takes it), but very literally is designed to reject the need for circumcision. For someone in Christ, the acceptance of the soteriological necessity of circumcision is allowing oneself to be mutilated (3:2; κατατομήν), and reflects Paul's former life lived "in the flesh" rather than his present, privileged life "in Christ" (3:3). Frankly, there is really nothing portrayed about the "downward" movement of Paul's life mirroring the first half of Christ's story in the hymn.[8] Instead, Paul's insistence is that he has moved up and his standing in Christ is a superlative position (3:8), and he now contrasts life lived in two spheres, in the sphere of the "flesh" versus in the sphere of Christ. Paul does not want the Philippian Christians to let themselves be circumcised, thus disparaging circumcision as life lived "in the flesh." It is not a privilege Paul lays aside, but a decisive direction that he wants his followers in Philippi to eschew at all costs, a "mutilation" (3:2). Their present standing—and their future hope, as the passage goes on to draw out—is wrapped up in their relationship with Christ and specifically in their rejection of circumcision. None of this is remotely related to the ethical issue of Philippians 2, which involves regarding one another within the community more highly than oneself.

Fee thinks Paul alludes to how Christ is "found in human likeness" (2:7) when he expresses his desire to be "found in Christ" (3:9).[9] This "echo" is strained. The hymn's depiction of Christ finds several phrases to capture Christ's downward descent of becoming human. Paul's desire to "be found" in Christ (εὑρεθῶ ἐν αὐτῷ) is a part of his soteriological corrective to preempt a Judaizing message from penetrating the Philippian church (3:2). Paul's hope is not in "his own righteousness" (another critique of his former life in Judaism) but in his standing "in Christ," the only source of righteousness. In other words, just because the verb "find" is used again does not mean there is some supposed literary allusion. Instead, its quite different usage in the two cases demonstrates that there is nothing like an "echo," intended or otherwise.

Neither is Christ taking the "form" (μορφή) of a slave (2:7) alluded to when Paul mentions being "conformed" (συμμορφιζόμενος) to Christ's death (3:10). The participle has a distant etymological relationship with the noun, but the two hardly relate to one another in their current usage. Christ's obedience to God as a slave to a master results ultimately in his death, but in the context of 2:5–7 his taking of the slave form is contrasted with his former status when he "was in the form of God" (ἐν μορφῇ θεοῦ ὑπάρχων). Paul's desire to be conformed to Christ's death and resurrection indicates Paul's understanding of the gospel rather than reflecting any intentional patterning of himself after Christ's story. He does not go on to depict such a biography for himself. Rather, he understands his position in Christ to cause him to identify with the gospel, Christ's acts becoming efficacious for Paul as he puts his faith in Christ (cf. Gal. 2:19–20). Hooker's notion of "interchange" (i.e., Christ became as we are so we can become as he is) allows a more precise relationship, soteriologically speaking, between chapters 2 and 3, and it is in this sense that it can be rightly said that "Paul's own manner of life is in conformity with the Gospel of the Cross which he sets out in chapter 2."[10] Hooker's is a theological rather than a literary observation.

Another correspondence that breaks down under further scrutiny is the comparison of Christ's and Paul's humility. Christ "humbles himself" (ἐταπείνωσεν, 2:8) in his obedience to the path that brought him to the crucifixion. This is then compared with Paul's knowing "what it is like to be humbled" (ταπεινοῦσθαι, 4:12; cf. 2:3; 3:21). But Paul does not mention his "humbling" in relation to his renunciation of his Jewish past, but rather as he depicts life in eschatological anticipation (3:21), and again in 4:12 as partially expressive of the missionary conditions of the faithful Christian life (which also include times of abundance). These verbal similarities do not create the impression that Paul is like Christ; on the contrary, Christ took on the lowly conditions of human existence in his incarnation (2:8), which Paul hopes will be transformed in the consummation (3:21).

Another implied correspondence may be found in the portrayal of Christ's exaltation by God (2:9–11) in parallel with Paul's expected exaltation out of his own suffering and death (1:20–23; 3:10–11, 14, 21).[11] As God is the agent in Christ's exaltation (2:9–11), so he is the deliverer of the Philippians (1:28) and of Paul together with the Philippians (3:20–21, though the agent here is identified as "the Lord Jesus Christ"). The experience of Christ's humility now/vindication later creates a positive expectation of the future for Paul and the Philippians that is intended to bring them eschatological comfort in light of 3:20–21. Nevertheless, the exaltation of Christ is accomplished by God in 2:9–11 and cannot be viewed as an ethical *Vorbild* (example) for the Philippians to pattern themselves after as Paul has himself (*Urbild* [archetype] is the more appropriate term in this case, as Käsemann has pointed out[12]).

2. THE *CRUX INTERPRETUM* OF 1 CORINTHIANS 11:1

A wholly different approach to the relationship between Christ's story and Paul's example in Philippians 2—3 is through the lens of what is considered Paul's well established linkage of his own personal example with the model of Christ: "This imitation pattern in Philippians 2—3 recalls Paul's call in 1 Cor. 11:1, 'Be imitators of me, as I am of Christ.' "[13] This would appear to provide a window into Paul's mind, allowing us a clear and convincing glimpse of how Paul conceives of the relationship of his own example with the ethical model of Christ. But this only holds if we read 1 Cor. 11:1 as most interpreters have, "Follow my example, as I *follow the example* of Christ" (NIV). This rendering, however, adds the words I have placed in italics, and ignores the soteriological significance of the cipher "of Christ" in the Corinthian correspondence. These factors should remove consideration of 1 Cor. 11:1 as a lens to interpret what Paul is doing in Philippians.[14]

The NRSV is better with "Be imitators of me, as I am of Christ." (μιμηταί μου γίνεσθε καθὼς κἀγὼ Χριστοῦ). Properly interpreted, this crux does not support the "Paul's example mirrors Christ's life" line of thinking. My reading of this verse is nuanced this way: "Imitate my example that I have portrayed in 1 Corinthians, because I am possessed by my master, Christ." There are several observations that I draw upon to support this rendering: (1) "of Christ" has a distinctive usage in Paul's conversation with the Corinthians, akin to the soteriological significance that the phrase "in Christ" takes on in the Pauline epistles; (2) Paul's literary use of his own personal example is at the heart of every single pastoral issue he treats in 1 Corinthians, but he makes no explicit use of Christ's example in 1 Corinthians; (3) and finally, Paul's paradigmatic self-portrayal in Philippians has several components, none of which can be characterized by "Be humble as I am." This nullifies any suggestion that Paul has consciously crafted his self-portrayal after the hymn's portrait of Christ. I shall take these up in turn.

The Distinctive Usage of "of Christ" in 1 Corinthians

"Of Christ" in 1 Corinthians is shorthand for belonging to Christ or being "in Christ" in a single, undivided church (1 Cor. 1:12; 2:16; 3:23; 6:15; 7:22; 12:27; 15:23; cf. 2 Cor. 10:1, 7). This cipher, by its extensive usage in the letter, takes on the weight of a technical term so that by the time we read 1 Cor. 11:1 the sense is that since Paul is "in Christ" or "belongs to Christ," he is a model of the quintessential Christian. In an entirely similar call to imitation in 1 Cor. 4:15, Paul likewise grounds himself as an exemplary model as their spiritual father "in Christ." In the same way, the call to imitation of Paul in Phil. 3:17 is based upon Paul's standing in Christ (cf. Phil. 1:1, 8, 13, 20–21; 3:7–10, 12). Against this some interpreters have suggested that the compound "co-imitators" (συμμιμηταί) in Phil. 3:17 should be taken as "be co-imitators with me [of Christ]."[15] Against this reading, adding in "with me" is a strained use of the genitive, the phrase "of Christ" must be supplied, and Paul proceeds to mention his own example but not Christ's (3:17b). A more plausible translation is, "join together in imitating me," which looks to the letter's thematic call to unity for reinforcement. Paul's ethical example is appropriate because of his existence "in Christ," and the Philippians are able to emulate him because they too are "in Christ" (e.g., Phil. 2:1, 5).

The Absence of Explicit Use of Christ's Example in 1 Corinthians

Paul's use of his own example is a striking, unifying feature of 1 Corinthians. Every major assertion that he makes is grounded in his explicit self-portrayal as a model to be imitated, whether as a literal model (as in 1 Cor. 3—4; chaps. 7, 9, and 14), or in a paradigmatic use of "I" as a literary feature of the epistle (as in 1 Cor. 5:3–4; 6:12; chap. 13).[16] In contrast with this high profile usage of his own example, Christ's explicit example is nowhere employed in 1 Corinthians. This is a striking omission but proves nothing by itself. Taken in tandem with the other two points which are being argued in this section of the essay, it weighs against the NIV rendering of 1 Cor. 11:1. This is not to say that Christ's example is never used in ethical admonition by Paul. It is, but sparingly and briefly in just a few places (Rom. 15:1–3; 2 Cor. 8:9; cf. Eph. 4:32–5:1). If we add to these Phil. 2:5–8, all use Christ's example in a very limited way to extol the virtue of his self-abasement out of regard for benefiting others.[17]

How Paul Appeals to His Own Example in Philippians

In this essay I am not denying that the Christ hymn is partly used for exemplification, nor am I denying that Paul's self-portrayals are paradigmatic. On the contrary, Paul perhaps models at least six things for the Philippians:

a. Self-renunciation of confidence "in the flesh," that is, in opposition to Judaizing requirements (3:4–10).
b. Affirmation of confidence "in Christ" (3:4–11).

c.   Eschatological reserve as one who has accepted the eschatological "not yet" of life in Christ (3:11–14, 20–21), perhaps set against Judaizing perfectionism or a tendency toward an over-realized eschatology (cf. 1:6, 10–11, 19–21; 2:8–11, 16, 19, 23–24; 4:5, 19–20).

d.   Eschatological encouragement, parenetically providing his own example as one who continues to pursue "the goal for the prize of the heavenly call of God in Christ Jesus" (3:14), a confidence he had earlier expressed (1:24–26) to supply further motivational stimulus for the Philippians to press on amid their struggles.

e.   Contentment arising from trusting prayer (1:3–11; 4:6–9; cf. Acts 16:13, 16, 25).

f.   Paul's regulative example to be obeyed. Paul does not conceive of his own example as one option among many, but rather as the regulative type for his followers. This is partly implied, since who he is vis-à-vis the community determines how his rhetoric will be heard. But the theme is explicit in 3:17–18, where Paul's example and those who "walk" according to his way are contrasted with the "many" who "walk" as "enemies of the cross." We can combine his comment in 2:12 with this: "Therefore, my beloved, just as you have always obeyed me, not only in my presence, but much more now in my absence . . . " [NRSV]. In 3:15 conformity to Paul's way is implied, and those who dissent will be enlightened by God (3:16; see also 4:1–2). Thus, while Paul's self-presentation is paradigmatic as an ethical pattern for the Philippians, there remains an implied assertion of authority to ensure their conformity to Paul's modeled way of thinking and living.[18]

Even though Paul models all these things for the Philippians, absent is a paradigmatic self-presentation of himself as one who has humbled himself as they should so they can become like Christ. Except for (d) above, it is difficult to see how much of Paul's explicit self-portrayal reflects the imagery or language of the hymn.

3. PAUL'S ETHICAL EXAMPLE
GROUNDED "IN CHRIST"

In a creative display of literary analysis, Paul Minear suggests that the singing of the hymn in the worship of the church is formative for Paul's own self-exemplification and the overall theological teaching and ethical appeal of the letter. He appeals to the putative verbal echoes mentioned above, what he identifies as the "grammar of correlations" and "an extensive pattern of parallels." He asserts, "It is not out of order, then, to suggest that these parallels may have been clarified in Paul's own mind through singing that hymn."[19] It is worth pondering.

But the question remains, How is Paul's ethical example in Philippians 3 grounded in Phil. 2:5–11? I think Fowl's nuanced understanding better reflects the relationship of the two: "Paul offers an account of his own life in 3:2–16 as a manifestation of a form of practical reasoning based on the story of Christ in 2:6–11" (p. 148 above). His self-exemplification is "really an account of how his perspective or point of view was transformed through his encounter with Christ."

In other words, Paul's ethical example is grounded in Christ's soteriological accomplishment (as in 1 Cor. 11:1). Paul is not simply lining up "like behaviors": Christ models the Christian life, Paul mirrors Christ's example, and the Philippians are to follow suit. Rather, Paul's own ethical example in Philippians 3 is grounded in the soteriological implications of the hymn. Now, as a result of Christ's exalted position (2:9–11), Paul's life has been transformed and his adoration of Christ is central for his life, salvation, and eschatological hope as he details in 3:2–21. Christ's motivation of humility in the hymn provides the mindset that the Philippians are to emulate in their community relations,[20] but they are enabled to have "Christ's mind" and obey him because they are "in Christ" (2:1–5).[21]

To adapt Minear's imaginative suggestion, it is not the Philippians' and Paul's repetitive singing of the model of Christ that empowers them to live out the life of Christ under his heavenly commonwealth. It is the adoration of Christ and the reminder of the power supplied by his resurrection for those who are "in Christ" that enables their ethical response. The recounting of Christ's glorious destiny and exalted state in 2:9–11 is what Paul explicitly identifies as the ground for ethical obedience: "in order that I may know him, and the power of his resurrection" (3:10). It is precisely because the Philippians, like Paul, are "in Christ" and have his resurrection power available to them that they are able to think as Christ desires and Paul exhorts, "think this way among yourselves, which also [you are enabled to think because you are] in Christ Jesus" (2:5).

NOTES

1. E.g., Wayne A. Meeks, "The Man from Heaven in Paul's Letter to the Philippians," in *The Future of Early Christianity: Essays in Honor of Helmut Koester,* ed. Birger Pearson (Minneapolis: Fortress Press, 1991), 329–36; Stephen Fowl, *The Story of Christ in the Ethics of Paul: An Analysis of the Function of the Hymnic Material in the Pauline Corpus,* JSNTSS 36 (Sheffield: JSOT Press, 1990); Paul S. Minear, "Singing and Suffering in Philippi," in *The Conversation Continues: Studies in Paul and John in Honor of J. Louis Martyn,* ed. R. T. Fortna and B. R. Gaventa (Nashville: Abingdon Press, 1990), 202–19; Gordon D. Fee, *Paul's Letter to the Philippians,* NICNT (Grand Rapids: Eerdmans, 1995).

2. E.g., Morna D. Hooker, "Philippians 2:6–11," in *Jesus und Paulus,* FS W. G. Kümmel, ed. E. E. Ellis and E. Grässer; (Göttingen: Vandenhoeck & Ruprecht, 1975), 151–64; William S. Kurz, "Kenotic Imitation of Paul and of Christ in Philippians 2 and 3," in *Discipleship in the New Testament,* ed. Fernando F. Segovia (Philadelphia: Fortress Press, 1985), 103–26; Minear, "Singing and Suffering in Philippi"; F. Gregory Bloomquist, *The Function of Suffering in Philippians,* JSNTSup 78 (Sheffield: JSOT Press, 1993), 135, 168.

3. Kurz, "Kenotic Imitation," 105.

4. Fee, *Philippians,* 314.

5. J. Paul Sampley, "Reasoning from the Horizons of Paul's Thought World: A Comparison of Galatians and Philippians," in *Theology and Ethics in Paul and His Interpreters: Essays in Honor of Victor Paul Furnish,* ed. Eugene Lovering and Jerry Sumney (Nashville: Abingdon Press, 1996), 114–31 (127).

6. "This letter's most comprehensive purpose is the shaping of a Christian *phronēsis,* a practical moral reasoning that is 'conformed to [Christ's] death' in hope of his resurrection" (Meeks, "The Man from Heaven," 333).

7. N. T. Wright, "Jesus Christ is Lord: Philippians 2:5–11," in *The Climax of the Covenant: Christ and the Law in Pauline Theology* (Minneapolis: Fortress Press, 1993), 56–98 (88). As in some of the examples below, this supposed "echo" is more a matter of Wright's English rendering than its Greek referent.

8. Contra Fee, *Philippians,* 315.

9. Ibid.

10. Hooker, "Philippians 2:6–11," 156.

11. Morna D. Hooker, "Interchange in Christ," *JTS* 22 (1971): 349–61 (356–57); Bloomquist, *Function of Suffering,* 112–14.

12. Ernst Käsemann, "Kritische Analyse von Phil. 2:5–11," in *Exegetische Versuche und Besinnungen* 1 (Göttingen: Vandenhoeck & Ruprecht, 1960), 51–95 (81); and see Robert Morgan's chapter above.

13. Kurz, "Kenotic Imitation," 106. Also, Christian Wolff, "Niedrigkeit und Verzicht in Wort und Weg Jesu und in der apostolischen Existenz des Paulus," *NTS* 34 (1988): 183–96; Stanley K. Stowers, "Friends and Enemies in the Politics of Heaven," in *Pauline Theology* 1, ed. J. Bassler (Minneapolis: Fortress Press, 1991), 105–21 (120).

14. E.g., Morna D. Hooker, "A Partner in the Gospel: Paul's Understanding of His Ministry," in *Theology and Ethics in Paul and His Interpreters: Essays in Honor of Victor Paul Furnish,* ed. Eugene Lovering and Jerry Sumney (Nashville: Abingdon Press, 1996), 83–100 (93). Richard Hays appeals to 1 Thess. 1:6 as the crux for interpreting Philippians, "You became imitators of us and the Lord," but this is not an ethical call to emulation. Rather, "imitation" here is a statement of comparison and identification, for in this context Paul is not saying, "Become like me and Christ in our humility," but "Your experience of suffering reflects ours also—be encouraged" (Richard B. Hays, *The Moral Vision of the New Testament* [San Francisco: HarperCollins, 1996], 31).

15. W. F. McMichael, " 'Be ye followers together of Me': Συμμιμηταί μου γίνεσθε— Phil. 3:17," *ExpTim* 5 (1893–94): 287; Hooker, "A Partner in the Gospel," 93–94.

16. Margaret M. Mitchell, *Paul and the Rhetoric of Reconciliation: An Exegetical Investigation of the Language and Composition of 1 Corinthians* (Louisville, Ky: Westminster/John Knox Press, 1992), 54 (esp. chap. 4); and see my "Paul's Paradigmatic 'I' and 1 Corinthians 6:12," *JSNT* 59 (1995): 39–58.

17. See Victor Paul Furnish, *Theology and Ethics in Paul* (Nashville: Abingdon Press, 1968), 218–23.

18. Abraham J. Malherbe, "Hellenistic Moralists and the New Testament," *ANRW* II.26.1, 267–333 (285–86); contra Willis P. de Boer, *The Imitation of Paul: An Exegetical Study* (Kampen: J. H. Kok, 1962), 184–87.

19. Minear, "Singing and Suffering in Philippi," 207.

20. So Peter T. O'Brien, "The Gospel and Godly Models in Philippians," in *Worship, Theology and Ministry in the Early Church: Essays in Honor of Ralph P. Martin,* ed. M. Wilkins and T. Paige, JSNTS 87 (Sheffield: JSOT Press, 1992), 273–84.

21. A balance struck by Hooker, "Philippians 2:6–11," 156.

BIBLIOGRAPHY

Anderson, G. A., and M. E. Stone, eds. *A Synopsis of the Books of Adam and Eve*. Early Judaism and Its Literature 5. Atlanta: Scholars Press, 1994.

Barclay, J. M. G. *Jews in the Mediterranean Diaspora from Alexander to Trajan (323 BCE–117 CE)*. Edinburgh: T. & T. Clark, 1996.

Barrett, C. K. *From First Adam to Last*. London: A. & C. Black, 1962.

———. *Paul: An Introduction to His Thought*. Louisville, Ky.: Westminster/John Knox Press, 1994.

Basevi, C., and J. Chapa. "Philippians 2:6–11: The Rhetorical Ethical Appeal in Philippians." In *Rhetoric and the New Testament*, ed. S. E. Porter and T. H. Olbrecht, 338–56. Sheffield: JSOT Press, 1993.

Bauckham, R. *The Climax of Prophecy: Studies on the Book of Revelation*. Edinburgh: T. & T. Clark, 1993.

———. "Jesus, Worship of." *ABD* 3: 812–19.

———. *The Theology of the Book of Revelation*. Cambridge: Cambridge University Press, 1993.

———. "The Worship of Jesus in Apocalyptic Christianity." *NTS* 27 (1980–81): 322–23.

Berger, Klaus. *Formgeschichte des Neuen Testaments*. Heidelberg: Quelle & Meyer, 1984.

———. "Hellenistische Gattungen im Neuen Testament." *ANRW* 2.25.2 (1984), 1031–1432 (esp. 1178–89).

Bergmeier, R. "Weihnachten mit und ohne Glanz: Notizen zu Johannesprolog und Philipperhymnus." *ZNW* 85 (1994): 47–68.

Black, D. A. "The Authorship of Philippians 2:6–11: Some Literary-Critical Observations," *Criswell Theological Review* 2 (1988): 269–89.

Bloomquist, F. Gregory. *The Function of Suffering in Philippians* JSNTSS 78. Sheffield: JSOT Press, 1993.

Bonnard, P. *L'Epître de Saint Paul aux Philippiens*. Neuchâtel: Delachaux & Niestlé, 1950.

Borsch, F. H. "Further Reflections on the Son of Man." In *The Messiah*, ed. J. H. Charlesworth, et al., 130–44. Minneapolis: Fortress Press, 1992.

Bousset, Wilhelm. *Kyrios Christos: Geschichte des Christusglaubens von den Anfängen des Christentums bis Irenaeus*. Göttingen: Vandenhoeck & Ruprecht, 1913; Zweite Auflage 1921. Eng. trans. by John E. Steely: *Kyrios Christos*. Nashville and New York: Abingdon Press, 1970.

Briggs, S. "Can an Enslaved God Liberate? Hermeneutical Reflections on Philippians 2:6–11." *Semeia* 47 (1989): 137–53.

Brockington, L. H. "The Septuagintal Background to the New Testament Use of doxa." In

Studies in the Gospels: Essays in Memory of R. H. Lightfoot, ed. D. E. Nineham, 1–8. Oxford: Blackwell, 1957.

Bruce, A. B. *The Humiliation of Christ.* Edinburgh: T. & T. Clark, 1881.

Bruce, F. F. *Philippians.* San Francisco: Harper & Row, 1983.

Caird, G. B. "The Development of the Doctrine of Christ in the New Testament." In *Christ for Us Today,* ed. N. Pittenger. London: SCM Press, 1968.

―――. *New Testament Theology.* Completed and edited by L. D. Hurst. Oxford: Clarendon Press, 1996.

Casey, P. Maurice. *From Jewish Prophet to Gentile God: The Origins and Development of New Testament Christology.* Cambridge: James Clark & Co., 1991.

―――. "The Deification of Jesus." *SBL 1994 Seminar Papers,* 697–714.

Castelli, E. *Imitating Paul: A Discourse of Power.* Louisville, Ky.: Westminster/John Knox Press, 1991.

Cerfaux, L. *Le Christ dans la Théologie de St. Paul.* 1951; ET, New York: Herder, 1962.

Chester, A. "Jewish Messianic Expectations and Mediatorial Figures and Pauline Christology." in *Paulus und antike Judentum,* ed. M. Hengel and U. Heckel. WUNT 58. Tübingen: Mohr (Siebeck), 1991.

Clark, G. H. *Philippians.* Trinity Papers 47. Hobbs, N.Mex.: Trinity Foundation, 1996.

Clarke, W. K. Lowther. "The Epistle to the Philippians." In *New Testament Problems: Essays—Reviews—Interpretations,* 141–50. London: SPCK, 1929.

Craddock, F. *Philippians.* Interpretation. Atlanta: John Knox Press, 1985.

Cranfield, C. E. B. "Some Comments on Professor J. D. G. Dunn's *Christology in the Making,* with Special Reference to the Evidence of the Epistle to the Romans." In *The Glory of Christ in the New Testament: In Memory of G. B. Caird,* ed. L. D. Hurst and N. T. Wright, 265–80. Oxford: Clarendon Press, 1987.

Cullmann, O. *The Christology of the New Testament.* London: SCM Press, 1963.

Davis, C. J. *The Name and Way of the Lord.* JSNTSup 129. Sheffield: JSOT Press, 1996.

Dawe, Donald G. "A Fresh Look at the Kenotic Christologies." *SJT* 15 (1962): 337–49.

de Boer, Willis P. *The Imitation of Paul: An Exegetical Study.* Kampen: J. H. Kok, 1962.

Dibelius, M. *An die Thessalonicher, an die Philipper.* HzNT. Tübingen: Mohr (Siebeck), [2]1923, [3]1937.

Dunn, J. D. G. *Christology in the Making: A New Testament Inquiry into the Origins of the Doctrine of the Incarnation.* London: SCM Press, [1980] 1989.

―――. "Pauline Christology: Shaping the Fundamental Structures." In *Christology in Dialogue,* ed. R. F. Berkey and S. A. Edwards, 96–107. Cleveland: Pilgrim Press, 1993.

―――. "Why Incarnation? A Review of Recent New Testament Scholarship." In *Crossing the Boundaries,* ed. S. E. Porter, 235–56. Leiden: E. J. Brill, 1994.

―――. *The Partings of the Ways.* London: SCM Press, 1991.

Edwards, James R. "Ernst Lohmeyer—ein Schlusskapitel," *Evangelische Theologie* 56/4 (1996): 320–42.

Eltester, Friedrich-Wilhelm. *Eikon im Neuen Testament.* BZNW 23. Berlin: Alfred Töpelmann, 1958.

Esking, Erik. *Glaube und Geschichte in der theologischen Exegese Ernst Lohmeyers: Zugleich ein Beitrag zur Geschichte der neutestamentlichen Interpretation.* Acta Seminarii Neotestamentici Upsaliensis 18. Kopenhagen: Ejnar Munksgaard; Lund: Gleerups, 1951.

Fee, G. D. "Philippians 2:5–11: Hymn or Exalted Pauline Prose?" *Bulletin for Biblical Research* 2 (1992): 29–46.

―――. *Paul's Letter to the Philippians.* NICNT. Grand Rapids: Eerdmans, 1995.

Feinberg, Paul D. "The Kenosis and Christology: An Exegetical-Theological Analysis of Philippians 2:6–11." *Trinity Journal* 1 (1980): 21–46.

Fitzmyer, Joseph A. "The Aramaic Background of Philippians 2:6–11." *CBQ* 50 (1988): 470–83.

————. "The Semitic Background of the New Testament Kyrios-Title." In idem, *A Wandering Aramean,* 115–42. SBLMS 15. Missoula, Mont.: Scholars Press, 1979.

Fossum, J. E. *The Name of God and the Angel of the Lord.* WUNT 36. Tübingen: Mohr (Siebeck), 1985.

Fowl, Stephen. *The Story of Christ in the Ethics of Paul: An Analysis of the Function of the Hymnic Material in the Pauline Corpus.* JSNTSup 36. Sheffield: Sheffield Academic Press, 1990.

France, R. T. "The Worship of Jesus: A Neglected Factor in Christological Debate?" In *Christ the Lord,* ed. H. H. Rowdon. Leicester: InterVarsity Press (1982): 17–36.

Furness, J. M. "Behind the Philippian Hymn." *ExpTim* 79 (1967–68): 178–82.

Furnish, Victor Paul. *Theology and Ethics in Paul.* Nashville: Abingdon Press, 1968.

Gamber, Klaus. "Der Christus-Hymnus im Philipperbrief in liturgiegeschichtlicher Sicht." *Biblica* 51 (1970): 369–76.

Georgi, D. "Der vorpaulinische Hymnus, Phil. 2:6–11." In *Zeit und Geschichte,* 263–93. Tübingen: Mohr (Siebeck), 1964.

Gibbs, J. G. "The Relation between Creation and Redemption according to Phil. II 5–11." *NT* 12 (1970): 273.

Greenlee, J. H. *An Exegetical Summary of Philippians.* Dallas, Tex.: Summer Institute of Linguistics, 1992.

Grelot, P. "Deux notes critiques sur Philippiens 2,6–11." *Biblica* 54 (1973): 169–86.

Gundry, R. H. "Style and Substance in 'The Myth of God Incarnate' according to Philippians 2:6–11." In *Crossing the Boundaries: Essays in Biblical Interpretation in Honour of Michael D. Goulder,* ed. Stanley E. Porter, Paul Joyce and David E. Orton. 271–93. Biblical Interpretation Series 8. Leiden: E. J. Brill, 1994.

Habermann, J. *Präexistenzaussagen im Neuen Testament.* Frankfurt: Peter Lang, 1990.

Harvey, Anthony. "Christ as Agent." In *The Glory of Christ in the New Testament,* ed. L. D. Hurst and N. T. Wright, 239–50. Oxford: Clarendon Press, 1987.

Harvey, J. "A New Look at the Christ Hymn in Philippians." *Expository Times* 76 (1964–65): 336.

Hawthorne, G. F. *Philippians.* WBC 43. Waco, Tex.: Word, 1983.

————. *The Presence and the Power: The Significance of the Holy Spirit in the Life and Ministry of Jesus,* 199–226. Dallas, Tex.: Word, 1991.

————. "The Imitation of Christ: Discipleship in Philippians." In *Patterns of Discipleship in the New Testament,* ed. R.N. Longnecker. Grand Rapids: Eerdmans, 1996.

————. "Philippians." *DPL* 707–13.

Haufe, Günter. *Gedenkvortrag zum 100. Geburtstag Ernst Lohmeyers.* Greifswalder Universitätsreden n.F. 59. Greifswald, 1991.

Hay, D. H. *Glory at the Right Hand: Psalm 110 in Early Christianity.* SBLMS 18. Nashville: Abingdon Press, 1973.

Hays, Richard B. *The Moral Vision of the New Testament.* San Francisco: HarperCollins, 1996.

Hengel, Martin. "Hymns and Christology." In idem, *Between Jesus and Paul,* trans. J. Bowden, 78–96. London: SCM Press, 1983.

————. "Christological Titles in Early Christianity." In *The Messiah,* ed. J. H. Charlesworth, 425–48. Minneapolis: Fortress Press, 1992.

————. "Sit at My Right Hand!" In idem, *Studies in Early Christology*, 119–225. Edinburgh: T. & T. Clark, 1995.

————. "The Song about Christ in Earliest Worship." In idem, *Studies in Early Christology*, 227–91. Edinburgh: T. & T. Clark, 1995.

Henry, P. "Kènose." *Dictionnaire de la Bible*. Supplément 5 (1957), 7–161.

Heriban, J. *"Retto fronein e kenosi": Studio esegetico su Fil 2,1–5, 6–11*. Biblioteca di scienze religiose 51. Rome: LAS, 1983.

Hofius, O. *Der Christushymus Philipper 2:6–11*. WUNT 17. Tübingen: Mohr (Siebeck), (1976) 1991.

Hooker, Morna D. "Interchange in Christ." *JTS* 22 (1971): 349–61.

————. "Philippians 2, 6–11." In *Jesus und Paulus: Festschrift für W.G. Kümmel*, ed. E. E. Ellis and Erich Grässer, 151–64. Göttingen: Vandenhoeck & Ruprecht, 1975. Reprint in *From Adam to Christ: Essays on Paul*, 80–100. Cambridge: Cambridge University Press, 1990.

————. "A Partner in the Gospel: Paul's Understanding of His Ministry." In *Theology and Ethics in Paul and His Interpreters: Essays in Honor of Victor Paul Furnish*, ed. Eugene Lovering and Jerry Sumney, 83–100. Nashville: Abingdon Press, 1996.

Hoover, R. W. "The Harpagmos Enigma: A Philological Solution." *Harvard Theological Review* 56 (1971): 95–119.

Howard, George. "Phil. 2:6–11 and the Human Christ." *CBQ* 40 (1978): 368ff.

Hurst, L. D. "Reenter the Pre-existent Christ in Philippians 2:5–11?" *NTS* 32 (1986): 449–57.

Hurtado, L. W. "Jesus as Lordly Example in Philippians 2:5–11." In *From Jesus to Paul: Studies in Honour of Francis Wright Beare*, ed. P. Richardson and J. C. Hurd, 113–26. Waterloo, Ont.: Wilfred Laurier University Press, 1984.

————. *One God, One Lord*. Philadelphia: Fortress Press, 1988.

————. "Pre-existence." *DPL*, 743–46.

Hutter-Wolandt, Ulrich. "Theologie als Wissenschaft: Zu Leben und Werk Ernst Lohmeyers (1890–1946): Mit einem Quellenanhang." *Jahrbuch für Schlesische Kirchengeschichte* 69 (1990): 1–46. Reprinted in Hutter-Wolandt, *Die evangelische Kirche Schlesiens im Wandel der Zeiten: Studien und Quellen zur Geschichte einer Territorialkirche*, 237–81; Veröffentlichungen der Forschungsstelle Ostmitteleuropa an der Universität Dortmund, Reihe B 43. Dortmund: Forschungsstelle Ostmitteleuropa, 1991.

Jeremias, J. "Zur Gedankenführung in den paulinischen Briefen." In *Studia Paulina in Honorem J. de Zwaan*, ed. J. N. Sevenster and W. C. van Unnik, 146–54. Haarlem: Bohn, 1953.

Jervell, J. *Imago Dei: Gen. i. 26f. im Spätjudentum und in den Paulinischen Briefen*. FRLANT 76. Göttingen: Vandenhoeck & Ruprecht, 1960.

Käsemann, Ernst. "Kritische Analyse von Phil. 2, 5–11." *ZTK* 47 (1950): 313–60. Reprinted in E. Käsemann, *Exegetische Versuche und Besinnungen* 1:51–95. Göttingen: Vandenhoeck & Ruprecht, 1960. Trans. by Alice F. Carse, "A Critical Analysis of Philippians 2:5–11," in *God and Christ: Existence and Province (Journal for Theology and Church* 5 [1968]: 45–88).

Kennel, Werner. *Frühchristliche Hymnen? Gattungskritische Studien zur Frage nach den Liedern der frühen Christenheit*. WMANT 71. Göttingen: Vandenhoeck & Ruprecht, 1995.

Knight, J. A. *Philippians, Colossians and Philemon*. Kansas City, Mo.: Beacon Hill, 1985.

Kögel, J. *Christus der Herr*. Göttingen, 1908.

Kraftchick, Steven. "A Necessary Detour: Paul's Metaphorical Understanding of the Philippian Hymn." *Horizons in Biblical Theology* 15 (1993): 9.

Krentz, Edgar. "Epideiktik and Hymnody: The New Testament and Its World." *Biblical Research* 90 (1995): 50–97.

————. *Galatians, Philippians, Philemon, 1 Thessalonians*. Minneapolis: Augsburg Publishing House, 1985.

Kurz, William S. "Kenotic Imitation of Paul and of Christ in Philippians 2 and 3." In *Discipleship in the New Testament*, ed. Fernando F. Segovia, 103–26. Philadelphia: Fortress Press, 1985.

Kuschel, K. J. *Born before All Time? The Dispute over Christ's Origin*. London: SCM Press, 1992.

————. *Philippians, Colossians, Philemon*. St. Louis: Concordia Publishing House, 1992.

Lattke, Michael. *Hymnus: Materialen zu einer Geschichte der antiken Hymnologie*. NTOA 19. Freiburg: Universitätsverlag; Göttingen: Vandenhoeck & Ruprecht, 1991.

Lightfoot, J. B. *St. Paul's Epistle to the Philippians*, 109–15. London: Macmillan, 1927.

Lohmeyer, Ernst. *Die Briefe an die Philipper, an die Kolosser und an Philemon*. KEK 9. Göttingen: Vandenhoeck & Ruprecht, 1930. 9th ed. (drawing on Lohmeyer's handwritten papers), ed. Werner Schmauch, 1953.

————. *Grundlagen Paulinischer Theologie*. Tübingen: Mohr (Siebeck), 1929. Reprint, Nendeln, Liechtenstein: Kraus, 1966.

————. *Kyrios Jesus: Eine Untersuchung zu Phil. 2,5–11*. Sitzungsberichte der Heidelberger Akademie der Wissenschaften, Philosophisch-historische Klasse, Jahrgang 1927/1928, 4. Abhandlung. Heidelberg: Carl Winter, Universitätsverlag, Zweite Auflage, 1961.

"Lohmeyer, Ernst, † (1890–1946)." In Ernst Lohmeyer, *Vorträge und Aufsätze, 1925–1962*, ed. Karlfried Fröhlich, 663–66. Tübingen: Mohr (Siebeck); Zurich: Zwingli, 1966.

Loofs, F. "Das altkirchliche Zeugnis gegen die herrschende Auffassung der Kenosestelle (Phil. 2:5 bis 11)." *Theologische Studien und Kritiken* 100 (1927–28).

Losie, Lynn Allan. "A Note on the Interpretation of Phil 2:5." *ExpTim* 90 (1978–79): 52–54.

Malherbe, Abraham J. "Hellenistic Moralists and the New Testament." *ANRW* II.26.1, 267–333.

Marrow, S. B. "A Christological Paraenesis: Philippians 2:5–11." *Word and Spirit* 5 (1983): 61–74.

————. "Obedience and Lordship." *Bible Today* 23 (1985): 377–82.

Marshall, J. "Paul's Ethical Appeal in Philippians." In *Rhetoric and the New Testament*, ed. S. E. Porter. Sheffield: JSOT Press, 1993.

Martin, Ralph P. *Carmen Christi: Philippians ii. 5–11 in Recent Interpretation and in the Setting of Early Christian Worship*. SNTSMS 4. Cambridge University Press, 1967. Revised editions, Grand Rapids: Eerdmans, 1983; Downers Grove, Ill.: InterVarsity Press, 1997 as *A Hymn of Christ*.

————. "Hymns, Hymn Fragments, Songs, Spiritual Songs." In *Dictionary of Paul and His Letters*, ed. Gerald F. Hawthorne, Ralph P. Martin, and Daniel G. Reid, 419–23. Leicester and Downers Grove, Ill.: InterVarsity Press, 1993.

————. "Morphe in Philippians 2:6–11." *ExpTim* 70 (1958–59): 183.

Meeks, Wayne A. "The Man from Heaven in Paul's Letter to the Philippians." In *The Future of Early Christianity: Essays in Honor of Helmut Koester*, ed. Birger Pearson, 329–36. Minneapolis: Fortress Press, 1991.

Melick, R. R. *Philippians, Colossians, Philemon*. Nashville: Broadman Press, 1991.

Merkelbach, R. "Zwei Beiträge zum Neuen Testament." *Rheinisches Museum für Philologie* 134 (1991): 346–51.

Minear, Paul S. "Singing and Suffering in Philippi." In *The Conversation Continues: Studies in Paul and John in Honor of J. Louis Martyn,* ed. R. T. Fortna and B. R. Gaventa, 202–19. Nashville: Abingdon Press, 1990.

Motyer, J. A. *The Message of Philippians.* Downers Grove, Ill.: InterVarsity Press, 1984.

Moule, C. F. D. "Further Reflexions on Philippians 2:5–11." In *Apostolic History and the Gospel: Biblical and Historical Essays Presented to F.F. Bruce on His 60th Birthday,* ed. W.W. Gasque and Ralph P. Martin, 264–76. Exeter: Paternoster Press, 1970.

Müller, U. B. *Der Brief des Paulus an die Philipper.* THKNT. Leipzig: Evangelische Verlagsanstalt, 1993.

———. "Der Christushymnus Phil 2:6–11." *ZNW* (1988): 17–44.

Oakes, Peter. "Philippians: From People to Letter." *Tyndale Bulletin* 47 (1996): 371–74.

O'Brien, P. T. *The Epistle to the Philippians.* NIGTC. Grand Rapids: Eerdmans, 1991.

———. "The Gospel and Godly Models in Philippians." In *Worship, Theology and Ministry in the Early Church: Essays in Honor of Ralph P. Martin,* ed. M. Wilkins and T. Paige, 273–84. JSNTSS 87. Sheffield: JSOT Press, 1992.

O'Connor, Jerome Murphy. "Christological Anthropology in Phil. 2:6–11." *RB* 83 (1976): 25–50.

O'Neill, J. C. "The Source of the Christology in Colossians." *NTS* 26 (1980): 87–100.

———. "Hoover on Harpagmos Reviewed, with a Modest Proposal Concerning Philippians 2:6." *HTR* 81 (1988): 445–49.

Otto, Wolfgang, ed. *Freiheit in der Gebundenheit: Zur Erinnerung an den Theologen Ernst Lohmeyer.* Göttingen: Vandenhoeck & Ruprecht, 1990.

Patton, Corrine L. "Adam as the Image of God: An Exploration of the Fall of Satan in the Life of Adam and Eve." *SBL 1994 Seminar Papers,* 294–300.

Philonenko, Marc, ed. *Le Trône de Dieu.* WUNT 2. Reihe 69. Tübingen: Mohr (Siebeck), 1993.

Pietersma, A. "Kyrios or Tetragram: A Renewed Quest for the Original Septuagint." In *De Septuaginta,* 85–102. Mississauga, Ont.: Benben Publications, 1984.

Schenk, W. *Die Philipperbrief des Paulus: Kommentar.* Stuttgart: W. Kohlhammer, 1984.

Schmauch, Werner, ed. *In Memoriam Ernst Lohmeyer.* Stuttgart: Evangelisches Verlagswerk, 1951.

Schoonenberg, Piet. " 'He Emptied Himself'—Philippians 2, 7." In *Who Is Jesus of Nazareth?* 47–66. Concilium 11. New York: Paulist Press, 1966.

Schumacher, H. *Christus in seiner Präexistenz und Kenose,* 1. Rome: Pontifical Biblical Institute, 1914.

Schweizer, E. *Erniedrigung und Erhöhung bei Jesus und seinen Nachfolgern.* Zurich: Zwingli, 1955.

Scroggs, Robin. *The Last Adam: A Study in Pauline Theology.* Oxford: Blackwell, 1966.

Seyoon, Kim. *The Origin of Paul's Gospel.* WUNT 2. Reihe 4. Tübingen: Mohr (Siebeck), 1981.

Silva, M. *Philippians.* WEC. Chicago: Moody Press, 1988.

Stanton, G. N. "Incarnational Christology in the New Testament." In *Incarnation and Myth: The Debate Continued,* 153ff. London: SCM Press, 1977.

Steenburg, D. "The Case Against the Synonymity of Morphe and Eikon." *JSNT* 34 (1988): 77–86.

———. "The Worship of Adam and Christ as the Image of God." *JSNT* 39 (1990): 77–93.

Stowers, Stanley K. "Friends and Enemies in the Politics of Heaven." In *Pauline Theology,* 1, ed. J. Bassler, 105–21. Minneapolis: Fortress Press, 1991.

Sykes, S. W. "The Strange Persistence of Kenotic Christology." In *Being and Truth: Essays in Honour of John Macquarrie,* ed. Alistair Kee and Eugene T. Long, 349–75. London: SCM Press, 1986.

Talbert, C. H. "The Problem of Pre-existence in Philippians 2:6–11." *JBL* 86 (1967): 150.

Thekkekara, M. "A Neglected Idiom in an Overstudied Passage (Phil 2:6–8)." *Louvain Studies* 17 (1992): 306–14.

Thielman, F. *Philippians.* NIV Application Commentary. Grand Rapids: Zondervan, 1995.

Trudinger, P. "A Down-to-Earth Ascension? A Note on Philippians 2:6–9." In *Faith and Freedom* 44 (1991): 126–29.

———. "Making Sense of the Ascension: The Cross as Glorification." *St. Mark's Review* 133 (1988): 11–13.

Wagner, G. "Le scandale de la Croix expliqué par le Chant du Serviteur d'Esaïe 53: Réflexion sur Philippiens 2/6–11." *Etudes Théologiques et Religieuses* 61 (1986): 177–87.

Wanamaker, C. A. "Philippians 2:5–11: Son of God or Adamic Christology?" *NTS* 33 (1987): 179–93.

Wansink, C. S. *Chained in Christ.* Sheffield: Sheffield Academic Press, 1996.

Way, David. *The Lordship of Christ: Ernst Käsemann's Interpretation of Paul's Theology.* Oxford: Oxford University Press, 1991.

Weiss, Johannes. "Beiträge zur paulinischen Rhetorik." In *Theologische Studien* (FS for Bernhard Weiss), 190ff. Göttingen: Vandenhoeck & Ruprecht, 1897.

Witherington, Ben, III. *Friendship and Finances in Philippi: The Letter of Paul to the Philippians.* Valley Forge, Pa.: Trinity Press International, 1994.

———. *Jesus the Sage: The Pilgrimage of Wisdom.* Minneapolis: Fortress Press, 1994.

Wolff, Christian. "Niedrigkeit und Verzicht in Wort und Weg Jesu und in der apostolischen Existenz des Paulus." *NTS* 34 (1988): 183–96.

Wong, T. Y-C. "The Problem of Pre-existence in Philippians 2, 6–11." *Ephemerides Theologicae Lovanienses* 62 (1986): 267–82.

Wright, N. T. "ἁρπαγμός and the Meaning of Philippians 2:5–11," *JTS* n.s. 37 (1986), 321–52.

———. "Jesus Christ Is Lord: Philippians 2:5–11." In *The Climax of the Covenant: Christ and the Law in Pauline Theology,* 56–98. Edinburgh: T. & T. Clark, 1991; Minneapolis: Fortress Press, 1992.